Thomas Charleston

List of the tax payers of the city of Charleston for 1860

Thomas Charleston

List of the tax payers of the city of Charleston for 1860

ISBN/EAN: 9783337713706

Printed in Europe, USA, Canada, Australia, Japan

Cover: Foto ©ninafisch / pixelio.de

More available books at **www.hansebooks.com**

LIST

OF THE

TAX PAYERS

OF THE

CITY OF CHARLESTON

FOR

1860

CHARLESTON:
STEAM-POWER PRESSES OF EVANS & COGSWELL,
No. 3 Broad and 103 East Bay Streets.
1861.

LIST OF THE TAX PAYERS

OF THE

CITY OF CHARLESTON FOR 1860.

		TAXES.
Abrahams, A. H.		
Real Estate..................$3,000		$42 00
Abrahams, A. H. & Son		
Stock of Goods..................5,000	70 00	
Commissions..................1,000	25 00	95 00
Abrahams, A. H., in trust		
Real Estate..................1,300		18 20
Abrahams, C. T., in trust for children		
Real Estate..................1,000		14 00
Adams, J. L.		
Real Estate..................8,000		112 00
Adams, W S.		
Real Estate..................10,000	140 00	
Stock of Goods..................6,000	84 00	
Slaves..................3	9 00	
Horse..................1	10 00	243 00
Adams, E. L.		
Real Estate..................25,000	350 00	
Interest on Bonds, &c..................140	3 50	
Slaves..................12	36 00	
Carriage..................1	30 00	
Horses..................2	20 00	
Dog..................1	2 00	441 50
Adams & Frost		
Commissions..................31,108		777 70
Addison, Jno. and sister		
Real Estate..................2,000		28 00
Addison, Edward		
Real Estate..................5,800	81 20	
Slaves..................2	6 00	87 20

			TAXES.
Addison, George			
Real Estate...................2,800			39 20
Addison, Jas. R.			
Real Estate..................15,500	217	00	
Slaves 10	30	00	
Carriage....................1	30	00	
Horses 4	40	00	317 00
Addison, Jas. R., Trustee Mrs. E. A.			
Real Estate..................32,000	448	00	
Slaves 11	33	00	481 00
Addison, Jas. R., Trustee			
Slaves.....................2			6 00
Addison, J R. & W P Shingler, Trustees			
Real Estate...................10,000	....		140 00
Addison, Jos. S.			
Real Estate....................5,000	70	00	
Slave 1		3	73 00
Addison, Mary			
Slave 1			3 00
Adger, Estate James			
Real Estate................101,500 00	1,421	00	
Interest on Bonds, &c. 2,724 16	68	10	
Slaves 3	9	00	
Shipping 45,000 00	337	50	1,835 60
Adger, Robert			
Real Estate..................30,300	424	20	
Interest on Bonds, &c..............280	7	00	
Slaves....................17	51	00	
Carriage....................1	30	00	
Shipping 1,500	11	25	
Horses 3	30	00	
Dog.......................1	2	00	555 45
Adger, Jane Ann			
Real Estate..................18,000	252	00	
Interest on Bonds, &c. 384	8	70	
Slaves 2	6	00	266 70
Adger, James & Co.			
Income 8,542	....		213 55
Adger, Susan D.			
Real Estate..................22,500	315	00	
Interest on Bonds,&c..............375	9	30	
Slaves 4	12	00	336 30
Adger, Estate William			
Slave 1			3 00

TAXES.

Adger, Robt. & Co.
  Stock of Goods..................152,800   2,129 20
  Horses 2   20 00   2,159 20
Adger, James
  Real Estate..........................20,000   280 00
  Slave 1   3 00
  Carriage 1   30 00
  Horses 2   20 00
  Dog 1   2 00   335 00
Adger, J E.
  Real Estate..........................12,000   168 00
  Slaves 4   12 00
  Carriage 1   30 00
  Horses 2   20 00   230 00
Adger, J E. & Co.
  Stock of Goods....................65,200   912 80
Agency, Mercantile
  Interest on Bonds, &c..........283 00   7 07
  Income............................1,679 79   41 99   49 06
Ahrens, C. D.
  Real Estate............................8,000   112 00
  Stock of Goods......................4,000   56 00
  Carriage 1   20 00   188 00
Ahrens, H.
  Stock of Goods 200   2 80
Ahrens, John
  Real Estate............................1,200   16 80
Aiken, Wm.
  Real Estate.........................281,100   3,955 40
  Slaves 14   42 00
  Carriage 1   30 00
  Horses....................................2   20 00   4,027 40
Aiken, J D.
  Real Estate..........................28,500   399 00
  Slaves 7   21 00
  Carriage 1   30 00
  Horses....................................2   20 00   470 00
Aiken, H. K.
  Interest on Bonds, &c...............700   17 50
  Slaves 4   12 00
  Carriage............................... 1   20 00
  Horse...................................... 1   10 00   59 50
Aiken, H. K. & Co.
  Commissions.......................2,500   62 50
Aimar, Thomas
  Dog 1   2 00

		TAXES.
Aimar, Thomas, Trustee		
Real Estate.................2,500	35 00	
Slave.................1	3 00	38 00
Aimar, G. R.		
Stock of Goods.................2,500	35 00	
Dog.................1	2 00	
Slave.................1	3 00	40 00
Ainger, Joseph M.		
Real Estate.................10,000	140 00	
Slaves.................8	24 00	164 00
Air, Estate Miss A. S.		
Slaves.................2	....	6 00
Akin, Estate Eliza		
Real Estate.................4,000	....	56 00
Albergotti, Mrs. S. W		
Slaves.................6	....	18 00
Alberti, E. R.		
Real Estate.................10,000	140 00	
Slave.................1	3 00	
Carriage.................1	20 00	
Horse.................1	10 00	173 00
Albers, H. H.		
Slaves.................5	....	15 00
Albers, H. T.		
Stock of Goods.................500	....	7 00
Albers, John		
Stock of Goods.................400	5 60	
Dog.................1	2 00	7 60
Albrecht, Dora G., agent		
Real Estate.................3,000	....	42 00
Albrecht, Lewis		
Real Estate.................800	....	11 20
Aldert, Thomas		
Slave.................1	....	3 00
Aldert, Sikke		
Real Estate.................4,000	56 00	
Interest.................140	3 50	
Slaves.................7	21 00	80 50
Aldrich, T. R.		
Carriage.................1	20 00	
Income.................500	12 50	32 50
Alexander, H. D.		
Interest.................35	88	
Slave.................1	3 00	3 88

TAXES.

Alexander, Samuel, Trustee
    Real Estate............5,500   77 00
    Slaves..................2   6 00   83 00
Alexander, R. N., Trustee
    Slave..................1   3 00
    Dog....................1   2 00   5 00
Alexander, Samuel
    Interest.............285   7 13
    Dog....................1   2 00   9 13
Alexander, John D.
    Slaves.................2   6 00
    Dogs...................2   4 00   10 00
Alexander, J. M.
    Real Estate...........2,500   ....   35 00
Alexander, Hannah
    Slaves.................9   ....   27 00
Alison, Lavinia
    Slaves.................3   ....   9 00
Allan, James
    Real Estate..........800   11 20
    Stock of Goods....1,200   16 80
    Slaves.................2   6 00   34 00
Allan, Alexander
    Real Estate.........5,000   70 00
    Slave..................1   3 00   73 00
Allemong, Mary T.
    Real Estate........14,500   203 00
    Interest............460   11 50   214 50
Allen, Thomas P
    Real Estate........16,200   226 80
    Interest on Bonds, &c......1,320   33 00
    Dividends...........300   7 50
    Slaves.................9   27 00
    Carriages..............2   40 00
    Horses.................3   30 00   364 30
Allender, Ann P
    Real Estate.........8,500   119 00
    Slaves................21   63 00   182 00
Alley, Jno. B. P
    Real Estate.........5,000   70 00
    Slave..................1   3 00
    Dog....................1   2 00   75 00
Alston, R. A., Agent James McLean
    Real Estate.........5,500   ....   77 00
Alston, in trust for Mrs. A. R. Mitchell
    Slaves.................6   ....   18 00

		TAXES.

Alston, Robt. A.
 Real Estate..................2,400 33 60
 Slaves 9 27 00
 Income..................1,740 43 50 104 10

Alston, Mrs. C. M. and A. L.
 Real Estate..................15,000   210 00

Alston, Joseph, Jr.
 Real Estate..................9,000 126 00
 Slaves 5 15 00 141 00

Alston, Charles, Sr.
 Real Estate..................22,000 308 00
 Dividends..................500 12 50
 Slaves 17 51 00
 Carriage..................1 30 00
 Carriage..................1 20 00
 Horses 4 40 00
 Dog..................1 2 00 463 50

Alston, R. F. W
 Real Estate..................35,000 490 00
 Slaves 10 30 00
 Carriage..................1 30 00
 Horses........................3 30 00
 Dog..................1 2 00 582 00

Alston, W A.
 Real Estate..................15,000 210 00
 Slaves 2 6 00 216 00

Alston, Mrs. John Ashe
 Slaves 10 30 00
 Carriage..................1 30 00
 Horses........................2 20 00
 Dog..................1 2 00 82 00

Ambler, D. A.
 Real Estate..................5,000 70 00
 Stock of Goods..................3,000 42 00 112 00

Amme, D. A.
 Stock of Goods..................7,000 98 00
 Slaves 2 6 00
 Dogs........................2 4 00 108 00

Amme, C.
 Real Estate..................8,000 112 00
 Slaves 4 12 00 124 00

Ancker, G. V
 Real Estate..................14,000 196 00
 Slaves 5 15 00 211 00

Ancker, G. V., & Co.
 Income..................2,000 .... 50 00

                                                                TAXES.

Ancrum, Jane
 Real Estate.....................6,500 91 00
 Slaves..........................12 36 00 127 00
Ancrum, Mrs. H. H.
 Slaves...........................4 .... 12 00
Ancrum, J H.
 Slaves..........................25 .... 75 00
Anderson, D.
 Real Estate.....................1,800 25 20
 Slaves...........................6 18 00 43 20
Andrews, Estate M.
 Real Estate.....................5,500 77 00
 Slave............................1 3 00 80 00
Angel, Martha
 Real Estate.....................5,000 70 00
 Slaves..........................20 60 00 130 00
Annelly, Miss A. L.
 Real Estate.....................4,000 56 00
 Slave............................1 3 00
 Carriage.........................1 30 00
 Horses...........................2 20 00
 Dog..............................1 2 00 111 00
Annelly, Miss A. N.
 Real Estate.....................4,000 56 00
 Slaves...........................4 12 00 68 00
Antony, Estate Mary
 Real Estate.....................1,500 21 00
 Slaves...........................6 18 00 39 00
Apler, D.
 Real Estate.....................1,600 22 40
 Stock of Goods..................500 7 00
 Carriage.........................1 20 00
 Horse............................1 10 00
 Dog..............................1 2 00 61 40
Arant, C.
 Slaves...........................3   9 00
Archer, Elizabeth M.
 Real Estate.....................1,500   21 00
Arms, Estate Sarah C.
 Real Estate.....................7,000 98 00
 Slaves...........................6 18 00 116 00
Armstrong, Susan S. & Estate A.
 Real Estate.....................2,500 35 00
 Slaves...........................3 9 00 44 00

		TAXES.
Armstrong, Archibald		
Dogs........2		4 00
Armstrong, D. F.		
Slave........1		3 00
Armstrong, Emma		
Slave........1	....	3 00
Armstrong, Jno. A.		
Horses........4	....	40 00
Armstrong, James		
Real Estate........7,500	....	105 00
Arnau, W D. P		
Stock of Goods........500	....	7 00
Arnau, W D. P., & Wife		
Slaves........3		9 00
Arnold, Richard		
Real Estate........13,000	182 00	
Slaves........2	6 00	
Carriage........1	20 00	208 00
Arnold, Mrs. S. T.		
Real Estate........2,000	28 00	
Slaves........3	9 00	37 00
Arnold, Louisa		
Slaves........7		21 00
Artman, John		
Real Estate........8,000	112 00	
Slaves........4	12 00	
Carriage........1	20 00	
Horse........1	10 00	
Dog........1	2 00	156 00
Artman, Mrs. M. G.		
Real Estate........4,000	56 00	
Slaves........3	9 00	65 00
Artman, Mary E.		
Slave........1	....	3 00
Artope, G. P		
Real Estate........14,000	196 00	
Slaves........14	42 00	238 00
Artope, Mrs. E. P		
Carriage........1	20 00	
Horse........1	10 00	30 00
Artope, Trust Estate Emma L.		
Real Estate........1,200	16 80	
Slaves........4	12 00	28 80

                                                                    TAXES.
Ash, Jno. S.
    Real Estate..........................29,000   406 00
    Slaves...................................12   36 00
    Carriage................................1   30 00
    Horses..................................2   20 00   492 00
Ashe, Henry
    Stock of Goods....................1,000   14 00
Ashby, Trust Estate Sarah H.
    Real Estate..........................1,500   21 00
    Slaves 2   6 00   27 00
Ashby, L. P
    Real Estate...........................1,500   21 00
Ashby, Thos.
    Slaves...................................15   45 00
Ashhurst, John
    Stock of Goods..................18,000   252 00
Ashley, Alice
    Real Estate..........................12,000   168 00
Association, Building
    Real Estate..........................14,000   196 00
Association, Theatre
    Real Estate..........................20,000   280 00
Atkinson, C. & Co.
    Stock of Goods....................1,700   23 80
    Interest on Bonds, &c............1,200   30 00
    Income...............................5,800   145 00   198 80
Auld, Estate Dr. Isaac
    Real Estate..........................3,000   42 00
    Slave..................................1   3 00   45 00
Austin. Earles
    Slaves 6   18 00
Austin, Robt.
    Real Estate..........................3,000   42 00
    Slaves 3   9 00
    Income...............................5,600   140 00
    Horse 1   10 00   201 00
Auten, Peter W
    Slave..................................1   3 00
Avielhe, Alidah
    Slave..................................1   3 00
Averill, C. N.
    Stock of Goods....................1,250   17 50
    Carriage................................1   20 00
    Commissions......................1,455   36 38
    Horse 1   10 00   83 88

		TAXES.
Avery, Estate Anson		
Real Estate.................5,000	....	70 00
Axson, Wm. J		
Real Estate.................4,000	56 00	
Slaves 6	18 00	74 00
Axson, Estate Ann		
Slaves 4		12 00
Axson, Mrs. Eliz'th M.		
Slaves 3		9 00
Aytes, John		
Real Estate................1,500	21 00	
Slave 1	3 00	24 00
Bachman, Rev John		
Real Estate.................7,000	98 00	
Slaves..............................4	12 00	
Carriage............................1	30 00	
Horses..............................2	20 00	160 00
Bachman, Rev. John, Trustee		
Slave................................1		3 00
Bachman, Rev. J and wife		
Interest..........................210	5 25	
Slave................................1	3 00	8 25
Backes, Francis		
Real Estate.................7,500	....	105 00
Backus, F		
Stock of Goods..........1,250	....	17 50
Bacot, R. H.		
Slaves 8	24 00	
Dog 1	2 00	26 00
Bacot, R. D.		
Shipping 2,000	15 00	
Commissions................1,500	37 50	
Horse................................1	10 00	62 50
Bacot, Elizabeth H., Mary D. and Estate H. G.		
Slaves 2	....	6 00
Bacot, Harriet S.		
Interest............................70	1 75	
Slaves 3	9 00	10 75
Bacot, R. Wainwright		
Real Estate.................7,000	98 00	
Slaves 3	9 00	
Commissions................3,824	95 60	
Dog 1	2 00	204 60
Bacot, Maria R.		
Slaves 4		12 00

		TAXES.
Bacot, Elizabeth H.		
Slave..................1		3 00
Bacot, Mary D.		
Slave..................1		3 00
Badger, Mary B.		
Real Estate..........2,000	28 00	
Slave..................1	3 00	31 00
Baggett, J H.		
Real Estate..........200	....	2 80
Bahntge, H.		
Slave..................1	....	3 00
Bahntge, F. W		
Stock of Goods.........400	5 60	
Horse..................1	10 00	15 60
Bailey, S. M.		
Real Estate..........24,000	....	336 00
Bailey, J. A., Trustee		
Slave..................1	....	3 00
Bailie, J. G.		
Real Estate..........12,000	168 00	
Stock of Goods........30,000	420 00	588 00
Baker, John		
Real Estate..........4,000	....	56 00
Baker, H. F & Co.		
Stock of Goods.........2,600	36 40	
Carriage..................1	20 00	
Commissions..........3,000	75 00	
Horse..................1	10 00	141 40
Baker, L. B.		
Real Estate..........4,500	63 00	
Slaves..................3	9 00	72 00
Baker, Charles E.		
Real Estate..........7,000	98 00	
Dog..................1	2 00	100 00
Baker, A. F		
Slaves..................5	....	15 00
Baker, E. B., Trustee		
Slave..................1	....	3 00
Baker, Estate Ann M.		
Real Estate..........5,000	....	70 00
Baker, R. L., Trustee		
Slave..................1	....	3 00
Baker, R. L. & J C.		
Slaves..................38		114 00

		TAXES.
Baker, J. Russell		
Slaves............3	9 00	
Commissions............735 56	18 39	27 39
Baker, J. Russell, Agent		
Slaves............6	....	18 00
Baker, Susan W		
Slaves............36		108 00
Baker, Mary B.		
Real Estate............5,000	70 00	
Slaves............15	45 00	115 00
Baker, Miss E. M.		
Slaves............4		12 00
Baker, Trust Estate Mary Ann		
Real Estate............2,300	....	32 20
Baker, John		
Real Estate............2,000	....	28 00
Ball, Estate Mrs. E. St. J.		
Real Estate............11,500	161 00	
Slaves............7	21 00	182 00
Ball, W J., Guardian		
Slaves............3	....	9 00
Ball, W J.		
Slaves............8	24 00	
Carriage............1	30 00	
Horses............2	20 00	
Dogs............3	6 00	80 00
Ball, Eliza C.		
Real Estate............18,000	252 00	
Interest on Bonds, &c............400	10 00	
Slaves............40	120 00	
Carriage............1	30 00	
Horses............2	20 00	432 00
Ball, Mrs. M. L.		
Slaves............6	....	18 00
Ball, E. N		
Real Estate............10,000	140 00	
Slaves............6	18 00	
Carriage............1	30 00	
Horse............1	10 00	198 00
Ball, Estate Elizabeth		
Real Estate............3,000	42 00	
Slaves............2	6 00	48 00

		TAXES.

Ballard, Joseph
 Real Estate..................9,500 133 00
 Interest on Bonds, &c........35 88
 Slaves..........................11 33 00
 Commissions..................300 7 50
 Horse 1 10 00
 Dog 1 2 00 186 38

Bancroft, W G.
 Stock of Goods............56,000 784 00

Bancroft, James
 Real Estate..................2,800 39 20
 Slaves...........................3 9 00 48 20

Bancroft, James Jr.
 Real Estate.................13,000 182 00
 Stock of Goods............18,500 259 00
 Slave.............................1 3 00 444 00

Banger, C. R.
 Stock of Goods..............500 .... 7 00

Bank, Planter's and Mechanic's
 Real Estate................68,000 952 00
 Dog................................1 2 00 954 00

Bank, Union
 Real Estate.................45,000 .... 630 00

Bank, People's
 Real Estate.................28,000 392 00

Bank, State
 Real Estate.................50,000 700 00

Bank, Farmers' and Exchange
 Real Estate.................30,000 .... 420 00

Bank, South-Western Railroad
 Real Estate.................28,000 .... 392 00

Bank, South Carolina
 Real Estate.................25,000 .... 350 00

Bank, Charleston
 Real Estate.................85,000 .... 1,190 00

Banks, Hugh R.
 Real Estate..................8,000 112 00
 Slaves............................8 24 00
 Carriage.........................1 30 00
 Horses............................2 20 00 186 00

Banks, H. R., in trust
 Dividends..................3,000 75 00

Banks, H. R., Trustee H. C. Bee
 Slaves ....6 .... 18 00

		TAXES.
Banks, Miss Virginia		
Slaves 7		21 00
Baralaro, Antonio		
Stock of Goods.........200		2 80
Barbot, P J.		
Real Estate.........6,000	84 00	
Interest on Bonds, &c......315	7 88	
Slave.........1	3 00	
Dogs 2	4 00	98 88
Barbot, Mrs. C. F. A.		
Real Estate.........15,000	210 00	
Interest on Bonds, &c......500	12 50	
Slaves.........17	51 00	
Dog.........1	2 00	275 50
Barfield, Trust Estate Eleanor A.		
Real Estate.........13,000 00	182 00	
Interest on Bonds, &c......60 40	1 51	
Slaves.........3	9 00	
Carriage.........1	20 00	
Horse.........1	10 00	222 51
Bargeman, B.		
Real Estate.........5,000	70 00	
Stock of Goods.........2,000	28 00	
Slaves.........5	15 00	
Dogs.........2	4 00	117 00
Baring, Charles		
Slave.........1		3 00
Barjoni, John		
Stock of Goods.........150		2 10
Barker, Theo. G.		
Income.........1,200		30 00
Barker, Saml. G.		
Real Estate.........10,600	148 40	
Slaves.........12	36 00	
Carriage.........1	30 00	
Carriage.........1	20 00	
Horses.........3	30 00	264 40
Barker, Estate H. C.		
Slaves.........6		18 00
Barkley, James B.		
Carriage.........1	20 00	
Horse.........1	10 00	
Dogs.........2	4 00	34 00
Barnwell, J L.		
Income.........600		15 00

TAXES.

Barnwell, Edwd. Jr.
 Real Estate..................18,000 252 00
 Slaves.............................16   48 00
 Carriage............................1   30 00
 Carriage............................1   20 00
 Commissions..................3,400 85 00
 Horses..............................3   30 00 465 00

Barnwell, Edwd. H.
 Slave................................1   3 00
 Carriage............................1   20 00
 Income..........................2,000 50 00
 Horse...............................1   10 00
 Dogs................................2   4 00 87 00

Barr, James
 Real Estate....................2,200 .... 30 80

Barrett, Estate Isaac
 Real Estate..................158,500 2,219 00
 Interest on Bonds, &c.........1,295 32 38
 Slaves.............................12   36 00 2,287 38

Barrett, Rachel J.
 Real Estate..................20,000 .... 280 00

Barrett, Jacob
 Real Estate..................44,000 616 00
 Interest on Bonds, &c.........10,450 261 25
 Slaves.............................46   138 00
 Carriage............................1   30 00
 Horses..............................2   20 00 1,065 25

Barrett & Drake
 Stock of Goods..............3,215 45 01
 Slave................................1   3 00
 Commissions....................350   8 75 56 76

Barron, Miss E.
 Slaves.............................10 .... 30 00

Barrow, David
 Real Estate....................7,000 98 00
 Slaves..............................5   15 00 113 00

Bart, C.
 Real Estate....................8,000 112 00
 Stock of Goods................500   7 00 119 00

Bartlett, Elizabeth A.
 Slaves..............................9   27 00

Bartlett & Stroub
 Stock of Goods..............7,200   100 80

Bartless, W H., Trustee
 Real Estate....................3,000 42 00
 Slave................................1   3 00 45 00

		TAXES.

Barton, Mrs. Sarah and Children
    Real Estate..........................2,000   28 00
    Slave....................................1   3 00   31 00

Bass, H. S.
    Real Estate..........................1,500   21 00
    Slave....................................1   3 00   24 00

Bassett, Oran.
    Real Estate..........................2,500   ....   35 00

Bates & Daniels
    Real Estate..........................3,000   ....   42 00

Bates, Edwin & Co.
    Real Estate..........................15,000   210 00
    Stock of Goods....................16,000   224 00   434 00

Baurmeister, G. C.
    Commissions........................3,600   ....   90 00

Baxter, Jane R.
    Slaves..................................2   ....   6 00

Bay, Gracia
    Real Estate..........................15,100   211 40
    Interest on Bonds, &c..........140   3 50
    Slaves..................................4   12 00   226 90

Baynard, W G.
    Real Estate..........................14,000   196 00
    Interest on Bonds, &c..........140   3 50
    Slaves..................................16   48 00
    Carriage...............................1   30 00
    Horses.................................3   30 00
    Dog......................................1   2 00   309 50

Beach, E. M.
    Real Estate..........................15,000   210 00
    Slaves..................................4   12 00
    Carriage...............................1   30 00
    Horses.................................2   20 00   272 00

Beach & King
    Real Estate..........................8,000   ....   112 00

Beatie, James
    Real Estate..........................9,000   126 00
    Slaves..................................8   24 00   150 00

Beckmann, C. J
    Real Estate..........................5,000   70 00
    Slaves..................................10   30 00   100 00

Beckmann, J. O.
    Real Estate..........................3,000   42 00

Beckmann, Chas. H.
    Slave....................................1   ....   3 00

			TAXES
Beckmann, Mrs. E. R.			
Real Estate............................2,200	30 80		
Slaves.......................................4	12 00	42 80	
Beckmann, W W			
Stock of Goods........................300	4 20		
Slave...1	3 00		
Dog..1	2 00	9 20	
Bee, Bernard E., Trustee			
Slave...1		3 00	
Bee, B. E.			
Slaves..4	....	12 00	
Bee, Mary F			
Slaves.......................................2		6 00	
Bee, Kezia			
Slave..1	....	3 00	
Bee, George W., Trustee			
Slaves..3		9 00	
Bee, James M.			
Real Estate............................8,000	....	112 00	
Bee, John B. and Wife, in trust			
Real Estate............................1,200	....	16 80	
Bee, Susan			
Slaves..2		6 00	
Bee, Wm. C.			
Real Estate..........................15,000	210 00		
Interest on Bonds, &c............1,282	32 05		
Slaves.......................................14	42 00		
Carriage....................................1	30 00		
Horses.......................................3	30 00		
Dogs..2	4 00	348 05	
Bee, Wm. C., & Co.			
Interest on Bonds, &c...............700	17 50		
Commissions......................14,642	368 05	385 55	
Bee, Robert R.			
Real Estate..........................17,000	238 00		
Slaves.....................................29	87 00		
Carriage....................................1	20 00		
Horses......................................2	20 00	365 00	
Bee, H. L., & R. A.			
Slave..1		3 00	
Bee, John James			
Real Estate............................3,000	42 00		
Slaves..2	6 00	48 00	
Bee, Wm. J			
Real Estate............................3,500		49 00	

		TAXES.
Bee, Benjamin C.		
Real Estate..................2,500		35 00
Bee, Mrs. M. S.		
Real Estate..................4,500	63 00	
Slaves............................9	27 00	90 00
Bee, James R.		
Dog...............................1		2 00
Bee, Mrs. J. S.		
Slaves.............................6	....	18 00
Beesley, John		
Real Estate.....................700	....	9 80
Behre, C. H.		
Stock of Goods................500		7 00
Behrens, Lewis		
Stock of Goods................600		8 40
Beile, Mrs. A. M.		
Real Estate..................9,500	133 00	
Slaves............................2	6 00	139 00
Belcher, Estate Mary A.		
Slaves............................2		6 00
Belin, A. H.		
Real Estate.................20,000	280 00	
Interest on Bonds, &c..........4,147	103 68	
Dividends.........................235	5 88	
Slaves...........................11	33 00	
Carriage..........................1	30 00	
Horses............................2	20 00	
Dogs.............................2	4 00	476 56
Bell, Samuel		
Real Estate..................3,000	42 00	
Slaves............................6	18 00	60 00
Bell, John		
Slave.............................1		3 00
Bell, Mrs. M. J. M.		
Real Estate.................36,000	504 00	
Slaves............................7	21 00	
Carriage..........................1	30 00	
Horses............................2	20 00	575 00
Bell, Wm.		
Slaves............................7	21 00	
Carriage..........................1	30 00	
Carriage..........................1	20 00	
Horses............................2	20 00	91 00

TAXES.

Bell, Dorinda
 Real Estate...................9,000 126 00
 Slaves...........................4 12 00 138 00

Bellinger, Dr. John
 Real Estate...................11,500 161 00
 Interest on Bonds, &c..........862 21 55
 Slaves...........................13 39 00
 Carriage..........................1 30 00
 Carriage..........................1 20 00
 Income........................6,000 150 00
 Horses............................3 30 00 451 55

Bellinger, Estate M. R.
 Interest on Bonds, &c........714 17 85

Bellinger, Estate E. C.
 Slaves...........................22 66 00

Belser, Louisa
 Real Estate...................15,000 210 00
 Slaves............................7 21 00 231 00

Benjamin, Mrs. H. J
 Real Estate...................2,500 35 00
 Slaves............................9 27 00 62 00

Benjamin, S. A.
 Stock of Goods................300 .... 4 20

Bennett, Thomas
 Real Estate..................278,200 3,894 80
 Slaves...........................31 93 00
 Carriage..........................1 30 00
 Horse 2 20 00 4,037 80

Bennett, W J.
 Real Estate...................30,000 420 00
 Slaves...........................77 231 00
 Carriage..........................1 20 00
 Horses............................2 20 00 691 00

Bennett, S. P
 Real Estate....................2,000 28 00
 Slaves............................3 9 00
 Carriage..........................1 20 00
 Commissions....................500 12 50 69 50

Bennett, Estate Jane M.
 Interest on Bonds, &c......2,334 50 58 36
 Slaves............................7 21 00 79 36

Bennett, Mrs. C. E.
 Slaves............................3 .... 9 00

Bennett, C. G.
 Real Estate...................3,000 42 00

			TAXES
Bennett, I. S. K.			
Slaves	8	24 00	
Carriage	1	20 00	
Horses	2	20 00	64 00
Bennett & Rhett			
Commissions	4,000		100 00
Bennett, Margaret			
Slave	1		3 00
Bennett, S. B., in trust			
Slave	1		3 00
Bennett, T. B., Trustee			
Slave	1		3 00
Bennett, T. B.			
Slaves	6	18 00	
Carriage	1	20 00	
Horse	1	10 00	48 00
Benoist, Estate Natalie			
Real Estate	23,300		326 20
Benseman, F W			
Real Estate	8,000	112 00	
Slaves	6	18 00	130 00
Benson, Estate Lawrence			
Real Estate	14,100		197 40
Benson, Estate L., (life estate in Mrs. Thwing.)			
Real Estate	8,500		119 00
Benter, J. C.			
Stock of Goods	300		4 20
Bentham, Estate R.			
Real Estate	12,000	168 00	
Slaves	8	24 00	192 00
Berrje, Charles			
Stock of Goods	800		11 20
Berry, Maria			
Real Estate	2,000		28 00
Berry, Wm. A			
Real Estate	1,500		21 00
Berry, Capt. M.			
Real Estate	10,000		140 00
Betjamann, John			
Real Estate	2,500		35 00
Bevin, John K.			
Real Estate	11,200	156 80	
Slaves	3	9 00	
Horse	1	10 00	175 80

23

		TAXES.
Bevin, John K., in trust		
Real Estate............1,500		21 00
Bianchi, A.		
Real Estate............5,000	70 00	
Stock of Goods............600	8 40	78 40
Bicaise, Benj. P		
Real Estate............6,000	84 00	
Stock of Goods............200	2 80	
Slaves 4	12 00	
Dog 1	2 00	100 80
Bickley, John, and wife		
Real Estate............22,000	308 00	
Interest on Bonds, &c.............210	5 25	
Slaves 18	54 00	
Carriage 1	30 00	
Horses............2	20 00	417 25
Bickley, Trust Estate Mary, and Julia A. F		
Slaves 4		12 00
Billings. Mrs. Julia		
Real Estate 300		4 20
Bingley, Mrs. Selina		
Slaves 2	....	6 00
Bingley. Trust Estate Jane G.		
Real Estate............2,000	....	28 00
Binns, John		
Real Estate 2,100	29 40	
Slave............1	3 00	32 40
Birch, Mrs. C. A.		
Real Estate............3,500	49 00	
Interest on Bonds, &c............1,172	29 30	
Slaves 7	21 00	
Dog 1	2 00	101 30
Bird, Wm.		
Slaves 2	....	6 00
Bird, Mrs. M. N. C.		
Slaves 4	....	12 00
Bird, C. H.		
Stock of Goods 3,000	....	42 00
Bird, Trust Estate Mary M.		
Real Estate............6,000	84 00	
Slaves 7	21 00	105 00
Bird, Wm., and others, Trustees		
Slave............1		3 00
Birnie, Wm. & S. Mowrey, Jr.		
Real Estate............10,000	....	140 00

TAXES.

Birnie, Wm.
 Real Estate......................23,000 322 00
 Interest on Bonds, &c............3,135 78 38
 Slaves 12 36 00
 Carriage 1 30 00
 Horses....................................2 20 00
 Dog..1 2 00 488 38

Bischoff, Henry
 Real Estate......................22,000 308 00
 Slaves 7 21 00
 Carriage 1 20 00
 Shipping 5,000 37 50 386 50

Bischoff, Henry & Co.
 Stock of Goods...................10,000 .... 140 00

Bischoff, Albert
 Real Estate......................43,500 609 00

Bissell, T. L. & J B.
 Stock of Goods....................3,000 42 00
 Carriage 1 20 00
 Horse 1 10 00 72 00

Bissell, J L., Sen., Agent C. E. Bissell
 Slaves 6 18 00

Bize, R.
 Real Estate........................3,000 42 00
 Slaves 5 15 00 57 00

Black, A. W
 Real Estate......................10,500 147 00
 Slaves 3 9 00
 Dog..1 2 00 158 00

Black, Rebecca
 Real Estate........................4,500 63 00

Black, A. Foster
 Real Estate ....600 .... 8 40

Black, F. C. & S. C.
 Stock of Goods....................5,360 75 04
 Slave 1 3 00 78 04

Black, S. C.
 Slave 1 3 00
 Dog..1 2 00 5 00

Black, Estate F. C.
 Interest on Bonds, &c..............300 7 53
 Slave 1 3 00 10 53

Black, Mrs. M. A.
 Slaves.....................................9 27 00

		TAXES.
Black. Geo. W		
Real Estate..........20,000	280 00	
Slaves..........23	69 00	
Carriage..........1	20 00	
Horse..........1	10 00	
Dog..........1	2 00	381 00
Blackham. William		
Real Estate..........1,800		25 20
Blacklock, Jno. F.		
Real Estate..........32,500	455 00	
Interest on Bonds, &c..........422	10 55	
Slaves..........3	9 00	
Carriage..........1	30 00	
Horses..........3	30 00	534 55
Blacklock, Jno. F. Trustee		
Slaves..........4		12 00
Blacklock, in trust		
Real Estate..........3,000	42 00	
Slaves..........4	12 00	54 00
Blackman, James		
Horse..........1		10 00
Blackman, Joseph		
Slaves..........3	....	9 00
Blackwell, Anna C.		
Slaves..........2		6 00
Blackwood, Harriet		
Real Estate..........8,000	....	112 00
Blair, Mrs. Isabella		
Slaves..........5		15 00
Blake. Estate Edward		
Slaves..........2		6 00
Blake, Julius A.		
Dog..........1		2 00
Blake, Estate C. L.		
Real Estate..........8,000	112 00	
Interest on Bonds, &c..........350	8 75	
Slave..........1	3 00	123 75
Blake, Joseph		
Slaves..........2		6 00
Blake, John		
Real Estate..........12,300	172 20	
Slaves..........6	18 00	190 20
Blake, Daniel		
Slaves..........2	6 00	
Carriage..........1	30 00	
Horses..........2	20 00	56 00

			TAXES.
Blake, Jno. in trust			
Real Estate............1,800			25 20
Blake, Daniel, Guardian			
Real Estate............20,000	280	00	
Slaves 3	9	00	
Carriage 1	30	00	
Carriage 1	20	00	
Shipping 4,000	30	00	
Horses............4	40	00	
Dog............1	2	00	411 00
Blakley, J. M.			
Slaves 4	......		12 00
Blamyer, Estate Wm.			
Slaves 7			21 00
Blanchard, S.			
Real Estate............1,200	......		16 80
Blanding, Wm.			
Real Estate............16,000	224	00	
Interest on Bonds, &c............116	2	90	226 90
Blank, J			
Stock of Goods............500	......		7 00
Blase, C. L.			
Real Estate............9,500	133	00	
Stock of Goods............500	7	00	
Slave 1	3	00	
Dog............1	2	00	145 00
Bliss, T. W			
Real Estate............2,000	28	00	
Stock of Goods............600	8	40	
Slave 1	3	00	
Carriage 1	20	00	
Horse............1	10	00	69 40
Bliss, T. W., Trustee			
Real Estate............8,500			119 00
Block, H. W			
Real Estate............1,500	21	00	
Stock of Goods............250	3	50	24 50
Blohme, J. C.			
Real Estate............13,500			189 00
Blondeau, E.			
Real Estate............3,500	77	00	
Slaves 2	6	00	83 00
Blum, Estate J C.			
Real Estate............52,100	729	40	
Slaves 23	69	00	798 40

		TAXES.

Blum, F. C.
    Real Estate..........................21,400   299 60
    Slaves 15   45 00
    Carriage 1   30 00
    Horses..................................2   20 00   394 60

Blum, F C. & Son
    Commissions......................2,400   60 00

Blum, Mrs. Esther
    Real Estate..........................33,400   467 60
    Slaves 2   6 00
    Carriage 1   30 00
    Horses..................................2   20 00
    Dog......................................1   2 00   525 60

Blum, John A.
    Real Estate..........................6,500   91 00
    Slaves 5   15 00   106 00

Blum, Robert A.
    Real Estate..........................5,000   70 00
    Slaves 11   33 00   103 00

Boag, Mrs. E. M.
    Slaves 7   21 00

Boag, Theo. G.
    Dog......................................1   ....   2 00

Bober, T.
    Stock of Goods....................200   ....   2 80

Bode, D.
    Real Estate 800   11 20

Bohles, Estate M. A.
    Real Estate 750   24 50

Bohles, Est. Luder E.
    Real Estate..........................5,500   77 00
    Slaves 2   6 00   83 00

Boinest, Margaret H.
    Slaves 9   ....   27 00

Bolger, Henry H.
    Real Estate..........................3,000   ....   42 00

Bolger, M., in trust
    Real Estate..........................1,500   21 00
    Stock of Goods....................500   7 00
    Dog......................................1   2 00   30 00

Bolles, A.
    Real Estate..........................5,000   70 00
    Slaves 2   6 00   76 00

Bollmann, B., in trust A. Theling
    Real Estate..........................2,500   35 00

		TAXES.

Bollmann Brothers
    Stock of Goods 8,000   112 00
    Slaves......6   18 00
    Carriage......1   20 00
    Dog......1   2 00   152 00

Bonneau, Eliza M.
    Real Estate......6,500   91 00
    Interest on Bonds, &c......1,260   31 50
    Slaves......4   12 00
    Dog......1   2 00   136 50

Bonnell, Frances
    Slave......1   3 00

Bonnell, John
    Real Estate......15,000   210 00
    Stock of Goods......15,000   210 00
    Slaves......5   15 00   435 00

Bonnell, Thomas
    Real Estate......5,000   70 00
    Slaves......2   6 00   76 00

Bonnell, Amelia D.
    Slave......1   3 00

Bookin, Jno. H.
    Stock of Goods......700   ....   9 80

Boone, Trust Estate M. C.
    Real Estate......1,800   25 20
    Slaves......4   12 00   37 20

Booth, Estate M.
    Real Estate......5,800   ....   81 20

Boring, W H.
    Real Estate......6,200   86 80
    Stock of Goods......2,200   30 80
    Slaves......5   15 00
    Dog......1   2 00   134 60

Bornemann, J H.
    Stock of Goods......300   ....   4 20

Bornemann, Fred'k.
    Stock of Goods......300   4 20

Bornemann, F. W
    Real Estate......3,000   42 00

Borner, F C.
    Stock of Goods......2,100   29 40
    Carriage......1   20 00   49 40

Bosch, Jno. F.
    Stock of Goods......800   11 20
    Dog......1   2 00   13 20

		TAXES.

Boudo, Estate H.
 Real Estate ....8,000 .... 112 00
Bourke, Ormsby
 Real Estate................1,000 .... 14 00
Boutelle, Charles
 Slaves 4   12 00
Boutiton, Margaret
 Slaves ....3 .... 9 00
Bowen, O. A.
 Slaves 2 6 00
 Carriage 1 30 00
 Horses 2 20 00
 Dog 1 2 00 58 00
Bowen, Foster & Co.
 Stock of Goods............26,000   364 00
Bowen, Mrs. M. W
 Slaves 2 6 00
 Carriage 1 20 00
 Horse 1 10 00 36 00
Bowers, John E.
 Commissions 970 84 24 27
 Dog 1 2 00 26 27
Bowie, Jas. S.
 Real Estate.................7,000 98 00
 Slaves 7 21 00
 Carriage 1 20 00
 Horse 1 10 00
 Dog 1 2 00 151 00
Bowie, J. S. & L.
 Real Estate................30,000 .... 420 00
Bowie, J. S. & L. & Co.
 Stock of Goods...............77,000 .... 1,078 00
Bowie Brothers & Co.
 Commissions ....8,900 .... 222 50
Bowie, Langdon
 Slaves 5 15 00
 Carriage 1 20 00
 Horse 1 10 00 45 00
Bowie, Jno. A.
 Interest on Bonds, &c............2,000 50 00
 Slaves 6 18 00 68 00
Bowman, Estate Miss M. H.
 Interest on Bonds, &c..............365 ...... 9 03
Bowman, Geo. A.
 Slaves ....4 .... 12 00

		TAXES.
Bowman, Miss E. L.		
Interest on Bonds, &c............1,633	40 83	
Slaves 15	45 00	
Dog 1	2 00	87 83
Bowman, T. B.		
Slave 1	3 00	
Shipping...............................600	4 50	7 50
Box, Mrs. K.		
Slave 1		3 00
Boyce, Estate P J		
Real Estate........................11,000	154 00	
Slaves 6	18 00	172 00
Boyce, Jas. P		
Real Estate..........................7,000	....	98 00
Boyce, Sam'l P		
Real Estate........................30,000	....	420 00
Boyden, John J		
Real Estate..........................2,500	35 00	
Dog..1	2 00	37 00
Boyden, Mrs. M. E.		
Real Estate..........................1,500	21 00	
Slaves.......................................9	27 00	48 00
Boylan, Joseph		
Horse 1	....	10 00
Boyle, Cornelia		
Slaves.....................................12	....	36 00
Boyle, M. E.		
Slaves.....................................11	....	33 00
Boyle, Trust Estate Mrs. M. L.		
Real Estate..........................1,000	14 00	
Slave 1	3 00	17 00
Boylston, Henry Sen.		
Real Estate..........................3,200	44 80	
Interest on Bonds, &c..............750	18 75	
Slaves.....................................11	33 00	
Carriage....................................1	20 00	
Dog..1	2 00	118 55
Boylston, J Reid		
Slaves.......................................2		6 00
Bradford, William		
Slaves.......................................2	....	6 00
Bradley, J C.		
Slaves.......................................5	15 00	
Horse 1	10 00	25 00

			TAXES.
Bradley, Wm. A.			
Real Estate	3,000	42 00	
Slave	1	3 00	
Dog	1	2 00	47 00
Bradley, A H.			
Real Estate	1,200		16 80
Bradwell, Isaac			
Slave	1	....	3 00
Brady. P., Sen.			
Real Estate	3,000	....	42 00
Brady, P			
Real Estate	3,500	49 00	
Slaves	4	12 00	
Dog	1	2 00	63 00
Brady & McDonell			
Stock of Goods	20,000	....	280 00
Brady, Catherine			
Real Estate	2,200		84 00
Brahe, A. H. & Co.			
Stock of Goods	6,000	....	84 00
Brahe, D.			
Real Estate	6,000	....	84 00
Brailsford, Dr. Wm. M.			
Slaves	3	....	9 00
Brailsford, W R.			
Real Estate	2,000	28 00	
Income	835	20 88	48 88
Brailsford, Anna L.			
Slaves	6	....	18 00
Brailsford, Dr. R. M.			
Slave	1	3 00	
Carriage	1	20 00	
Income	800	20 00	43 00
Brailsford, Mrs. E. A.			
Slaves	3	....	9 00
Brailsford, Anna L. and W G. Carere			
Real Estate	4,000	....	56 00
Branch, Jno, L.			
Real Estate	4,000	56 00	
Slave	1	3 00	
Income	1,389 98	34 74	
Dog	1	2 00	95 74
Brant, H. F			
Real Estate	2,500	35 00	
Stock of Goods	400	5 60	
Slaves	6	18 00	58 60

			TAXES.
Brant. James L.			
Slave	1		3 00
Brant, T. C			
Horse	1	10 00	
Dog	1	2 00	12 00
Brant. Mrs. D. S. M.			
Stock of Goods	300		4 20
Brant, Mrs. L.			
Real Estate	1,000		14 00
Branford, Mrs. C. G.			
Real Estate	19,100	267 40	
Slaves	2	6 00	
Dog	1	2 00	275 40
Branford. C L.			
Slave	1		3 00
Brauer. W A.			
Stock of Goods	500	7 00	
Horse	1	10 00	17 00
Brawley Jno. H.			
Stock of Goods	5,000		70 00
Breaker. C M.			
Slaves	4		12 00
Breaker, Trust Estate of Mrs. J A. R. and children			
Real Estate	3,000		42 00
Bredemann. William			
Real Estate	4,000	56 00	
Slaves	2	6 00	62 00
Breden, M.			
Stock of Goods	200		2 80
Breeden. M.			
Stock of Goods	300		4 20
Bredenburg, Jno. H.			
Real Estate	14,500	203 00	
Stock of Goods	2,000	28 00	
Horse	1	10 00	
Dog	1	2 00	243 00
Bredenburg. J. J			
Stock of Goods	500	7 00	
Dog	1	2 00	9 00
Bredenburg. L.			
Real Estate	2,500	35 00	
Stock of Goods	800	11 20	
Slaves	2	6 00	
Dog	1	2 00	54 20

		TAXES.
Breur, M.		
Stock of Goods......600		8 40
Brewster, C R.		
Real Estate......29,400	411 60	
Slaves......4	12 00	
Carriage......1	30 00	
Horses......2	20 00	
Dog......1	2 00	475 60
Brewster, C. R. and W S.		
Income......2,750		68 75
Brewster, C. R., Trustee		
Slave......1		3 00
Brickwedel. J. H. & Co.		
Stock of Goods......5,000		70 00
Briggs. David		
Real Estate......8,500	119 00	
Slave......1	3 00	
Dog......1	2 00	124 00
Brightman, Mrs. S. A.		
Slaves......4	....	12 00
Bringewarth, William		
Stock of Goods...... ...300		4 20
Brisbane. A. H.		
Real Estate......3,500	49 00	
Slaves......14	42 00	
Carriage......1	20 00	
Horse......1	10 00	121 00
Brisbane, Miss E.		
Slaves......4	....	12 00
Brisbane, Miss M.		
Real Estate......3,000	42 00	
Slave......1	3 00	45 00
Brissenden, Henry J.		
Real Estate......1,500	21 00	
Dog......1	2 00	23 00
Bristoll, T. M.		
Real Estate......13,000	182 00	
Dog......1	2 00	184 00
Bristoll, T. M. & Co.		
Stock of Goods......23,000		322 00
Bristoll, W B.		
Stock of Goods......6,500	....	91 00
Broadfoot, John		
Real Estate......4,000	....	56 00

			TAXES.
Brock, Jacob			
Real Estate	4,000		56 00
Brocklebanks, Estate William			
Real Estate	3,000		42 00
Brodie, Mrs. E. M.			
Slaves	5		15 00
Brodie, Robert H.			
Slaves	4		12 00
Brodie, Robert			
Real Estate	20,500		287 00
Brodie, Ann H.			
Real Estate	1,800		25 20
Brodie, J. W & Son			
Slaves	5	15 00	
Carriage	1	20 00	
Commissions	5,000	125 00	
Horse	1	10 00	
Dog	1	2 00	172 00
Brookbanks, William			
Stock of Goods	300	4 20	
Horse	1	10 00	
Dog	1	2 00	16 20
Brooks, Sarah			
Stock of Goods	500		7 00
Broughton, T. Alexander			
Interest on Bonds, &c.	875	10 30	
Carriage	1	20 00	
Income	412	21 88	
Horse	1	10 00	
Dog	1	2 00	64 18
Brower, Wm.			
Real Estate	1,800	25 20	
Dog	1	2 00	27 20
Brown, Mrs. Eliza			
Real Estate	5,000	70 00	
Slaves	2	6 00	76 00
Brown, Trust Estate S C and children			
Real Estate	10,000	140 00	
Slaves	13	39 00	
Carriage	1	20 00	
Horse	1	10 00	209 00
Brown, Thomas K.			
Real Estate	2,000	28 00	
Slaves	13	39 00	
Horses	3	30 00	97 00

TAXES.

Brown, George W
   Real Estate..........................27,500   385 00
   Slaves......................................10   30 00
   Carriage....................................1   30 00
   Carriage....................................1   20 00
   Horses......................................3   30 00   495 00

Brown, George W., Trustee Mrs. Hyams
   Slaves.......................................2   6 00

Brown & Palma
   Stock of Goods....................25,000   350 00

Brown, S. K.
   Real Estate..........................2,500   35 00

Brown, S. K., Trustee
   Real Estate............................600   8 40

Brown, W S.
   Real Estate..........................5,000   70 00
   Income................................1,000   25 00   95 00

Brown, A. McD.
   Slaves.......................................7   21 00
   Carriage....................................1   20 00
   Horse.......................................1   10 00
   Dog...1   2 00   53 00

Brown, Mrs. M. E.
   Slaves.......................................4   ....   12 00

Brown, James W
   Real Estate..........................6,400   89 60
   Stock of Goods.....................5,000   70 00
   Slaves.......................................4   12 00
   Carriage....................................1   20 00
   Commissions.......................1,500   37 50
   Horse.......................................1   10 00
   Dog...1   2 00   241 10

Brown, Eliza
   Slaves.......................................3   9 00

Brown, Trust Estate Mary
   Real Estate.........................10,500   147 00
   Interest on Bonds, &c..............148   3 70   150 70

Brown, Emilie
   Real Estate..........................3,000   42 00
   Slaves.......................................2   6 00   48 00

Brown, B. H.
   Real Estate.........................12,000   168 00
   Slaves......................................12   36 00   204 00

Brown, Estate Magdalen
   Real Estate..........................1,500   21 00

TAXES.

Brown, Robt. E.
 Slaves 2   6 00
 Commissions.....................1,200   30 00   36 00
Brown, Estate George
 Real Estate......................20,000   280 00
 Slaves...5   15 00
 Carriage 1   20 00
 Horse 1   10 00
 Dog...1   2 00   327 00
Brown, Mrs. Catherine
 Real Estate........................9,000   126 00
 Slaves 6   18 00   144 00
Brown, James M.
 Slaves...2   6 00
 Dog...1   2 00   8 00
Brown, A. H.
 Real Estate......................10,000   140 00
 Slaves 17   51 00
 Carriage 1   30 00
 Carriage..1   20 00
 Horses 3   30 00
 Dog...1   2 00   273 00
Brown, A. H., Trustee
 Slaves..5   15 00
Brown & Porter
 Real Estate........................5,000   70 00
 Income............................10,000   250 00   320 00
Brown, Estate John
 Real Estate........................1,500   ....   21 00
Brown, A. S.
 Real Estate........................3,000   ....   42 00
Brown, Susan
 Slaves..2   ....   6 00
Brown, Ellen L., in trust
 Real Estate........................5,000   70 00
 Slaves 6   18 00   88 00
Brown, Mrs. Lavinia
 Real Estate........................5,000   70 00
 Slaves 5   15 00   85 00
Browne, Julius P., Jr.
 Horse 1   10 00
 Dog...1   2 00   12 00
Browne, Ann M.
 Real Estate........................5,500   ....   77 00

TAXES.

Browne, James
   Real Estate..................6,000   84 00
Browne, G. B.
   Real Estate..................6,000   84 00
   Slaves 2   6 00   90 00
Browne & Calder
   Stock of Goods............35,000   490 00
Brownfield, J. W
   Slaves.............................25   75 00
Browning, A. F.
   Real Estate.................27,200   380 80
   Stock of Goods............40,000   560 00
   Slaves............................12   36 00
   Carriage...........................1   20 00
   Horse..............................1   10 00
   Dog................................1   2 00   1,008 80
Browning, A. F., Trustee
   Slave..............................1   ....   3 00
Brownlee, Estate E.
   Slave..............................1   3 00
Brummer, J. H.
   Stock of Goods..............500   7 00
   Dog................................1   2 00   9 00
Bruning & Jager
   Stock of Goods............4,000   ....   56 00
Brunjes, Wm.
   Real Estate.................16,000   224 00
   Stock of Goods..............400   5 60
   Dog................................1   2 00   231 60
Bruns, Henry M.
   Real Estate..................9,000   126 00
   Slaves.............................8   24 00
   Carriage...........................1   20 00
   Horse..............................1   10 00
   Dog................................1   2 00   182 00
Bruns, Dr. J. Dickson
   Slaves.............................3   9 00
   Carriage...........................1   20 00
   Income..........................500   12 50
   Horse..............................1   10 00
   Dog................................1   2 00   53 50
Bruns, John
   Stock of Goods..............400   ....   5 60
Brunsen, C. H.
   Stock of Goods..............100   1 40

TAXES.

Bryan, Trust Estate Geo. S. & R. L.
 Real Estate............9,500 133 00
 Slaves..................4 12 00 145 00
Bryan, Geo. S., Trustee
 Slave...................1 3 00
Bryan, W J.
 Slaves..................3 9 00
Bryant, Mrs. Sarah
 Slaves..................2 6 00
Buck, Lewis
 Stock of Goods........800 11 20
 Dog....................1 2 00 13 20
Buckheit, P
 Real Estate..........3,500 49 00
 Slaves.................2 6 00
 Carriage...............1 20 00
 Dog....................1 2 00 77 00
Bucking. Jno. H.
 Real Estate..........1,200 16 80
Buckley, James
 Stock of Goods........500 7 00
Budd, T. S. & T. G.
 Stock of Goods......4,500 63 00
 Commissions........11,000 275 00 338 00
Budd, Thomas S.
 Slaves.................3 9 00
 Carriage...............1 20 00
 Horse..................1 10 00
 Dog....................1 2 00 41 00
Budd, T. G., Trustee
 Real Estate..........8,000 112 00
Budds, J. D.
 Real Estate..........2,500 35 00
 Dog....................1 2 00 37 00
Buero, E.
 Stock of Goods........300 4 20
Buero, Angelo
 Stock of Goods........300 4 20
Buerhaus, Louisa
 Real Estate..........3,000 42 00
 Slave..................1 3 00 45 00
Buggle, John
 Stock of Goods........300 4 20
 Slave..................1 3 00 7 20

			TAXES.
Buhré D.			
Real Estate	2,000	28 00	
Stock of Goods	800	11 20	39 20
Buist, George			
Real Estate	13,000	182 00	
Slaves	16	48 00	
Carriage	1	20 00	
Horse	1	10 00	
Dog	1	2 00	262 00
Buist, Martha			
Slaves	2		6 00
Buist, Trust Estate and Wife,			
Real Estate	9,000	126 00	
Interest on Bonds, &c	250	6 25	132 25
Buist, Henry			
Real Estate	8,000	112 00	
Slaves	5	15 00	
Carriage	1	20 00	
Income	4,000	100 00	
Horse	1	10 00	
Dogs	2	4 00	261 00
Bull, E.			
Real Estate	9,000		126 00
Bull, Wm. Izard			
Real Estate	12,000	168 00	
Slaves	23	69 00	
Carriage	1	30 00	
Horses	3	30 00	
Dog	1	2 00	299 00
Bull, Miss L. A.			
Real Estate	2,500		35 00
Bullwinkel, D.			
Stock of Goods	500		7 00
Bullwinkel, D.			
Stock of Goods	700	9 80	
Slave	1	3 00	12 80
Bullwinkel, H.			
Real Estate	7,000		98 00
Bullwinkel, H.			
Real Estate	8,000	112 00	
Stock of Goods	1,200	16 80	
Slaves	7	21 00	
Carriage	1	20 00	
Dog	1	2 00	171 80
Bullwinkel, John D.			
Stock of Goods	1,000		14 00

			TAXES.
Bullwinkel. John H.			
Real Estate	4,000	56 00	
Stock of Goods	300	4 20	60 20
Bullwinkel, Jno. H.			
Real Estate	3,000	42 00	
Stock of Goods	300	4 20	46 20
Bulow. Estate J. J.			
Slaves	5		15 00
Bulow. Estate Thos. L.			
Real Estate	42,300	592 20	
Slaves	2	6 00	598 20
Bunch, Dennis D.			
Real Estate	2,000	28 00	
Slaves	6	18 00	46 00
Bunger. C			
Stock of Goods	500		7 00
Burch. Jno. R.			
Real Estate	800		11 20
Burckmyer. Jno. C			
Real Estate	18,000	252 00	
Slaves	5	15 00	
Carriage	1	20 00	
Horse	1	10 00	
Dog	1	2 00	299 00
Burckmyer & Moffett			
Stock of Goods	6,000	84 00	
Commissions	1,600	40 00	124 00
Burckmyer. Jno. A.			
Real Estate	5,500	77 00	
Stock of Goods	22,000	308 00	
Slaves	7	21 00	406 00
Burckmyer. C. L.			
Real Estate	11,000	154 00	
Slaves	4	12 00	
Shipping	4,000	30 00	
Dog	1	2 00	198 00
Burdell's children. T. J.			
Real Estate	3,000		42 00
Burdell. T. J.			
Slave	1		3 00
Burdell's children, Estate J E.			
Real Estate	1,600		22 40
Burdell. Emma			
Slaves	3		9 00

                                                                TAXES.
Burden, W B.
    Carriage 1   20 00
    Horse 1   10 00
    Dog 1   2 00   32 00
Burden, Estate K.
    Slaves 11   33 00
Burden, Trust Estate K. and Mary
    Slaves 12   36 00
Burgess, Mrs. M. E.
    Slaves 3   9 00
Burie, Joshua
    Real Estate 2,000   28 00
Burk, Jno. H.
    Real Estate 4,500   63 00
Burk, Saml.
    Real Estate 200   ....   2 80
Burke, A. J.
    Real Estate 800   11 20
    Stock of Goods 300   4 20
    Slave 1   3 00   18 40
Burke, James
    Stock of Goods 8,000   112 00
Burke, Jno., Trustee
    Slave 1   3 00
Burlington, Ann
    Slave 1   ....   3 00
Burn, Estate Wm.
    Real Estate 3,500   49 00
    Slaves 2   6 00
    Dogs 2   4 00   59 00
Burn, Henry, Sen.
    Real Estate 3,000   ....   42 00
Burn, Geo. W
    Real Estate 1,700   23 80
    Slaves 4   12 00   35 80
Burnett, A. W
    Slaves 21   63 00
    Carriage 1   30 00
    Horses 2   20 00   113 00
Burnham, R. W
    Real Estate 80,000   112 00
    Stock of Goods 2,700   37 80
    Slaves 2   6 00
    Dog 1   2 00   157 80

			TAXES.

Burns, Jno.
 Real Estate......................3,500 49 00
 Slave..................................1 3 00 52 00
Burns, D. M.
 Real Estate......................5,000   70 00
Burrows, Saml.
 Slaves 8   24 00
Burrows, Mary and Sarah
 Slaves 2   6 00
Burrows, Frederick
 Slave 1   3 00
Burrows, Henry, Trustee
 Slave 1   3 00
Busch, Estate Stephen
 Real Estate......................2,700 37 80
 Stock of Goods 400 5 60 43 40
Busch, J D.
 Real Estate......................1,000 14 00
 Horse 1 10 00
 Dog 1 2 00 26 00
Busé, J. F
 Stock of Goods................500   7 00
Butler, R. M
 Real Estate......................5,000 70 00
 Slaves 4 12 00 82 00
Butler & Bee
 Real Estate......................12,000 168 00
 Stock of Goods................10,000 140 00
 Slave 1 3 00
 Commissions....................7,700 192 50 503 50
Butterfield, H. L.
 Real Estate......................50,000 700 00
 Slaves 4 12 00 712 00
Byrns, Garatt
 Real Estate......................2,000   28 00
Cade, Walter
 Real Estate......................3,000 42 00
 Slave 1 3 00
 Horse 1 10 00 55 00
Cade, Henry L.
 Real Estate......................2,000 28 00
 Dog 1 2 00 30 00
Cadow, McKenzie & Co
 Stock of Goods................62,000 868 00
 Slaves 2 6 00
 Dog 1 2 00 876 00

			TAXES.
Cahill, John			
Real Estate	1,200		16 80
Cain, Dr. D. J			
Dividends	195	4 88	
Slaves	6	18 00	
Carriages	2	40 00	
Income	7,000	175 00	
Horses	3	30 00	
Dog	1	2 00	269 88
Calder, William			
Real Estate	80,000	1,120 00	
Slaves	6	18 00	1,138 00
Calder, Estate James			
Real Estate	11,000	154 00	
Slaves	5	15 00	169 00
Calder, A.			
Slaves	5	15 00	
Carriage	1	20 00	
Horse	1	10 00	45 00
Calderbank, N.			
Real Estate	1,500	21 00	
Interest on Bonds, &c	100	2 50	
Slave	1	3 00	26 50
Caldwell, James M.			
Slaves	12	36 00	
Carriage	1	30 00	
Carriage	1	20 00	
Horses	3	30 00	
Dogs	3	6 00	122 00
Caldwell, Mrs. Ann T.			
Real Estate	9,000		126 00
Caldwell, Blakely & Co.			
Slave	1	3 00	
Commissions	15,123 63	378 01	381 01
Caldwell, Robert			
Real Estate	8,000	112 00	
Horse	1	10 00	122 00
Caldwell & Robinson			
Real Estate	4,000	56 00	
Commissions	23,000	575 00	631 00
Caldwell, R. & A. P & Co.			
Real Estate	17,000	238 00	
Stock of Goods	8,000	112 00	
Interest on Bonds, &c	168	4 20	
Slaves	6	18 00	
Carriage	1	20 00	
Commissions	5,000	125 00	517 20

                                                                    TAXES.

Caldwell, Wm. S.
   Interest on Bonds, &c 140   3 50
Caldwell, John W
   Real Estate 2,200   30 80
   Shipping 16,200   121 50   152 30
Caldwell, John W & Son
   Income 10,000   250 00
Callahan, Wm.
   Real Estate 2,200   30 80
   Stock of Goods 300   4 20
   Slave 1   3 00   38 00
Cambridge, Ann M.
   Real Estate 2,700   37 80
   Slaves 22   66 00   103 80
Cambridge, Ann, Trustee
   Slave 1   ....   3 00
Cambridge, Ann M., Trustee
   Slave 1   ....   3 00
Cameron, George S.
   Real Estate 85,000   .... 1,190 00
Cameron & Co.
   Real Estate 20,000   280 00
   Slave 1   3 00
   Horse 1   10 00   293 00
Cameron, Archibald, Trustee
   Real Estate 4,500   ....   63 00
Cammer, Estate F. S.
   Real Estate 3,000   42 00
Cammer, Estate H. W
   Slaves 4   ....   12 00
Campbell, Ellen
   Real Estate 11,000   154 00
   Slaves 2   6 00   160 00
Campbell, Rev. J B.
   Real Estate 11,000   154 00
   Interest on Bonds, &c 945   23 62
   Slaves 2   6 00
   Dog 1   2 00   185 62
Campbell, W M.
   Stock of Goods 7,000   98 00
   Slave 1   3 00
   Commissions 4,300   107 50   208 50
Campbell, I. M., Trustee
   Slave 1   3 00

			TAXES.
Campbell, Dr. I. M.			
Real Estate	8,000	112 00	
Slaves	11	33 00	
Carriage	1	20 00	
Income	500	12 50	
Horse	1	10 00	
Dog	1	2 00	189 50
Campbell, Wm. L., Trustee			
Slave	1		3 00
Campbell, James B.			
Real Estate	3,000	42 00	
Slaves	6	18 00	
Carriage	1	20 00	
Income	4,000	100 00	
Horse	1	10 00	190 00
Campbell, A.			
Slaves	7	21 00	
Dog	1	2 00	23 00
Campbell, Mary			
Real Estate	2,800		39 20
Campsen, Henry			
Real Estate	3,000	42 00	
Dog	1	2 00	44 00
Campsen, J			
Real Estate	11,000	154 00	
Slaves	3	9 00	
Carriage	1	20 00	
Dogs	2	4 00	187 00
Canalé, A.			
Interest on Bonds, &c	250	6 25	
Slaves	3	9 00	
Commissions	900	22 50	37 75
Candler, Edward			
Income	100		2 50
Cannaday, James			
Real Estate	1,500		21 00
Cannet, Mrs. L. M.			
Slaves	2		6 00
Canning, C.			
Real Estate	3,000	42 00	
Dog	1	2 00	44 00
Cannon, George, Administrator			
Slave	1		3 00
Cannon, Catharine A., Trustee			
Real Estate	1,000		14 00

TAXES.

Cannon, Catharine A.
  Real Estate................1,600   22 40
  Slaves..........................2   6 00   28 40
Cannon, Margaret
  Real Estate................1,500   21 00
  Slave 1   3 00   24 00
Canter, Judith
  Real Estate................1,500   21 00
Canter, D. & J.
  Stock of Goods............3,500   49 00
Cantwell, Mrs. Elizabeth G., Guardian
  Real Estate................3,500   49 00
  Slaves..........................4   12 00   61 00
Capdeville, Mary
  Real Estate................2,500   35 00
  Slave 1   3 00   38 00
Capers, Thos. Farr
  Real Estate...............15,000   210 00
  Slaves........................15   45 00
  Carriage.......................1   30 00
  Carriage.......................1   20 00
  Horses.........................3   30 00
  Dogs...........................2   4 00   339 00
Capers & Heyward
  Commissions................5,000   125 00
Capers, Mrs. M. E.
  Slave 1   3 00
Capers, Wm.
  Slaves.........................2   6 00
Capers, F. W and others, Trustees
  Slaves.........................2   6 00
Capers, Estate Wm.
  Slaves.........................2   6 00
Capp, Geo. W
  Real Estate..................600   8 40
Carberry, John
  Real Estate................4,000   56 00
  Slave 1   3 00   59 00
Carere, Wm. G.
  Slaves.........................2   6 00
Carere, Wm. G. and A. L. Brailsford
  Real Estate 400   5 50
Carere, Estate Charles
  Real Estate................6,000   84 00
  Slaves.........................6   18 00   102 00

			TAXES.
Carere, Wm. G., Trustee			
Real Estate	1,200		16 80
Carere, Eliza F			
Real Estate	7,000	98 00	
Slaves	10	30 00	
Carriage	1	20 00	
Horse	1	10 00	158 00
Carere, Dr. M. E.			
Real Estate	26,900	376 60	
Slaves	4	12 00	
Carriage	1	20 00	
Shipping	5,600	42 00	
Income	4,000	100 00	
Horse	1	10 00	560 60
Carey, E. M.			
Real Estate	10,000	140 00	
Stock of Goods	2,500	35 00	
Slaves	7	21 00	
Carriage	1	20 00	
Horse	1	10 00	
Dog	1	2 00	228 00
Carey, James			
Real Estate	2,000		28 00
Carew, Trust Estate E. W			
Interest on Bonds, &c	642		16 05
Carew, Jno. E.			
Real Estate	6,500	91 00	
Slaves	17	51 00	
Carriage	1	30 00	
Horses	3	30 00	202 00
Carmalt, J. W			
Real Estate	4,500	63 00	
Slave	1	3 00	
Horse	1	10 00	
Dogs	2	4 00	80 00
Carmalt & Briggs			
Stock of Goods	15,000	210 00	
Shipping	1,200	9 00	
Horse	1	10 00	229 00
Carney, Peter			
Real Estate	900		12 60
Carnihan, Jno.			
Real Estate	3,200	44 80	
Slaves	6	18 00	62 80
Carpenter, Maria			
Real Estate	4,000		56 00

TAXES.

Carpenter, Trust Estate Margaret
　Real Estate..........................3,500　　49 00
　Slaves ....2　　 6 00　　55 00
Carr, Charles D.
　Real Estate.....................13,000　　　　　　 182 00
Carr, Charles D. & Co.
　Real Estate.....................13,000　 182 00
　Stock of Goods..................5,000　　70 00
　Slaves..8　　24 00　 276 00
Carr, Charles D., Trustee
　Slaves..2　　　　　　　6 00
Carr, H. W., Trustee
　Slave ....1　　　　　　　3 00
Carr, H. W
　Slave ....1　　　　　　　3 00
Carr, H. W., Agent for Piquet
　Slaves..2　　..........　　6 00
Carrington, Wm.
　Real Estate........................6,000　　84 00
　Slaves..7　　21 00
　Horse ....1　　10 00
　Dog ....1　　 2 00　 117 00
Carrington, Wm. & Co.
　Stock of Goods...................35,000　　　　　　 490 00
Carroll, James
　Real Estate........................5,500　　77 00
　Stock of Goods..................1,500　　21 00　　98 00
Carroll, Trust Estate E. A
　Slaves..9　　27 00
　Carriage ....1　　20 00
　Horses..2　　20 00　　67 00
Carson, Trustees, W A. & J. P.
　Interest on Bonds, &c............3,280　　82 00
　Slave ....1　　 3 00　　85 00
Carson, Mrs. C.
　Interest on Bonds, &c............1,500　　..........　　37 50
Carson, Mrs. Caroline
　Slaves..2　　..........　　6 00
Carsten, Catherine M.
　Real Estate........................7,000　　98 00
　Slave ....1　　 3 00
　Carriage ....1　　20 00
　Horse ....1　　10 00　 131 00

                                              TAXES.
Carsten. Wm. F
    Real Estate..................3,200   44 80
    Slave...........................1   3 00   47 80
Carswell, Dr. Wm. A.
    Slaves..........................7   21 00
Cart, Elizabeth C.
    Real Estate..................7,500   105 00
    Slaves..........................3   9 00   114 00
Cart, Frances G.
    Slave...........................1   3 00
    Carriage........................1   20 00
    Horse...........................1   10 00   33 00
Cart, Eliza and Laura
    Real Estate..................3,000   42 00
    Slave...........................1   3 00   45 00
Carter. A.
    Stock of Goods..............4,000   56 00
Carter, Solern
    Stock of Goods................300   4 20
    Horse...........................1   10 00   14 20
Carter. Nelson
    Stock of Goods.............12,000   168 00
Casey, Rose
    Real Estate..................3,000   ....   42 00
Casey. Jeremiah
    Real Estate....................700   ....   9 80
Casowich, B.
    Stock of Goods................200   ....   2 80
Cassidy, C. R.
    Real Estate..................3,000   42 00
    Slaves..........................2   6 00   48 00
Castamayna, Mrs. F
    Slave...........................1   3 00
Cater, T. M.
    Real Estate..................7,000   98 00
    Stock of Goods..............7,000   98 00
    Slaves..........................5   15 00
    Carriage........................1   20 00
    Commissions................2,000   50 00
    Horses..........................2   20 00
    Dog.............................1   2 00   303 00
4

		TAXES.

Caulier, Dr. Geo.
 Real Estate..................14,000 196 00
 Stock of Goods..................2,000 28 00
 Slaves...................2 6 00
 Carriage..................1 15 00
 Income..................1,000 25 00
 Horse..................1 10 00
 Dog..................1 2 00 282 00

Cay. Miss A.
 Slave..................1 .... 3 00

Cay. Jno. E., Trustee
 Slave..................1 3 00

Chaffee, O. J
 Real Estate..................55,500 777 00
 Interest on Bonds..................4,500 112 50
 Slaves..................6 18 00
 Carriage..................1 30 00
 Horses..................2 20 00
 Dog..................1 2 00 959 50

Chaffee, St. Armand, & Croft
 Stock of Goods..................20,000 280 00
 Slave..................1 3 00 283 00

Chaffee, Mrs. S. A.
 Slaves..................7 21 00

Chaffee & Knauff
 Stock of Goods..................2,000 28 00

Chaffee, Charles H., Trustee
 Slave..................1 3 00

Chalk, Jno. G.
 Real Estate..................6,000 84 00
 Slaves..................6 18 00
 Carriage..................1 20 00
 Horse..................1 10 00
 Dog..................1 2 00 134 00

Chamberlain, Charles V
 Real Estate..................12,000 168 00
 Slaves..................5 15 00
 Dog..................1 2 00 185 00

Chamberlain, Miler, & Co.
 Stock of Goods..................81,000 .... 1,134 00

Chambers, James S.
 Slaves..................5 15 00

Chambers, Jno. W
 Slave..................1 3 00
 Commissions..................1,300 32 50 35 50

			TAXES
Champlin, Samuel			
Dog	1		2 00
Champlin, Virginia			
Real Estate	2,000	28 00	
Slaves	2	6 00	34 00
Chanler, Elizabeth S.			
Slave	1		3 00
Charmer, Catharine E.			
Real Estate	600		8 40
Chapeau, Estate Mary			
Real Estate	18,600	260 40	
Slaves	13	39 00	299 40
Chapeau, Felix F. & Thos. T.			
Slaves	2		6 00
Chapin, Leonard			
Stock of Goods	15,000	210 00	
Horse	1	10 00	
Dog	1	2 00	222 00
Chapman, W H.			
Slaves	9	27 00	
Horse	1	10 00	
Dog	1	2 00	39 00
Chapman, Estate James			
Real Estate	19,000	266 00	
Slaves	19	57 00	
Dividends	490	12 25	
Carriage	1	20 00	
Horse	1	10 00	
Dog	1	2 00	367 25
Chapman, Miss L. C			
Slaves	3		9 00
Chapman, Miss Virginia			
Slaves	3		9 00
Chapman, Samuel			
Real Estate	5,000	70 00	
Slaves	6	18 00	88 00
Chapman, Perry E.			
Real Estate	3,000	42 00	
Slaves	3	9 00	51 00
Chapman, Robt. B.			
Income	1,800	45 00	
Commissions	980	24 50	69 50
Chapman, Miss A.			
Slave	1		3 00

		TAXES.
Chapman, Robert, Executor		
Slaves 4		12 00
Chazal, J. P		
Slaves 5	15 00	
Carriage 1	20 00	
Income 3,500	87 50	
Horse 1	10 00	132 50
Chazal, Estate J. P		
Real Estate 4,000	56 00	
Slaves 6	18 00	74 00
Chazal, J P., Trustee		
Slave 1		3 00
Cheeseborough, John		
Slaves 2		6 00
Cheeseborough, John, Trustee		
Real Estate 9,000	126 00	
Slaves 8	24 00	150 00
Cheney, E. and Wife		
Slaves 6		18 00
Cherrill, Mary Ann		
Stock of Goods 1,800	25 20	
Slaves 2	6 00	31 20
Chew, Thomas R.		
Real Estate 1,700	23 80	
Dog 1	2 00	25 80
Chevieux, Augustus F		
Real Estate 200	....	2 80
Chiffille, Estate Mrs. H. C.		
Slaves 2	....	6 00
Childs, Jane		
Real Estate 3,000	42 00	
Slaves 5	15 00	
Dog 1	2 00	59 00
Chisolm, Mrs. P H.		
Slaves 2	6 00	
Carriage 1	30 00	
Horses 2	20 00	56 00
Chisolm, Robt. T.		
Real Estate 15,000	210 00	
Slaves 3	9 00	
Carriage 1	30 00	
Horses 2	20 00	269 00
Chisolm, Estate J. M.		
Real Estate 10,000	140 00	
Slaves 7	21 00	161 00

			TAXES.
Chisolm, Robert T. and Sons			
Real Estate 75,000	1,050 00		
Slaves 61	183 00		
Horses 2	20 00	1,253 00	
Chisolm, Caspar A.			
Slave 1	3 00		
Carriage 1	20 00		
Horse 1	10 00	33 00	
Chisolm, R. G.			
Interest on Bonds, &c 400	10 00		
Slaves 1	3 00		
Horse 1	10 00	23 00	
Chisolm, Dr. J. J.			
Real Estate 10,000	140 00		
Slaves 5	15 00		
Carriage 1	30 00		
Horses 2	20 00	205 00	
Chisolm, A. H.			
Real Estate 25,000	....	350 00	
Chisolm, H. L.			
Slaves 4		12 00	
Chrietzburg, Mrs. J. C. and children			
Real Estate 8,000	....	112 00	
Chrietzburg, Mrs. Clara			
Real Estate 7,200	100 80		
Slave 1	3 00	103 80	
Christian, Peter			
Real Estate 1,000	....	14 00	
Christianson, Jasper			
Real Estate 10,000	140 00		
Slaves 8	24 00	164 00	
Christie, Ellen C.			
Real Estate 5,500	77 00		
Slaves 2	6 00	83 00	
Christopher, John			
Real Estate 800		11 20	
Chupien, Estate L. Y.			
Real Estate 5,000	70 00		
Interest on Bonds,&c 140	3 50		
Slaves 4	12 00	85 50	
Chupien, Theodore F.			
Real Estate 400	5 60		
Interest on Bonds,&c 140	3 50		
Income 500	12 50	21 60	

			TAXES
Church, J F.			
Real Estate	12,500	175 00	
Stock of Goods	1,500	21 00	
Slaves	3	9 00	
Carriage	1	20 00	
Horse	1	10 00	235 00
Clacius & Witte			
Stock of Goods	9,000		126 00
Clancy, Jno.			
Real Estate	3,000		42 00
Clancy, Mary Ann			
Slaves	3		9 00
Clark, Richard			
Real Estate	5,500	77 00	
Slaves	2	6 00	83 00
Clark, Rob't. A.			
Slaves	5	15 00	
Dog	1	2 00	17 00
Clark, Charles			
Real Estate	3,000	42 00	
Stock of Goods	500	7 00	49 00
Clark, Henry			
Real Estate	18,600	260 40	
Interest on Bonds,&c	700	17 50	
Slaves	18	54 00	
Horse	1	10 00	341 90
Clark, Josephine F			
Slaves	2		6 00
Clark, G. E.			
Stock of Goods	2,000		28 00
Clark, Mary Ann			
Slave	1		3 00
Clark, R. M.			
Slaves	3		9 00
Clark, Mary P			
Slaves	3		9 00
Clarke, D. O.			
Stock of Goods	300	4 20	
Commissions	15	38	4 58
Clarke, Mrs. H. R.			
Slaves	6		18 00
Clarke, J J Pringle			
Interest on Bonds, &c	3,000	75 00	
Slaves	3	9 00	84 00

		TAXES.

Clarkson, R. H.
    Real Estate 3,000   42 00
    Slaves 8   24 00
    Carriage 1   30 00
    Commissions 1,500   37 50
    Horses 2   20 00   153 50

Clausen, J. C. H.
    Real Estate 24,500   343 00
    Slaves 9   27 00
    Carriage 1   20 00
    Horses 3   30 00   420 00

Clausen, John C.
    Stock of Goods 400   5 60

Cleapor, Harriet and Emeline
    Slaves 4   12 00

Cleaper, Charles W., Trustee
    Real Estate 1,200   16 80

Cleary, Estate Catharine
    Slaves 8   24 00

Clement, Estate John
    Real Estate 3,000   42 00

Clement, J. P
    Slaves 6   18 00

Clifford, L. C.
    Real Estate 6,000   84 00
    Slaves 22   66 00
    Carriage 1   30 00
    Horses 2   20 00
    Dog 1   2 00   202 00

Clinton, Margaret W
    Slaves 8   24 00

Close, Anna
    Real Estate 2,500   35 00
    Slaves 1   3 00   38 00

Clotworthy, James
    Stock of Goods 500   7 00

Club, Charleston
    Real Estate 20,000   280 00

Clyde, Mary
    Real Estate 1,200   16 80

Coates, Wm. S.
    Horse 1   10 00
    Dog 1   2 00   12 00

Cobia, F J
    Real Estate 20,500   287 00
    Slaves 8   24 00   311 00

			TAXES.
Cobia. Ann			
Real Estate	1,500	21 00	
Slaves	2	6 00	27 00
Cobia. Henry			
Real Estate	13,500	189 00	
Interest on Bonds, &c	200	5 00	
Slaves	15	45 00	
Carriage	1	30 00	
Horses	2	20 00	
Dog	1	2 00	291 00
Cobia. Henry & Co.			
Real Estate	20,000	280 00	
Stock of Goods	23,000	322 00	
Slave	1	3 00	
Shipping	11,000	82 50	
Commissions	12,000	300 00	987 50
Cobia. Mary			
Real Estate	3,000	42 00	
Slaves	6	18 00	50 00
Cobia. Estate Ann			
Real Estate	800	11 20	
Slaves	4	12 00	23 20
Cobia. Sarah			
Real Estate	2,500	35 00	
Slaves	7	21 00	56 00
Cobia. Miss M. J.			
Interest on Bonds, &c	400	10 00	
Slaves	3	9 00	19 00
Coburn. P. K.			
Real Estate	3,500		49 00
Coburn. P. K., Trustee S. and wife			
Real Estate	8,500	119 00	
Slave	1	3 00	122 00
Cochran. C. B.			
Real Estate	5,000	70 00	
Interest on Bonds, &c	1,200	30 00	
Slaves	11	33 00	
Dog	1	2 00	135 00
Cochran. John C., in trust Mrs. J. J. Payne			
Real Estate	8,500		119 00
Cochran. John C.			
Real Estate	6,500	91 00	
Slaves	5	15 00	
Carriage	1	30 00	
Horses	2	20 00	
Dog	1	2 00	158 00

		TAXES.
Cochran, J. C. and Thomas R. Waring, in trust		
Slaves...................2		6 00
Coffin, Dr. A.		
Slave...................1		3 00
Coffin, G. M., Trustee W P Ravenel		
Slave...................1		3 00
Coffin, G. M., Trustee Anna M. Missroon		
Slaves...................4		12 00
Coffin, G. M., Trustee Miss Huger		
Interest on Bonds, &c...........232		5 80
Coffin, G. M., Trustee Miss M. L. Pinckney		
Slave...................1		3 00
Coffin, G. M., Trustee of H. Missroon's children		
Interest on Bonds, &c...........2,790		69 75
Coffin, G. M., Trustee Mrs. Holmes and Miss Thayer		
Interest on Bonds, &c...........1,082		27 05
Coffin, G. M., Trustee Mrs. Mary S. Peronneau		
Real Estate...........8,000	112 00	
Slaves...........5	15 00	
Dog...........1	2 00	129 00
Coffin, G. M., Trustee M. W Perenneau		
Interest on Bonds, &c...........160	4 00	
Slaves...........8	24 00	
Carriage...........1	20 00	
Dog...........1	2 00	50 00
Coffin, G. M.		
Real Estate...........8,000	112 00	
Slaves...........5	15 00	
Dog...........1	2 00	129 00
Coffin & Pringle		
Income...........15,193		379 83
Cogdell, R. W		
Real Estate...........4,500		63 00
Cogswell, Harvey		
Slaves...........2		6 00
Cogswell, Esther S.		
Interest on Bonds, &c...........500	12 50	
Slaves...........4	12 00	24 50
Cohen, J. S.		
Real Estate...........10,000	140 00	
Interest on Bonds, &c...........1,150	28 75	
Dividends...........300	7 50	
Slaves...........4	12 00	188 25
Cohen, Rinah S.		
Slaves...........2		6 00

			TAXES
Cohen. Estate S. J.			
Real Estate	15.400	215 60	
Interest on Bonds, &c	35	88	
Slaves	3	9 00	225 48
Cohen, Jacob			
Real Estate	4,000	56 00	
Slaves	15	45 00	
Carriage	1	20 00	
Horse	1	10 00	
Dog	1	2 00	133 00
Cohen. David D.			
Real Estate	24.500	343 00	
Slaves	5	15 00	
Carriage	1	20 00	
Horse	1	10 00	388 00
Cohen. Jacob & Son			
Commissions	2.500		62 50
Cohen. Joseph			
Real Estate	18.000		252 00
Cohen. Deborah H. and children			
Slaves	2		6 00
Cohen, J. Barrett. Trustee			
Real Estate	2.000		28 00
Cohen. P M., Attorney for C. M. Cohen			
Stock of Goods	1,000	14 00	
Slave	1	3 00	17 00
Cohen. P M., Trustee			
Real Estate	16.000		224 00
Cohen. Israel. Trustee			
Real Estate	1.200		16 80
Cohen. Mary E.			
Real Estate	14.200	198 80	
Slaves	5	15 00	
Carriage	1	30 00	
Horses	2	20 00	263 80
Cohen. P M., Trustee			
Slave	1		3 00
Cohen. Bella			
Slaves	3		9 00
Cohen. Mrs. M. L.			
Real Estate	5,000	70 00	
Slaves	5	15 00	85 00
Cohen. Mrs. H.			
Stock of Goods	150		2 10

			TAXES.
Cohen, Esther			
Slaves	7		21 00
Cohen, Louis			
Interest on Bonds, &c	2,500	62 50	
Slaves	2	6 00	68 50
Cohen, Isaac B., Trustee			
Slave	1		3 00
Cohen, John J.			
Real Estate	5,000	70 00	
Slaves	3	9 00	79 00
Cohen, Assigned Estate A. N., Jr.			
Real Estate	1,400		19 60
Cohrs, C. H.			
Slave	1		3 00
Cohrs, C. H., Trustee			
Slave	1		3 00
Colburn, J H.			
Slave	1		3 00
Colburn, Estate James S.			
Real Estate	13,200	184 80	
Slaves	9	27 00	211 80
Colburn, A. A.			
Real Estate	18,000	252 00	
Slaves	8	24 00	
Carriage	1	30 00	
Horses	2	20 00	326 00
Colcolough, James			
Horse	1		10 00
Colcock, Estate W H.			
Slaves	2		6 00
Colcock, W F.			
Slaves	24	72 00	
Carriage	1	30 00	
Horses	3	30 00	
Dogs	2	4 00	136 00
Colcock, R. H.			
Slaves	2	6 00	
Carriage	1	20 00	26 00
Colcock, C. J.			
Real Estate	10,000	140 00	
Interest on Bonds, &c	70	1 75	
Slaves	5	15 00	
Carriage	1	30 00	
Commissions	8,000	200 00	
Horses	2	20 00	
Dog	1	2 00	408 75

TAXES.

Colcock, Charles J., Trustee
 Interest on Bonds, &c...............70 1 75
 Slaves...............................2 6 00 7 75
Colcock, John
 Real Estate.....................8,000 112 00
 Slaves...............................4 12 00 124 00
Colcock, John, Trustee
 Slaves...............................3   9 00
Cole, George F.
 Real Estate.....................16,000 224 00
 Stock of Goods.................1,500 21 00
 Slaves...............................2 6 00 251 00
Coleman, Elizabeth
 Real Estate.....................2,000 28 00
 Slaves...............................1 3 00 31 00
Collins, P
 Real Estate.....................3,250   45 50
Collins, Patrick
 Real Estate.....................8,300   116 20
Collins, Edward
 Real Estate.....................5,100 71 40
 Dog..................................1 2 00 73 40
Colman, G. & J.
 Stock of Goods.................5,000   70 00
Colson, Charles
 Real Estate.....................12,100 169 40
 Stock of Goods.................4,550 63 70
 Slaves...............................6 18 00
 Carriage.............................1 20 00
 Horse................................1 10 00
 Dog..................................1 2 00 283 10
Company, Charleston Insurance & Trust
 Real Estate..................10,000 00 140 00
 Premiums of Insurance......86,192 88 1,077 41 1,217 41
Company, Charleston Floating Dry Dock & M. R.
 Real Estate.....................72,000   1,000 08
Company, New York Life Insurance, "Martin"
 Premiums of Insurance..........3,166   39 58
Company, Unity Fire Insurance
 Premiums of Insurance.........14,679   183 49
Company, Hampden Fire Insurance
 Premiums of Insurance............403   5 04
Company, North American Fire Insurance
 Premiums of Insurance..........1,421   17 76

	TAXES.
Company, Hartford Fire Insurance	
Premiums of Insurance 4,547	56 84
Company, N. E. Mutual Life Insurance	
Premiums of Insurance 1,167	14 59
Company, Ætna Insurance	
Premiums of Insurance 7,174	89 68
Company, Ætna Life Insurance	
Premiums of Insurance 1,147	14 34
Company, Connecticut Fire Insurance	
Premiums of Insurance 1,400	17 50
Company, Irving Fire Insurance	
Premiums of Insurance.............92	1 15
Company, Massasoit Insurance	
Premiums of Insurance............670	8 38
Company, Washington Fire Insurance	
Premiums of Insurance............725	9 06
Company, American Temperance Life Insurance	
Premiums of Insurance............650	8 13
Company, Resolute Fire Insurance	
Premiums of Insurance............540	6 75
Company, Northern Assurance	
Premiums of Insurance :.........3,300	41 25
Company, New York Life Insurance, "Taylor,"	
Premiums of Insurance 2,770	34 63
Company, British Commercial Life Insurance	
Premiums of Insurance 2,360	29 50
Company, North American Insurance	
Premiums of Insurance 1,120	15 25
Company, The Home Fire Insurance	
Premiums of Insurance 13,250	165 63
Company, Charleston Gas Light	
Capital Stock....................755,700	3,778 50
Company, Valley of Virginia	
Premiums of Insurance............ 972	12 15
Company, Augusta Insurance and Banking	
Premiums of Insurance 21,634	270 43
Company, Lorillard Fire Insurance	
Premiums of Insurance............419	5 24
Company, Royal Insurance	
Premiums of Insurance 15,500	193 75
Company, The Market Fire Insurance	
Premiums of Insurance 1,363	17 04
Company, Mercantile Fire Insurance	
Premiums of Insurance............770	9 63

	TAXES.
Company, The Lamar Insurance Premiums of Insurance 2,800	35 00
Company, Continental Insurance Premiums of Insurance 3,463	43 29
Company, The Springfield Premiums of Insurance 2,850	35 63
Company, The Hanover Insurance Premiums of Insurance............203	2 54
Company, Charter Oak Fire Insurance Premiums of Insurance............430	5 38
Company, Commercial Fire Insurance Premiums of Insurance............500	6 25
Company, The Merchants' Insurance Premiums of Insurance 1,640	20 50
Company, The Goodhue Fire Insurance Premiums of Insurance 710	8 88
Company, Phœnix Fire Insurance Premiums of Insurance.........1,200	15 00
Company, North Carolina Mutual Insurance Premiums of Insurance.........4,812	60 15
Company, Manhattan Life Insurance Premiums of Insurance 2,514	31 43
Company, City Fire Insurance Premiums of Insurance 1,374	17 18
Company, Southern Mutual Insurance Premiums of Insurance 19,427	242 84
Company, Southern Mutual Life Insurance Premiums of Insurance..........9,162	114 53
Company, Union Cotton Press Slaves......................................9	27 00
Company, Phœnix Insurance Premiums of Insurance......2,656 82	33 21
Company, Park Fire Insurance Premiums of Insurance.......436 51	5 46
Company, Humboldt Fire Insurance Premiums of Insurance.......333 58	4 17
Company, Fulton Fire Insurance Premiums of Insurance........332 37	4 15
Company, Liverpool and London Fire and Life Insurance Premiums of Insurance.........11,369	142 11
Company, N. E. Fire and Marine Insurance Premiums of Insurance........608 67	7 61
Company, Metropolitan Fire Insurance Premiums of Insurance 5,250	65 63

			TAXES.
Company, Security Insurance			
Premiums of Insurance..........3,975			49 69
Company, Adams Express			
Income.....................................4,007		100 18	
Horses..5		50 00	150 18
Company, South Carolina Cordage			
Real Estate.........................4,000			56 00
Company, South Carolina Insurance			
Real Estate..........................6,000		84 00	
Premiums of Insurance........70,560		882 00	966 00
Company, Fireman's Insurance			
Premiums of Insurance..........66,000		....	825 00
Company, Hazard Powder			
Stock of Goods...................4,835			67 69
Company, Cannonsboro' Wharf and Mill			
Real Estate.........................40,000		....	560 00
Company, Railroad Accommodation Wharf			
Real Estate.......................125,000		1,750 00	
Slaves..................................4		12 00	1,762 00
Comstock, D. B.			
Real Estate..........................2,500		35 00	
Slaves..................................6		18 00	
Horse..................................1		10 00	63 00
Condy, Estate Thomas D.			
Real Estate.........................18,200		254 80	
Slaves..................................2		6 00	260 80
Cone, Edward T.			
Stock of Goods 700		9 80	
Horse.................................. 1		10 00	19 80
Conner, George			
Stock of Goods........................500			7 00
Conner, H. W			
Real Estate.........................44,000		616 00	
Slaves..................................7		21 00	
Carriage..............................1		30 00	
Horses.................................2		20 00	687 00
Conner, H. W & Co.			
Commissions.....................8,500			212 50
Conner, James			
Income.............................2,500			62 50
Connor, Margaret			
Real Estate........................1,500		21 00	
Slave..................................1		3 00	24 00

                                                                    TAXES.

Coogan, P J
    Real Estate........................17,000   238 00
    Slave......................................1   3 00   241 00
Cook, Augustus
    Stock of Goods....................2,000   28 00
Cook, Mary E.
    Real Estate.........................5,000   70 00
    Slave......................................1   3 00   73 00
Cook, John A.
    Real Estate........................33,200   464 80
    Stock of Goods....................5,500   77 00
    Slaves...................................13   39 00   580 80
Cook, T. A.
    Slave......................................1   ....   3 00
Cook, G. S.
    Slave......................................1   3 00
    Carriage..................................1   20 00
    Horse......................................1   10 00   33 00
Cook, Francis
    Real Estate...........................600   ....   6 80
Cooke, Mary L.
    Slaves.....................................2   ....   6 00
Cooper, Mary
    Real Estate........................10,000   140 00
    Slaves.....................................4   12 00
    Carriage..................................1   20 00
    Horse......................................1   10 00   182 00
Cooper, Estate N.
    Real Estate........................12,500   175 00
    Slaves...................................12   36 00   211 00
Cooper, Assignee Estate G. W
    Real Estate.........................1,200   ....   16 80
Copes, James
    Real Estate........................69,800   977 20
    Slaves...................................22   66 00
    Horses....................................6   60 00   1,103 20
Copes, James, Trustee
    Real Estate...........................600   8 40
Corbett, Mary
    Slaves.....................................3   ....   9 00
Corbett, Louisa C. W
    Slaves...................................19   ....   57 00
Corbett, J N.
    Stock of Goods....................3,000   42 00

		TAXES.
Corbett, Estate John H.		
Slaves 4		12 00
Corbett, W B.		
Slaves 3		9 00
Corbett, John		
Real Estate..........5,200		72 80
Corcoran, James		
Real Estate..........2,500		35 00
Corcoran, T. D.		
Real Estate..........3,500	49 00	
Slaves 2	6 00	
Dog......................1	2 00	57 00
Corcoran, Thos.		
Real Estate..........1,500		21 00
Cordes, Geo.		
Stock of Goods......500	7 00	
Slaves 2	6 00	
Dog......................1	2 00	15 00
Cordes, Mrs. M. L.		
Slave....................1		3 00
Cordes, Theodore		
Real Estate..........3,000	42 00	
Stock of Goods...12,000	168 00	
Slaves 5	15 00	
Dog......................1	2 00	227 00
Cordova, M.		
Stock of Goods......100		1 40
Cordray, L. E.		
Slave....................1		3 00
Cordray, L. E., Trustee		
Slave....................1		3 00
Cordray's children, Thomas		
Real Estate..........4,000	56 00	
Slave....................1	3 00	59 00
Corkle, Catharine		
Slaves 2		6 00
Corrigan, Peter M.		
Stock of Goods....2,000	28 00	
Dog......................1	2 00	30 00
Cosgrove, James		
Horse...................1		10 00
Costa, Mrs. V		
Real Estate..........3,000	42 00	
Stock of Goods......200	2 80	
Slave....................1	3 00	47 80

5

		TAXES.
Costa, L.		
Real Estate...........................900		12 60
Costello, Daniel		
Stock of Goods........................200		2 80
Costello, Thomas		
Real Estate........................2,000		28 00
Coster, Estate J G.		
Real Estate.......................15,000		210 00
Coté, E.		
Stock of Goods..................10,100		141 40
Cothran, Jeffers & Co.		
Commissions......................3,122	78 05	
Horse 1	10 00	88 05
Courtenay, S. G.		
Real Estate.......................20,500		287 00
Courtenay, S. G. & Co.		
Stock of Goods...................18,000		252 00
Courtney, W C.		
Real Estate.......................14,000	196 00	
Slaves 3	9 00	205 00
Courtney, W C., Trustee		
Dividends............................243		608 00
Courtney & Tennent		
Real Estate.......................18,000	252 00	
Stock of Goods..................65,000	910 00	1,162 00
Courtney, John L.		
Real Estate 600		8 40
Covert, Sarah C.		
Real Estate........................3,700	....	51 80
Covert, Thomas W		
Slaves 3		9 00
Coward, Jesse J.		
Slaves 2		6 00
Coward, Estate James		
Slaves 3		9 00
Cowperthwait, E. R.		
Real Estate.......................12,000	168 00	
Stock of Goods....................9,000	126 00	
Slave 1	3 00	297 00
Cox, A. M.		
Slaves 4	....	12 00
Crafts, Margaret		
Slaves 9	....	27 00

			TAXES.

Crafts, George I.
 Slaves 13 39 00
 Carriage 1 20 00
 Horses.................................2 20 00 79 00

Crane, Boylston & Co.
 Stock of Goods................137,137 .... 1,919 91

Crane, J G.
 Real Estate.........................3,000 .... 42 00

Crandall, Estate Ann
 Real Estate..........................1,000 .... 14 00

Cranston, H.
 Real Estate.........................5,000 70 00
 Slaves 4 12 00 82 00

Creighton, John McP
 Slaves 12 36 00
 Carriage 1 30 00
 Horses.................................2 20 00
 Dog 1 2 00 88 00

Creighton, Ann
 Real Estate.........................8,000 112 00
 Interest on Bonds, &c...........5,096 127 40
 Slaves 30 90 00
 Carriage 1 30 00
 Horses.................................2 20 00 379 40

Crews, A. J
 Real Estate........................10,000 140 00
 Slaves 2 6 00
 Carriage 1 20 00
 Horse 1 10 00
 Dog 1 2 00 178 00

Crews, J. M., in trust for children
 Real Estate.........................1,600 22 40
 Dog 1 2 00 24 40

Cripps, Annie and Charlotte
 Real Estate.........................4,500 63 00
 Dog 1 2 00 65 00

Cripps, Annie
 Slaves 5   15 00

Cromley, C.
 Slaves 2   6 00

Cromwell, S. T.
 Real Estate.........................14,000 196 00
 Slave 1 3 00 199 00

Crook, Mrs. L. F.
 Real Estate.........................1,000 .... 14 00

			TAXES.

Cross, William
 Real Estate..........................2,500   35 00

Cross, M. W
 Slaves 7   21 00
 Dog......................................1   2 00   23 00

Cross, H. B.
 Slaves..................................3   9 00

Cross, M. W and brother
 Slaves..................................2   6 00

Crouch, Mrs. E. I. and children
 Real Estate..........................9,000   126 00
 Slaves................................12   36 00   162 00

Crow, Estate Mrs. M. B.
 Real Estate..........................2,200   ....   30 80

Cruikshanks, Estate Mary
 Real Estate..........................23,000   322 00

Cruikshanks, Estate William
 Real Estate..........................22,000   ....   308 00

Cruikshanks, Estate Samuel
 Real Estate..........................30,000   420 00
 Slaves..................................2   6 00   426 00

Cudworth, E. M.
 Real Estate..........................2,000   28 00

Cudworth, Catharine
 Real Estate..........................1,000   ....   14 00

Culbert, Estate John
 Real Estate..........................1,500   ....   21 00

Cullinane, P
 Stock of Goods 1,000   14 00

Culliton, N.
 Real Estate..........................5,500   77 00
 Slaves..................................2   6 00   83 00

Cummings, Thomas J
 Real Estate..........................3,000   42 00

Cummings, Margaret H.
 Real Estate..........................2,000   ....   28 00

Cummings, J. C.
 Real Estate..........................1,000   14 00

Cunningham, Andrew
 Real Estate..........................24,500   343 00
 Slaves................................14   42 00
 Carriage..............................1   20 00
 Horses.................................2   20 00
 Dog......................................1   2 00   427 00

		TAXES.
Cunningham, Rev. H. B.		
Slaves....................3		9 00
Cunningham, Estate R. M.		
Slaves....................8		24 00
Cunningham, Mrs. Ann		
Real Estate..........7,500	105 00	
Slaves....................7	21 00	126 00
Cunningham, George L.		
Horse....................1		10 00
Cunningham, John		
Slaves....................7	21 00	
Carriage.................1	20 00	
Dog......................1	2 00	43 00
Currant, E.		
Stock of Goods......5,000		70 00
Currie, John		
Stock of Goods......4,000		56 00
Curtis, James M.		
Real Estate..........5,000	70 00	
Slaves....................3	9 00	79 00
Curtis, Mrs. J. L.		
Real Estate..........3,000	42 00	
Slaves....................2	6 00	48 00
Curtis, Mary		
Real Estate..........1,600		22 40
Curtis, Mrs. Ann		
Real Estate..........4,000	....	56 00
Curtis, Dr. Thomas		
Slaves....................4		12 00
Curtis, Estate William		
Real Estate.........15,000		210 00
Cuthbert, Misses		
Interest on Bonds, &c....2,500	62 50	
Slaves....................2	6 00	68 50
Cuthbert, Lucius, Sen.		
Slaves....................2		6 00
Cuthbert, L.		
Slave....................1		3 00
Cuttino, Caroline		
Slave....................1		3 00
Cuyler, E. P		
Stock of Goods......6,000	84 00	
Slave....................1	3 00	
Carriage.................1	20 00	
Horse....................1	10 00	117 00

		TAXES.
Daggett, William L., Trustee		
Real Estate............1,500		21 00
Daggett, William L., Agent		
Real Estate............1,200	16 80	
Slave 1	3 00	19 80
Dail, E.		
Real Estate............1,500	21 00	
Dog............................1	2 00	23 00
Dallas, William		
Real Estate............2,800	39 20	
Dog............................1	2 00	41 20
Daly, Estate John		
Real Estate............9,000	126 00	
Slaves........................2	6 00	132 00
Daly, Edward		
Stock of Goods......10,000	140 00	
Carriage....................1	20 00	
Horse 1	10 00	
Dog............................1	2 00	172 00
Dangerfield, James, Trustee		
Slaves........................3		9 00
Darcy, Thomas		
Real Estate............3,100		43 40
Darrell, N. W		
Real Estate............10,000	140 00	
Slaves........................6	18 00	
Carriage....................1	20 00	
Horse 1	10 00	
Dog............................1	2 00	190 00
Davant, C. E., Trustee		
Slave..........................1		3 00
Davega, Isaac		
Real Estate............13,100		183 40
Davega, Mrs. G. J.		
Slaves........................2		6 00
Davega & Tobias		
Income....................1,200	....	30 00
Davega, Dr. C.		
Real Estate............2,000	28 00	
Carriage....................1	20 00	
Income.....................500	12 50	
Dogs..........................2	4 00	64 50
Davega & Chrietzberg		
Income.....................300	....	7 50

                                                                    TAXES.
David, R. L.
    Stock of Goods 3,000   42 00
    Slave....................................1   3 00   45 00
David & Epstein
    Stock of Goods..................3,000   42 00
Davidson, Thomas
    Slaves..................................2   6 00
Davidson, William
    Slaves..................................12   36 00
    Carriage...............................1   20 00
    Horse...................................1   10 00   66 00
Davie, Mrs. F
    Slaves..................................9   27 00
Davies, John S.
    Interest on Bonds, &c..............700   17 50
Davis, Amanda R.
    Slaves..................................6   18 00
Davis, Martha
    Real Estate.........................3,000   42 00
Davis, John
    Real Estate.........................5,000   70 00
Davis, D. W
    Real Estate.........................1,200   16 80
Davis, Zimmerman
    Interest on Bonds, &c..........946 63   23 66
    Slaves..................................5   15 00
    Dog......................................1   2 00   40 66
Davis, Mary Ann
    Real Estate.........................1,300   18 20
Davis, Estate Jacob
    Real Estate.........................1,800   25 20
Davis, Isaac B.
    Income..............................1,000   25 00
Davis, Isaac
    Real Estate.........................5,000   70 00
    Slaves..................................7   21 00
    Dog......................................1   2 00   93 00
Davis, R. C. & J.
    Shipping..........................25,300   189 75
Davis, W K., Trustee
    Slaves..................................6   18 00
    Dog......................................1   2 00   20 00
Davis, Geo. W
    Slaves..................................2   6 00

			TAXES.

Davis, Geo. Y.
    Slave........1........3 00
    Income........1,000........25 00........28 00
Davis, R. C.
    Slaves........8........24 00
    Carriage........1........15 00
    Horse........1........10 00........49 00
Davis, Jane
    Slaves........10........30 00
Dawson, the Misses
    Real Estate........5,500........77 00
    Slave........1........3 00........80 00
Dawson, T. O.
    Slaves........5........15 00
Dawson, Job
    Real Estate........3,500........49 00
    Slave........1........3 00........52 00
Dawson, E. J
    Real Estate........18,000........252 00
Dawson, Margaret A.
    Slaves........6........18 00
Dawson, Carolina
    Real Estate........4,500........63 00
    Slaves........9........27 00
    Dog........1........2 00........92 00
Dawson, A. V
    Real Estate........22,600........316 40
    Slaves........12........36 00
    Carriage........1........30 00
    Horses........2........20 00
    Dogs........2........4 00........406 40
Dawson & Blackman
    Real Estate........10,000........140 00
    Stock of Goods........4,000........56 00........196 00
Dawson, Joseph
    Real Estate........3,000........42 00
    Slaves........5........15 00
    Dog........1........2 00........59 00
Dawson, Dr. J. L.
    Real Estate........9,500........133 00
    Slaves........21........63 00
    Carriage........1........30 00
    Carriage........1........15 00
    Income........5,000........125 00
    Horses........3........30 00
    Dog........1........2 00........398 00

			TAXES.
Dawson, J. & F.			
Real Estate	22,100	309 40	
Stock of Goods	7,000	98 00	
Slaves	2	6 00	
Commissions	500	12 50	425 90
Dawson, Dr. J. E.			
Real Estate	6,425	89 95	
Slave	1	3 00	92 95
Dawson, Miss E. H.			
Slaves	6		18 00
Deas, E. A.			
Slaves	22		66 00
Deas, Trustee of Dr. and wife			
Real Estate	10,000		140 00
Deas, Miss A. O. H.			
Slaves	2		6 00
Deas, Miss S. T.			
Slaves	3		9 00
Deas, John			
Slave	1		3 00
Deas, Miss M. K.			
Interest on Bonds, &c	735	18 38	
Slave	1	3 00	21 38
Deas, children Thomas H.			
Slaves	18		54 00
Deckhoff, C., Trustee			
Slaves	2		6 00
De Cottes, Mrs. Alphonse			
Slaves	8		24 00
Deery, B.			
Real Estate	3,500	49 00	
Stock of Goods	500	7 00	56 00
De Hay. R. H.			
Slaves	4		12 00
Dehon, William			
Real Estate	14,000	196 00	
Interest on Bonds, &c	850	21 25	
Slaves	6	18 00	
Carriage	1	30 00	
Horses	2	20 00	
Dog	1	2 00	287 25
Dehon, Estate Sarah			
Real Estate	1,200		16 80
Deighen, John			
Real Estate	7,000	98 00	
Carriage	1	20 00	118 00

			TAXES.
Deignan, Charles			
Shipping	1,500		11 25
Deignan, Francis			
Real Estate	3,000	42 00	
Slaves	2	6 00	48 00
Deignan & Roberts			
Shipping	800		6 00
De Jongh, William F			
Real Estate	400		5 60
Delaporte, A.			
Horse	1		10 00
Deleon, H. H.			
Slave	1	3 00	
Commissions	4,738	118 45	121 45
De Lorme, William M., Trustee			
Slaves	3		9 00
Denaux, Thomas C.			
Slaves	2	6 00	
Dog	1	2 00	8 00
De Pass, S. C.			
Carriage	1	20 00	
Horse	1	10 00	30 00
Depository, Methodist Book			
Stock of Goods	9,000		126 00
Derwort, William H. H.			
Dog	1		2 00
De Saussure, H. A.			
Real Estate	17,000	238 00	
Interest on Bonds, &c	2,000	50 00	
Slaves	10	30 00	
Carriage	1	30 00	
Income	1,200	30 00	
Horses	2	20 00	398 00
De Saussure, Wilmot G.			
Real Estate	5,000	70 00	
Interest on Bonds, &c	61	1 53	
Slaves	4	12 00	
Carriage	1	30 00	
Horse	1	10 00	
Dog	1	2 00	125 53
De Saussure, C. A.			
Real Estate	5,000	70 00	
Slaves	5	15 00	
Commissions	2,500	62 50	
Dog	1	2 00	149 50

			TAXES.
De Saussure, Louis D.			
Real Estate	12,000	168 00	
Interest on Bonds, &c	2,718	67 95	
Slaves	9	27 00	
Carriage	1	30 00	
Commissions	10,988	274 58	
Horse	1	10 00	
Dog	1	2 00	579 53
De Saussure, Dr. H. W			
Real Estate	8,000 00	112 00	
Interest on Bonds, &c	114 24	2 86	
Slaves	14	42 00	
Carriage	1	20 00	
Income	3,500	87 50	
Horses	2	20 00	284 36
Desebrock, H.			
Stock of Goods	300		4 20
Desel, Estate C. L.			
Real Estate	11,000	154 00	
Slaves	18	54 00	
Carriage	1	30 00	
Horses	2	20 00	258 00
De Treville, Richard			
Real Estate	15,000	210 00	
Interest on Bonds, &c	800	20 00	
Slaves	7	21 00	
Income	1,500	37 50	288 50
De Treville, Robert			
Dog	1		2 00
De Veaux, J P			
Slaves	9	27 00	
Carriage	1	30 00	
Commissions	4,400	110 00	
Horses	2	20 00	
Dog	1	2 00	189 00
De Veaux, J. P., Jr.			
Slave	1		3 00
Devereux, N. & Son			
Real Estate	3,000	42 00	
Horse	1	10 00	52 00
Devereux & Egan			
Real Estate	2,800	39 20	
Slave	1	3 00	
Horse	1	10 00	52 20
De Vineau, E.			
Real Estate	8,500		119 00

			TAXES.
De Vineau, Elizabeth			
Slaves	3		9 00
Dewar, Estate William S.			
Real Estate	4,500	63 00	
Slave	1	3 00	66 00
Dewees, Thomas H.			
Real Estate	34,900	488 60	
Stock of Goods	8,000	112 00	600 60
Dewees, William			
Horse	1		10 00
Dewees, John			
Slaves	18	54 00	
Carriage	1	20 00	
Horse	1	10 00	84 00
Dewing, Hiram			
Slave	1	3 00	
Carriage	1	20 00	
Horse	1	10 00	33 00
Dewing & Thayer,			
Real Estate	18,000	....	252 00
De Witt, G.			
Stock of Goods	13,000	182 00	
Horse	1	10 00	192 00
Dibble, P V			
Stock of Goods	3,100	43 40	
Slave	1	3 00	
Dog	1	2 00	48 40
Dibble, Henrietta M.			
Real Estate	6,000	84 00	
Interest on Bonds, &c	182	4 55	
Slaves	7	21 00	
Dog	1	2 00	111 55
Dick, Mary J.			
Slave	1		3 00
Dickinson, Rachel			
Slaves	3	....	9 00
Dickson, Dr. S. H.			
Real Estate	8,000	112 00	
Slaves	4	12 00	124 00
Dieckhoff, C.			
Real Estate	14,100	197 40	
Stock of Goods	600	8 40	
Slaves	2	6 00	
Dog	1	2 00	213 80

			TAXES
Dieckhoff, C., Trustee			
Slaves	2		6 00
Diefenbach, C.			
Slaves	2		6 00
Diersen, William			
Real Estate	6,600	92 40	
Dog	1	2 00	94 40
Dierson, H. C.			
Stock of Goods	1,500		21 00
Dill, Joseph T.			
Real Estate	8,000	112 00	
Slaves	6	18 00	
Carriage	1	20 00	
Carriage	1	15 00	
Commissions	3,700	92 50	
Horse	1	10 00	
Dogs	2	4 00	271 50
Dingle, G. W			
Real Estate	15,000	210 00	
Slaves	2	6 00	216 00
Dingle, G. W., Trustee of Calder and children			
Real Estate	8,000		112 00
Disher, Robert W			
Real Estate	29,500	413 00	
Slaves	31	93 00	
Carriage	1	20 00	
Shipping	2,500	18 75	
Horses	4	40 00	584 75
Divine, Thomas			
Real Estate	6,000		84 00
Dixon, Thomas			
Slaves	12	36 00	
Dogs	2	4 00	40 00
Doar, Mrs. M. A.			
Slaves	3	9 00	
Dog	1	2 00	11 00
Doar, Estate C. M.			
Slaves	6		18 00
Doar, S. D.			
Real Estate	14,000	196 00	
Slaves	13	39 00	
Carriage	1	30 00	
Horses	2	20 00	285 00
Dobson, Estate O. L.			
Real Estate	24,000	336 00	
Slaves	3	9 00	345 00

		TAXES.
Dobson, Mrs. N. R.		
Real Estate..................7,000	98 00	
Slave.............................1	3 00	
Carriage.........................1	20 00	
Horse............................1	10 00	131 00
Dodge, William F.		
Stock of Goods..............950	13 00	
Commissions..................400	10 00	23 00
Doniphan, Elizabeth		
Slaves............................8		24 00
Doogan, Patrick		
Real Estate..................8,700	121 80	
Slaves............................2	6 00	
Dog..............................1	2 00	129 80
Dooley, Bridget, Trustee		
Real Estate..................1,000		14 00
Doran, William		
Real Estate..................4,000	56 00	
Slaves............................2	6 00	
Carriage.........................1	20 00	
Horse............................1	10 00	92 00
Dorbaum & Menke		
Stock of Goods..............600		8 40
Dorre, H.		
Real Estate.................22,000	308 00	
Stock of Goods..............400	5 60	
Dog..............................1	2 00	315 60
Dorrill, A.		
Real Estate..................2,800	39 20	
Slaves............................3	9 00	48 20
Doscher, John		
Stock of Goods..............300		4 20
Dothage, J		
Stock of Goods............1,000	14 00	
Slaves............................4	12 00	26 00
Dotterer, Thomas D.		
Slaves............................3	9 00	
Dog..............................1	2 00	11 00
Dotterer, Mary		
Real Estate..................8,000	112 00	
Interest on Bonds, &c.....1,000	25 00	
Slaves...........................12	36 00	
Carriage.........................1	30 00	
Horses...........................2	20 00	
Dog..............................1	2 00	225 00

		TAXES.
Dougherty, Estate John		
Real Estate.....17,300		242 20
Dougherty, Margaret		
Slaves.....5		15 00
Dougherty, Mary		
Slaves.....5		15 00
Dougherty, John		
Real Estate.....25,000	350 00	
Stock of Goods.....1,200	16 80	
Slaves.....7	21 00	
Shipping.....500	3 75	
Horse.....1	10 00	
Dog.....1	2 00	403 55
Douglass, Walter		
Real Estate.....3,000		42 00
Douglass, R. & Co.		
Real Estate.....22,500	315 00	
Slaves.....14	42 00	357 00
Douglass, M. Josephine		
Slaves.....14	....	42 00
Douglass, Caroline M. C.		
Slaves.....2		6 00
Dowd, Martin		
Real Estate.....12,000	168 00	
Slave.....1	3 00	171 00
Doyle, James		
Real Estate.....2,500		35 00
Doyle, John		
Real Estate.....2,000	....	28 00
Drago, Andrew		
Stock of Goods.....300		4 20
Drake & Moses		
Commissions.....2,500		75 00
Drake, C. C.		
Stock of Goods.....8,000		112 00
Drayton, Miss H. T.		
Real Estate.....4,500	63 00	
Slaves.....13	39 00	
Carriage.....1	30 00	
Horses.....2	20 00	152 00
Drayton, James S.		
Real Estate.....5,000	70 00	
Slaves.....21	63 00	
Dog.....1	2 00	135 00

TAXES.

Drayton, Thomas F
 Real Estate..........................1,000 14 00
 Slaves...................................13 39 00
 Carriage..................................1 20 00
 Horse.....................................1 10 00
 Dog.......................................1 2 00 85 00
Drayton, Martha S.
 Real Estate..........................8,000 112 00
 Slaves....................................4 12 00 124 00
Drayton, T. H. M. & John
 Real Estate..........................1,400 19 60
 Slaves...................................15 45 00 64 60
Drayton, J. G.
 Slaves....................................7 21 00
Dryer, C.
 Stock of Goods......................1,000 14 00
 Slave.....................................1 3 00 17 00
Droger, D.
 Real Estate..........................3,000 42 00
 Stock of Goods........................800 11 20 53 20
Drummond, John
 Real Estate..........................7,000 98 00
 Slaves....................................5 15 00 113 00
Du Bose, E. C.
 Slaves....................................2 6 00
Duc, H. A.
 Real Estate.........................29,100 407 40
 Stock of Goods......................1,000 14 00
 Interest on Bonds, &c 434 10 85
 Slaves....................................6 18 00
 Carriage..................................1 20 00
 Horse.....................................1 10 00 480 25
Duc, F. H.
 Stock of Goods........................500 7 00
 Horse.....................................1 10 00 17 00
Duffin, P
 Real Estate..........................2,000 28 00
Duffus, Mrs. John
 Real Estate..........................3,000 42 00
 Slaves....................................5 15 00
 Carriage..................................1 20 00
 Horse.....................................1 10 00 87 00
Duffus, James A.
 Real Estate..........................2,500 35 00
 Dog.......................................1 2 00 87 00

		TAXES.
Duffus, James A. and others, Trustees		
Slave..1		3 00
Duffus, Ann S.		
Real Estate.........................3,000	42 00	
Slaves...................................2	6 00	48 00
Dufort, J L.		
Real Estate.........................2,000	28 00	
Slave....................................1	3 00	31 00
Dufort, Pauline		
Slaves....................................2		6 00
Dufort, Elias		
Real Estate.........................5,500	77 00	
Horse....................................1	10 00	
Dog.......................................1	2 00	89 00
Dufort, A.		
Real Estate.........................3,000	42 00	
Dog.......................................1	2 00	44 00
Dukes, William C.		
Real Estate........................26,600	372 40	
Slaves...................................8	24 00	
Carriage................................1	30 00	
Horses..................................2	20 00	
Dog......................................1	2 00	448 40
Dukes, W C. and Sons		
Real Estate.........................2,000	28 00	
Commissions.....................19,050	476 25	504 25
Dukes, John R.		
Real Estate.........................7,250	101 50	
Slaves...................................7	21 00	122 50
Dukes, John R., Trustee		
Real Estate.........................6,500		91 00
Dukes, John R., Trustee of Dukes		
Real Estate....................1,200 00	16 80	
Interest on Bonds, &c..........54 50	1 36	
Slaves...................................4	12 00	30 16
Dukes, John R., Trustee of Carson		
Real Estate.........................5,000	70 00	
Slave....................................1	3 00	
Carriage................................1	20 00	
Horse....................................1	10 00	103 00
Dukes, T. C. H.		
Dividends.............................6	15	
Slave....................................1	3 00	
Carriage................................1	20 00	
Horses..................................2	20 00	
Dogs.....................................2	4 00	47 15

		TAXES.

Dukes, T. C. H., Administrator
    Real Estate..........................3,300   46 20
    Slave.......................................1   3 00   49 20

Dulin, R.
    Slaves......................................3   9 00

Duncan, Archibald
    Real Estate 700   ....   9 80

Dunham, Taft & Co.
    Stock of Goods...................35,000   490 00

Dunkin, B. F.
    Real Estate........................11,000   154 00
    Slaves.....................................5   15 00
    Carriage..................................1   30 00
    Horses.....................................2   20 00   219 00

Dunkin, A. H.
    Real Estate.........................6,500   91 00
    Interest on Bonds, &c............245   6 13
    Slaves.....................................2   6 00
    Income...............................1,300   32 50
    Dogs.......................................2   4 00   139 63

Dunkin, A. H., Trustee of Huger
    Real Estate..........................1,600   22 40
    Slaves....................................15   45 00   67 40

Dunkin, A. H., Trustee of Brown
    Interest on Bonds, &c........1,236 86   30 92
    Slaves......................................3   9 00   39 92

Dunn, Charles
    Real Estate..........................8,000   112 00
    Stock of Goods......................500   7 00   119 00

Dunn, John
    Real Estate..........................1,500   21 00
    Slaves......................................3   9 00   30 00

Dunn, Estate William
    Real Estate..........................3,000   ....   42 00

Dunneman, C.
    Real Estate..........................1,200   16 80
    Horse 1   10 00   26 80

Dunning, James
    Real Estate........................12,000   168 00
    Slaves....................................16   48 00
    Horses.....................................3   30 00
    Dog...1   2 00   248 00

Dunning, Margaret
    Real Estate..........................4,000   56 00

		TAXES.

Dupont, F.
    Stock of Goods....................1,500   21 00
    Slaves...............................3   9 00   30 00
Dupont, C. C., Administrator
    Real Estate.......................3,500   ....   49 00
Dupont, Dr. Wilfred
    Carriage...........................1   15 00
    Horse 1   10 00   25 00
Du Pré, Julia
    Real Estate.....................34,500   483 00
    Slaves.............................3   9 00   492 00
Dupree, Daniel A.
    Slaves.............................2   ....   6 00
Dupree, Trust Estate Isabella
    Real Estate........................800   11 20
Dupree, Estate J.
    Slaves.............................3   9 00
Dupree, Mary Ann
    Slaves.............................2   6 00
Duquercron, Mary A. and F H.
    Slave..............................1   ....   3 00
Duquercron, Miss P
    Real Estate.....................4,000   56 00
    Slaves.............................5   15 00   71 00
Duquercron, Leopold
    Real Estate.....................2,500   ....   35 00
Duryea, R. S.
    Real Estate.....................4,500   63 00
    Slave..............................1   3 00
    Income..........................1,000   25 00
    Dog................................1   2 00   93 00
Dusenbury, George
    Real Estate.....................3,000   ....   42 00
Dutrieux, Estate C.
    Real Estate.....................7,500   105 00
    Slaves.............................4   12 00   117 00
Duval, J. B. & Son
    Stock of Goods..................3,000   42 00
    Slaves.............................3   9 00
    Dog................................1   2 00   53 00
Earle, James P
    Real Estate....................44,500   623 00
    Slaves............................17   51 00
    Carriage...........................1   20 00
    Horse..............................1   10 00   704 00

		TAXES
Early, Catharine		
Real Estate........3,500		49 00
Early, John		
Stock of Goods........150	....	2 10
Early, Edward		
Real Estate........1,200		16 80
Eason, James M.		
Real Estate........14,500	203 00	
Slaves........6	18 00	
Dogs........2	4 00	225 00
Eason, J M. & Brother		
Real Estate........12,000	168 00	
Slaves........12	36 00	
Carriage........1	20 00	
Horse........1	10 00	234 00
Eason, Thomas D.		
Real Estate........5,000	70 00	
Slaves........5	15 00	
Dog........1	2 00	87 00
Eason, Estate J. J.		
Real Estate........600		8 40
Eason, Mary P and Caroline M.		
Slaves........3		9 00
Easterby, William H.		
Slaves........4	12 00	
Commissions........900	22 50	
Horse........1	10 00	44 50
Easterby, S. D.		
Real Estate........1,500	21 00	
Slaves........2	6 00	27 00
Eberhardt, E. W		
Stock of Goods........500	....	7 00
Eberhardt, C. H.		
Stock of Goods........600		8 40
Eckhard, Mary E.		
Slaves........2		6 00
Eden, John A.		
Slaves........2		6 00
Eddie, Alexander		
Real Estate........2,300	....	32 20
Eddie, Margaret and Children		
Real Estate........1,200	....	16 80
Edgerton, Richards & Co.		
Stock of Goods........15,000	....	210 00

85

			TAXES.
Edgerton, E. W			
Real Estate	10,000	140 00	
Slaves	16	48 00	
Horse	1	10 00	
Dogs	2	4 00	202 00
Edgerton & Richards			
Real Estate	26,000	364 00	
Interest on Bonds, &c	275	6 88	
Slaves	20	60 00	
Shipping	13,500	101 25	532 13
Edgerton, James E.			
Dog	1		2 00
Edings, Miss P E.			
Slaves	3		9 00
Edmondston, Charles			
Real Estate	5,000	70 00	
Slaves	6	18 00	88 00
Edmondston, Mrs. M. M.			
Real Estate	4,500	63 00	
Slave	1	3 00	66 00
Edmondston, L. A.			
Real Estate	1,300	18 20	
Slaves	5	15 00	
Carriage	1	30 00	
Income	4,000	100 00	
Horses	2	20 00	183 20
Edwards, Charles L.			
Real Estate	7,500	105 00	
Slaves	5	15 00	120 00
Edwards, Mrs. F B.			
Real Estate	4,500	63 00	
Slaves	2	6 00	69 00
Edwards, George B. and Elizabeth H.			
Real Estate	2,500		35 00
Edwards, James F			
Real Estate	7,000	98 00	
Slaves	5	15 00	113 00
Edwards, James F., Trustee of Gadsden			
Real Estate	9,000	126 00	
Slaves	15	45 00	171 00
Edwards, Evan			
Real Estate	5,000	70 00	
Slaves	8	24 00	
Dog	1	2 00	96 00
Edwards, Evan, Trustee			
Slaves	3		9 00

		TAXES.
Edwards, John J., Trustee		
Slave 1		3 00
Edwards, Mrs. C. L.		
Slaves 8		24 00
Edwards, Rebecca B.		
Slaves............10		30 00
Edwards, F M.		
Real Estate............5,000	70 00	
Slaves 5	15 00	
Carriage............1	20 00	
Income............200	5 00	
Horse 1	10 00	
Dog............1	2 00	122 00
Egan, John		
Real Estate............2,000	28 00	
Stock of Goods............800	11 20	
Slaves............2	6 00	45 20
Egleston, George W		
Slave 1	3 00	
Income............300	7 50	10 50
Egleston, T. R.		
Real Estate............5,000	70 00	
Slaves............4	12 00	82 00
Ebney, Trust Estate Mrs. S. E.		
Slaves............3		9 00
Ehney, Estate P M.		
Slave 1		3 00
Ehney, John		
Real Estate............285	....	3 99
Ehney, E. W., Trustee		
Slaves............2	....	6 00
Ehrich, Henry		
Real Estate............18,500	259 00	
Slaves............2	6 00	265 00
Ehrlich, Morris		
Stock of Goods............100	....	1 40
Ehrlich, Morris, Trustee of children		
Real Estate............1,000	....	14 00
Elfe, Albert		
Real Estate............34,700	485 80	
Slaves............15	45 00	
Carriages............2	40 00	
Horses............2	20 00	
Dog............1	2 00	592 80

		TAXES
Elfe, Miss M. A.		
Real Estate............4,000	56 00	
Interest on Bonds, &c............650	16 25	
Slaves............3	9 00	81 25
Elford, F P		
Real Estate............5,000	70 00	
Slaves............12	36 00	
Carriage............1	20 00	
Horses............2	20 00	146 00
Elliott, Thomas O.		
Real Estate............4,000	56 00	
Slave............1	3 00	59 00
Elliott, Juliet G.		
Real Estate............26,300	368 20	
Slaves............21	63 00	
Carriage............1	30 00	
Horses............2	20 00	
Dog............1	2 00	483 20
Elliott, Estate Gibbes L.		
Interest on Bonds. &c............4,000	100 00	
Slaves............13	39 00	139 00
Elliott, James H.		
Interest on Bonds, &c............938	23 45	
Slaves............11	33 00	
Carriage............1	20 00	
Horse............1	10 00	86 45
Elliott, W S.		
Real Estate............10,000	140 00	
Carriage............1	15 00	
Horses............2	20 00	
Dog............1	2 00	177 00
Elliott, W S., Trustee		
Slaves............7		21 00
Elliott, Sarah G., Trust Estate		
Interest on Bonds, &c............63	1 58	
Dividends............14	35	
Slave............1	3 00	4 93
Ellis, Benjamin		
Real Estate............1,200		16 80
Ellis, Elizabeth A.		
Slaves............2	....	6 00
Elsworth, J T.		
Real Estate............18,500	259 00	
Slaves............38	114 00	
Carriage............1	20 00	
Horse............1	10 00	
Dog............1	2 00	405 00

			TAXES.

Emery, Mrs. J E.
 Real Estate............2,500 35 00
 Slaves............2 6 00 41 00
Emery, J. R.
 Real Estate............4,000 56 00
 Slave............1 3 00 59 00
Emillinette, Miss A. C.
 Real Estate............1,500 21 00
 Slaves............2 6 00 27 00
England, Mrs. M.
 Real Estate............3,700 51 80
 Slaves............2 6 00 57 80
England, W J
 Real Estate............1,200 16 80
 Slaves............3 9 00 25 80
England, W J., in trust
 Real Estate............7,000 98 00
 Slaves............4 12 00 110 00
Englebert, George
 Real Estate............2,000   28 00
English, Harriet S.
 Real Estate............15,000 210 00
 Slaves............5 15 00
 Carriage............1 20 00
 Horse............1 10 00 255 00
Enslow, Joseph A.
 Slave............1 3 00
 Carriage............1 20 00
 Horse............1 10 00 33 00
Enston, William
 Real Estate............65,000 910 00
 Stock of Goods............20,000 280 00
 Interest on Bonds, &c............7,000 175 00
 Slaves............8 24 00
 Carriage............1 20 00 1,409 00
Enston, William, and Estate Gates
 Real Estate............110,000   1,540 00
Entelmann, F
 Real Estate............4,000 56 00
 Stock of Goods............1,200 16 80 72 80
Epping, J. P M.
 Real Estate............11,000   154 00
Esdorn, Frederick H.
 Real Estate............7,000 98 00
 Stock of Goods............800 11 20
 Slaves............3 9 00 118 20

                                                                    TAXES.

Esdra, Eugene
  Slave 1   3 00
  Horse 1 10 00   13 00
Estill, William
  Real Estate 3,000   42 00
Estill, A. D.
  Real Estate 200   2 80
  Interest on Bonds, &c 100   2 50   5 30
Evans, Benjamin F.
  Real Estate 6,000 84 00
  Slaves 5 15 00
  Carriage 1 20 00
  Horse 1 10 00
  Dog 1   2 00 131 00
Evans, Eliza
  Slaves 3   9 00
Evans, Robert
  Real Estate 3,500 49 00
  Horse 1 10 00   59 00
Evans, Jane E.
  Slaves 6   18 00
Evans, E. J
  Slaves 3   9 00
Evans, Dr. George
  Slaves 2   6 00
Evans, Estate James B.
  Real Estate 7,500   105 00
Faber, Dr. John C.
  Real Estate 8,000   112 00
Faber, John Lewis
  Real Estate 19,500   273 00
Faber, Joseph W
  Commissions 1,825 77   45 64
Faber, Maria C.
  Real Estate 13,200 184 80
  Slaves 13 39 00
  Carriage 1 30 00
  Horses 2 20 00 273 80
Faber, Mary M.
  Real Estate 19,000 266 00
  Slaves 7 21 00 287 00
Fabian, Mrs. L.
  Slaves 2   6 00

			TAXES.
Fairchild, Daniel			
Real Estate	16,000	224 00	
Slaves	13	39 00	
Carriage	1	20 00	
Horse	1	10 00	293 00
Fairchild & Hamlin			
Real Estate	13,000	182 00	
Commissions	2,500	62 50	244 50
Falk, J L. & Co.			
Stock of Goods	13,000		182 00
Falk, Abraham			
Real Estate	10,000	140 00	
Stock of Goods	4,000	56 00	
Slaves	2	6 00	202 00
Fanning, F D.			
Real Estate	16,000	224 00	
Stock of Goods	24,000	336 00	
Slave	1	3 00	563 00
Farley, John			
Slaves	3		9 00
Farley, Maria E.			
Slave	1		3 00
Farnum, Oliver			
Slaves	3	....	9 00
Farnum & Dotterer			
Real Estate	10,000	140 00	
Stock of Goods	12,000	168 00	308 00
Farrar, S. S.			
Real Estate	21,000	294 00	
Slaves	12	36 00	
Carriage	1	30 00	
Horses	3	30 00	
Dog	1	2 00	392 00
Farrar, S. S. & Brothers			
Real Estate	70,000	980 00	
Slaves	2	6 00	986 00
Farrar, S. S., Brothers & Co.			
Stock of Goods	70,000	980 00	
Shipping	2,500	18 75	
Dog	1	2 00	1,000 75
Farrar, J C.			
Slaves	9	27 00	
Dog	1	2 00	29 00
Fauconnet, Charles P			
Real Estate	1,600	....	22 40

			TAXES.
Fay, Estate Margaret			
Slaves	4		12 00
Faysoux, Miss H.			
Slaves	4		12 00
Fedtke, John H.			
Real Estate	450		6 30
Fehrenback, N			
Real Estate	16,700	233 80	
Slaves	5	15 00	
Dog	1	2 00	250 80
Feldmann, B.			
Stock of Goods	1,500		21 00
Felipe, J. Q.			
Stock of Goods	1,000	14 00	
Dog	1	2 00	16 00
Fenn, Trust Estate Mary B. and children			
Slaves	5		15 00
Feran, James			
Stock of Goods	300		4 20
Ferebee, Wilson			
Slaves	4		12 00
Ferguson, John			
Real Estate	6,000	84 00	
Slaves	2	6 00	90 00
Ferguson, Elizabeth			
Slaves	5		15 00
Ferrall, Thomas			
Real Estate	1,200		16 80
Ferrall, John J			
Real Estate	5,000	70 00	
Slaves	4	12 00	82 00
Ferrell, Miss M. C.			
Slaves	2		6 00
Ferrera, Martha			
Real Estate	3,000	42 00	
Slave	1	3 00	45 00
Ferette, John F.			
Stock of Goods	100		1 40
Feugas, H. P			
Real Estate	3,800	53 20	
Slaves	2	6 00	59 20
Ficken, John F.			
Real Estate	10,500	147 00	
Stock of Goods	5,000	70 00	
Slave	1	3 00	
Dogs	2	4 00	224 00

		TAXES.
Fiekling, Julius, (minor)		
Slaves.................4		12 00
Fields, Nathaniel		
Real Estate..........28,200	394 80	
Slaves.................7	21 00	
Dog....................1	2 00	417 80
Fields, Nathaniel, Trustee		
Slave..................1		3 00
Figeroux, B.		
Stock of Goods........3,500	49 00	
Slave..................1	3 00	
Dog....................1	2 00	54 00
Fillette, Mrs. A.		
Real Estate...........4,500	63 00	
Stock of Goods........1,500	21 00	
Slave..................1	3 00	87 00
Fillette, T.		
Slaves.................6		18 00
Fillidy, Trust Estate of M. E.		
Real Estate...........1,500	....	21 00
Fillion, Rev. Leon		
Interest on Bonds, &c....70	....	1 75
Finagin, Trust Estate of C. B.		
Real Estate...........1,500	21 00	
Slave..................1	3 00	
Dog....................1	2 00	26 00
Finagin, Thomas		
Real Estate...........1,600	22 40	
Slave..................1	3 00	25 40
Fincken, A.		
Real Estate...........2,300	32 20	
Stock of Goods..........400	5 60	37 80
Finegin, George		
Real Estate...........2,000	28 00	
Slave..................1	3 00	
Shipping..............500	3 75	34 75
Fink, H.		
Real Estate...........2,300	32 20	
Stock of Goods..........400	5 60	37 80
Finklen, Henrietta R.		
Slaves.................3		9 00
Finley, James		
Stock of Goods........1,550	21 70	
Dog....................1	2 00	23 70

		TAXES.
Finley, William Peronneau		
Slaves.....2		6 00
Finley, W W		
Real Estate 600	8 40	
Shipping 1,700	12 75	21 15
Fischer, E. J. H.		
Real Estate.....5,000	70 00	
Stock of Goods.....400	5 60	75 60
Fishburn, Robert		
Slaves.....15	45 00	
Carriage.....1	30 00	
Horses.....2	20 00	95 00
Fisher, Sarah, Executrix		
Real Estate.....10,000	140 00	
Slaves.....4	12 00	152 00
Fisher, Samuel W		
Real Estate.....5,000	....	70 00
Fitch, Dr. William M.		
Real Estate.....12,000	168 00	
Slaves.....14	42 00	
Carriage.....1	30 00	
Carriage.....1	20 00	
Income.....6,000	150 00	
Horses.....7	70 00	
Dogs.....2	4 00	484 00
Fitch, Dr. A.		
Slaves.....2	6 00	
Carriage.....1	20 00	
Income.....500	12 50	38 50
Fitts, John L.		
Real Estate.....1,500	21 00	
Slave.....1	3 00	24 00
Fitts, William M.		
Real Estate.....500	....	7 00
Fitts, William M., in trust		
Real Estate.....1,500		21 00
Fitzer, Thomas F.		
Real Estate.....1,000		14 00
Fitzpatrick, Timothy		
Horse.....1		10 00
Fitzsimons, Mrs. E. P		
Real Estate.....10,000	140 00	
Interest on Bonds, &c.....1,600	40 00	
Slaves.....4	12 00	
Carriage.....1	30 00	
Horses.....2	20 00	242 00

		TAXES.	

Flach, George W
    Stock of Goods.....................2,500   35 00
    Dog....................................1   2 00   37 00
Flagg, Mrs. M. E.
    Real Estate.........................11,000   154 00
    Slaves 9   27 00
    Carriage..............................1   30 00
    Horses................................2   20 00
    Dog....................................1   2 00   233 00
Flagg, Charles E. B.
    Interest on Bonds, &c...............44   1 10
    Income.............................1,400   35 00   36 10
Fleming, Richard and Doolen
    Real Estate.......................1,200   61 80
Fleming, D. F
    Slaves.................................3   9 00
    Carriage..............................1   30 00
    Horses................................2   20 00   59 00
Fleming, D. F. & Co.
    Stock of Goods..................30,000   420 00
Fleming, W H.
    Slaves.................................5   15 00
    Carriage..............................1   20 00
    Horse 1   10 00   45 00
Flemming, Peter
    Real Estate.......................2,000   28 00
Flinn, Dr. T. J
    Slaves.................................5   15 00
Flinn, Robert
    Real Estate.......................3,000   42 00
Fludd, Eliza
    Real Estate......................12,000   168 00
    Slaves.................................5   15 00
    Carriage..............................1   30 00
    Horses................................2   20 00   233 00
Flynn, John T.
    Stock of Goods......................300   4 20
Flynn, Mrs. M. A. T.
    Slaves.................................5   15 00
Flynn, John T., Trustee
    Slave 1   3 00
Flynn, Patrick
    Real Estate.......................1,800   25 20
Flynn, Thomas
    Interest on Bonds, &c..............300   7 50
    Slaves.................................5   15 00   22 50

			TAXES.
Fogartie, Arthur			
Real Estate	7,000		98 00
Fogarties & Stillman			
Stock of Goods	60,000	840 00	
Horse	1	10 00	850 00
Fogartie, Edward			
Real Estate	1,800	25 20	
Slaves	7	21 00	
Carriage	1	20 00	
Horse	1	10 00	
Dog	1	2 00	78 20
Fogartie, James' and Sarah's children			
Real Estate	3,000		42 00
Fogarty, Philip			
Stock of Goods	2,300	32 20	
Slaves	11	33 00	
Dog	1	2 00	67 20
Foissin, Mrs. M.			
Slaves	5		15 00
Foley, B.			
Real Estate	5,000	70 00	
Stock of Goods	12,000	168 00	
Slave	1	3 00	
Dog	1	2 00	243 00
Folger, E. J.			
Real Estate	2,000		28 00
Folker, Martha M. and sisters			
Real Estate	3,000		42 00
Folker, Mrs. O. F			
Slaves	9		27 00
Folker, O. F			
Slaves	3		9 00
Follin, G., Trustee			
Slaves	2	6 00	
Dog	1	2 00	8 00
Follin, G., Agent			
Stock of Goods	9,000		126 00
Foote, Eliza Ann			
Real Estate	3,500	49 00	
Slaves	2	6 00	55 00
Fora, L.			
Real Estate	2,000	28 00	
Stock of Goods	2,000	28 00	56 00
Forbes, Robert			
Real Estate	5,500	77 00	
Slaves	5	15 00	92 00

		TAXES.

Force, B. W
    Real Estate........8,000   112 00
    Slaves........2   6 00
    Dog........1   2 00   120 00

Force & Mitchell
    Stock of Goods........30,000   ....   420 00

Ford, J D.
    Carriage........1   20 00
    Commissions........1,640   41 00
    Horse........1   10 00
    Dog........1   2 00   73 00

Ford, Benjamin
    Real Estate........3,500   49 00
    Stock of Goods........5,000   70 00
    Slave........1   3 00
    Carriage........1   20 00
    Horse........1   10 00   152 00

Ford, Frederick A.
    Income........600   ....   15 00

Fordham, Jane
    Real Estate........2,500   35 00

Forrest, Rev. John
    Real Estate........5,000   70 00

Forsythe & McComb
    Stock of Goods........3,000   42 00

Forsythe, William C.
    Stock of Goods........4,200   ....   58 80

Forster, Mrs. Ann
    Interest on Bonds, &c........600   ....   15 00

Foster, Charles
    Slaves........14   ....   42 00

Foster, Amelia E.
    Real Estate........11,000   154 00
    Slaves........3   9 00   163 00

Foster, Dr. A. M.
    Real Estate........6,000   84 00

Fowler, Trust Estate of A. D. and wife
    Real Estate........1,500   21 00
    Slaves........6   18 00   39 00

Fowler, Miss C. L.
    Real Estate........1,600   22 40

Fowler, Mrs. Jesse P
    Real Estate........1,500   21 00
    Stock of Goods........600   8 40   29 40

			TAXES.
Fox, Mrs. Ann			
Real Estate	6,000	84 00	
Slave	1	3 00	87 00
Frampton, Dr. L. A.			
Real Estate	3,000		42 00
Franke, Charles D.			
Real Estate	4,000	....	56 00
Fraser, Charles			
Real Estate	13,000	182 00	
Interest on Bonds, &c.	1,120	28 00	
Slave	1	3 00	
Dogs	3	6 00	219 00
Fraser, Estate F G.			
Slaves	2		6 00
Fraser, H. D., in trust			
Slaves	3		9 00
Fraser, Miss M. J.			
Real Estate	16,000	224 00	
Slaves	10	30 00	254 00
Fraser, Frederick E.			
Slaves	6	18 00	
Commissions	4,300	107 50	
Dog	1	2 00	127 50
Fraser, John & Co.			
Real Estate	11,500	161 00	
Stock of Goods	40,000	560 00	
Slave	1	3 00	
Shipping	80,000	600 00	
Income	30,000	750 00	2,074 00
Fraser, F. E., Trustee of J H. & E. A. Ladson			
Real Estate	12,000	168 00	
Slaves	3	9 00	177 00
Frazer, Mrs. Sarah			
Slaves	16	....	48 00
Frazer, Trust Estate M. A.			
Slave	1	....	3 00
Frazer, Mrs. R. F.			
Slaves	4	....	12 00
Frazer, Mrs. R. L. D			
Slave	1		3 00
Frazer, John M., Trustee			
Slave	1	....	3 00
Frazer, Charles P and others, Trustees			
Slave	1	....	3 00

	TAXES.

Fredsberg, Joan Magnus
    Commissions..........................1,000   25 00

Freeman, Estate E.
    Slaves 7   ....   21 00

Fremter, Mary
    Slaves 3   ....   9 00

Frien, Thomas
    Stock of Goods.........................500   ....   7 00

Frieze, F.
    Stock of Goods.........................600   ....   8 40

Fripp, John A.
    Real Estate..........................12,000   168 00
    Slave 1   3 00   171 00

Fripp, William, Sr.
    Slaves 5   ....   15 00

Froneberger, C.
    Real Estate..........................12,000   168 00
    Slave 1   3 00   171 00

Frost, Dr. H. R.
    Real Estate..........................76,500   1,071 00
    Interest on Bonds, &c............1,600   40 00
    Slaves.......................................16   48 00
    Carriage....................................1   30 00
    Carriage....................................1   20 00
    Income.................................4,000   100 00
    Horses 4   40 00   1,349 00

Frost, H. R., Trustee
    Slaves 6   18 00

Frost, H. R., Trustee
    Slaves 5   ....   15 00

Frost, Edward
    Real Estate..........................23,000   322 00
    Interest on Bonds, &c............3,400   85 00
    Slaves.......................................12   36 00
    Carriage....................................1   30 00
    Carriage....................................1   20 00
    Horses.......................................3   30 00
    Dog..1   2 00   525 00

Frost, Thomas
    Interest on Bonds, &c........1,752 50   43 81
    Slaves 3   9 00   52 81

Frost, E. H.
    Slave...1   3 00
    Carriage....................................1   20 00
    Horse 1   10 00   33 00

			TAXES.
Fuller, E. N.			
Real Estate	7,500	105 00	
Interest on Bonds, &c.	1,000	25 00	
Slaves	15	45 00	
Carriage	1	20 00	
Horse	1	10 00	
Dog	1	2 00	207 00
Fuller, Benjamin			
Slaves	15		45 00
Fulmer, Ann			
Real Estate	1,000		14 00
Fulton, Catherine A.			
Real Estate	6,500		91 00
Funke, H. H.			
Real Estate	2,500		35 00
Furman, C. M.			
Real Estate	3,900	54 60	
Slaves	15	45 00	99 60
Furman, C. M., Trustee Alexander and Berger			
Interest on Bonds, &c.	175		4 38
Furman, C. M., Trustee Alexander and wife			
Real Estate	8,500	119 00	
Slaves	2	6 00	125 00
Furman & Spratt, Assignee of Gadsden			
Real Estate	125,400	1,755 60	
Slaves	40	120 00	1,875 60
Furman, Maria and Ann			
Slaves	6		18 00
Furman, Irvin, Trustee			
Slaves	2		6 00
Furst, D. H.			
Real Estate	4,500	63 00	
Dog	1	2 00	65 00
Furst, D. H., Trustee			
Slave	1		3 00
Gadsden, C. P.			
Real Estate	12,000 00	168 00	
Interest on Bonds, &c.	262 50	6 56	
Slaves	12	36 00	
Carriage	1	20 00	
Horse	1	10 00	240 56
Gadsden, Thomas			
Real Estate	6,000		84 00
Gadsden, Estate James			
Real Estate	13,400		187 60

			TAXES.
Gadsden, Alexander E.			
Real Estate	11,000	154 00	
Slaves	13	39 00	
Carriage	1	30 00	
Horses	2	20 00	243 00
Gadsden, Estate W S.			
Real Estate	11,800		165 20
Gadsden, T. N			
Carriage	1	20 00	
Horse	1	10 00	30 00
Gadsden, James			
Real Estate	10,000	140 00	
Interest on Bonds, &c	1,472	36 80	
Slaves	8	24 00	200 80
Gadsden, Fisher			
Slave	1		3 00
Gadsden, Laura, in trust			
Slaves	7		21 00
Gadsden, Ann			
Slaves	8		24 00
Gadsden, Elizabeth F.			
Interest on Bonds, &c	200	5 00	
Slaves	6	18 00	23 00
Gage, A., & Co.			
Real Estate	22,000	308 00	
Stock of Goods	4,000	56 00	
Carriage	1	15 00	
Horses	4	40 00	419 00
Gaillard, Cornelia M.			
Slaves	8		24 00
Gaillard, Frances			
Slaves	13		39 00
Gaillard, Estate Dr. P C.			
Real Estate	8,000	112 00	
Slaves	8	24 00	
Horse	1	10 00	146 00
Gaillard, Estate Theodore			
Real Estate	25,500	357 00	
Slave	1	3 00	360 00
Gaillard, P C.			
Interest on Bonds, &c	760	19 00	
Slaves	6	18 00	
Carriage	1	20 00	
Commissions	2,600	65 00	
Horse	1	10 00	
Dog	1	2 00	134 00

			TAXES.
Gaillard, Mrs. Susan E.			
Real Estate	4,500	63 00	
Slaves	19	57 00	
Dog	1	2 00	122 00
Gale, R. W			
Real Estate	3,500	49 00	
Stock of Goods	16,000	224 00	
Slaves	3	9 00	
Horse	1	10 00	292 00
Gamage, Mrs. E.			
Slave	1		3 00
Gamble, Mrs. C. L.			
Stock of Goods	2,000	....	28 00
Gambatti, A.			
Real Estate	2,500	35 00	
Slave	1	3 00	38 00
Gannon, Rodger			
Real Estate	5,500	77 00	
Stock of Goods	800	11 20	88 20
Gannon, Michael			
Slaves	3	9 00	
Carriage	1	20 00	
Dog	1	2 00	31 00
Gantt, Trust Estate James L. and wife			
Slaves	12	36 00	
Dog	1	2 00	38 00
Gantt, R. A.			
Slaves	2	....	6 00
Gantt, Trustee of S. A.			
Slaves	2		6 00
Gantt, Susan L.			
Slaves	4	....	12 00
Gantt, Susan A.			
Slaves	15	45 00	
Carriage	1	30 00	
Horses	2	20 00	
Dog	1	2 00	97 00
Gantt, Thomas J., Trustee			
Slave	1		3 00
Gantt, Trust Estate R. S. and wife			
Real Estate	5,000	70 00	
Slaves	4	12 00	82 00
Garbon, Estate G.			
Real Estate	6,500	....	91 00

			TAXES.
Gardelle, A.			
Slaves	5	15 00	
Commissions	4,000	100 00	
Dog	1	2 00	117 00
Garden, H. R.			
Slaves	3		9 00
Gardner, Mrs. E. M.			
Slaves	10		30 00
Garetty, Thomas			
Dog	1		2 00
Garetty, Thomas, Agent			
Real Estate	22,800	319 20	
Slaves	4	12 00	331 20
Garves, J			
Stock of Goods	900		12 60
Garey, E. A. J.			
Real Estate	4,000		56 00
Gates, Estate Thomas			
Real Estate	8,100	113 40	
Interest on Bonds, &c	126	3 15	116 55
Gatewood, William C.			
Real Estate	45,300	634 20	
Slaves	10	30 00	664 20
Gayer, Estate W J.			
Real Estate	25,000	350 00	
Slaves	7	21 00	371 00
Geddings, Dr. E.			
Real Estate	54,000	756 00	
Slaves	16	48 00	
Carriage	1	30 00	
Carriage	1	20 00	
Income	6,000	150 00	
Horses	3	30 00	1,034 00
Geddings, Dr. J T. M.			
Interest on Bonds, &c	350	8 75	
Slaves	2	6 00	
Carriage	1	20 00	
Income	1,500	37 50	
Horse	1	10 00	82 25
Geddes, Mrs. G. C.			
Slaves	7		21 00
Geffords, Matilda			
Real Estate	2,000		28 00

			TAXES.
Geiger, Dr. David			
Slaves	12	36 00	
Carriage	1	20 00	
Horse	1	10 00	
Dog	1	2 00	68 00
George, Reuben S.			
Real Estate	2,000		28 00
Gerard, Estate P G.			
Real Estate	5,000		70 00
Gerard, Elizabeth			
Slave	1		3 00
Gerardeau and wife, Trust Estate			
Real Estate	5,000		70 00
Geraghty, Thomas			
Real Estate	7,000		98 00
Geraty, Christopher			
Real Estate	13,000	182 00	
Stock of Goods	600	8 40	
Slave	1	3 00	193 40
Geraty, B.			
Real Estate	7,500	105 00	
Stock of Goods	600	8 40	
Slaves	6	18 00	131 40
Gerdes, Charles H.			
Stock of Goods	1,500		21 00
Gerdts, Henry			
Real Estate	19,000	266 00	
Slaves	4	12 00	
Carriage	1	20 00	
Horse	1	10 00	308 00
Gerdts, H. & Co.			
Stock of Goods	8,000		112 00
Gerkin, Henry			
Stock of Goods	550	7 70	
Dog	1	2 00	9 70
Gerkin, John			
Stock of Goods	400	5 60	
Carriage	1	20 00	
Horse	1	10 00	
Dog	1	2 00	37 60
Gervais, Jane Caroline			
Slave	1		3 00
Gervais, John L.			
Slaves	12	36 00	
Carriage	1	30 00	
Horses	2	20 00	86 00

		TAXES.
Getty, C. W., in trust		
Slave....1		3 00
Gibbes & Co.		
Real Estate....3,000		42 00
Gibbes, James S.		
Real Estate....14,000	196 00	
Slaves....9	27 00	
Carriage....1	30 00	
Shipping....1,500	11 25	
Horses....2	20 00	284 25
Gibbes, Mrs. C. S.		
Slaves....5		15 00
Gibbes, Misses H. L. and M. H.		
Slave....1		3 00
Gibbes, Mrs. C. S., in trust		
Slaves....11		33 00
Gibbes, James T.		
Slaves....2		6 00
Gibbes, Lewis R.		
Slaves....5	15 00	
Dog....1	2 00	17 00
Gibbes, L. R., Trustee		
Interest on Bonds, &c....105	2 63	
Slaves....39	117 00	119 63
Gibbes, Sarah P		
Real Estate....2,500		35 00
Gibbes, heirs of Estate George Gibbes, Jr.		
Real Estate....6,500		91 00
Gibbes, Allen S.		
Slaves....2	6 00	
Carriage....1	15 00	
Horse....1	10 00	31 00
Gibbes, Dr. E. A.		
Real Estate....15,700	219 80	
Slaves....25	75 00	294 80
Gibbes, Trust Estate Amelia S.		
Real Estate....5,000	70 00	
Slaves....14	42 00	
Carriage....1	30 00	
Horses....2	20 00	162 00
Gibbes, Ann		
Real Estate....5,000		70 00
Gibbes, Trust Estate A. W		
Real Estate....7,800	109 20	
Slaves....8	24 00	133 20

		TAXES.
Gibbes, Mrs. M. L.		
Slaves ..3		9 00
Gibbes, Miss E. C.		
Slave ..1		3 00
Gibbon, John		
Real Estate ..8,000	112 00	
Slaves ..3	9 00	121 00
Gibbon, John and George E.		
Stock of Goods ..7,000	98 00	
Commissions ..600	15 00	113 00
Gibbon, George E.		
Slaves ..2	6 00	
Dog ..1	2 00	8 00
Gibbon, George		
Real Estate ..64,700	905 80	
Interest on Bonds, &c ..943	23 58	
Slaves ..9	27 00	
Carriage ..1	30 00	
Horses ..2	20 00	
Dog ..1	2 00	1,008 38
Gibson, Estate James		
Real Estate ..6,600		92 40
Gibson, D. C.		
Slaves ..2		6 00
Gibson, D. C., Trustee		
Real Estate ..1,500		21 00
Gibson, D. C., Trustee		
Slaves ..2		6 00
Gibson, A. E.		
Real Estate ..8,000	112 00	
Interest on Bonds.&c ..240	6 00	
Slaves ..17	51 00	169 00
Gidiere, P R.		
Slaves ..4		12 00
Gidiere, J. J		
Real Estate ..6,000	84 00	
Slaves ..2	6 00	90 00
Gifford, Thomas		
Real Estate ..2,400	33 60	
Slaves ..3	9 00	42 60
Gilbert, E. M.		
Slaves ..4		12 00
Gilchrist, R. C.		
Real Estate ..6,500	91 00	
Interest on Bonds, &c ..117	2 93	93 93

			TAXES.
Gilchrist, R. C., Trustee of Radcliffe			
Slave 1			3 00
Gilchrist, R. C., Trustee			
Slaves..6			18 00
Gilchrist, R. C., Trustee of Jones			
Real Estate............................3,000			42 00
Gilchrist, R. C., Executor and Trustee			
Interest on Bonds,&c...............30		75	
Slaves 3		9 00	
Carriage......................................1		20 00	
Horse 1		10 00	39 75
Gildersleeve, Trust Estate E. L.			
Real Estate............................8,000		....	112 00
Giles, Robert			
Real Estate............................3,000		42 00	
Slaves 11		33 00	75 00
Gillespie, A. L.			
Slaves 4		....	12 00
Gilliland, W H.			
Real Estate..........................26,000		364 00	
Slaves 9		27 00	
Carriage......................................1		20 00	
Shipping 2,000		15 00	
Horse 1		10 00	
Dog..1		2 00	438 00
Gilliland, W H., Trustee			
Real Estate............................1,500		....	21 00
Gilliland, Howell & Co.			
Stock of Goods....................83,000		....	1,162 00
Gilliland, Estate William D.			
Real Estate............................8,000		112 00	
Slaves 2		6 00	118 00
Gillis, Francis			
Real Estate............................1,200			16 80
Gilman, Caroline			
Real Estate............................4,000		56 00	
Slave..1		3 00	59 00
Girardeau, Rev. John L.			
Real Estate............................5,000		70 00	
Slaves 10		30 00	
Dog..1		2 00	102 00
Girardeau, Mary F			
Slaves 7			21 00
Given, William & Co.			
Stock of Goods....................10,000			140 00

		TAXES.
Given, William		
Real Estate..........19,500	273 00	
Slave..........1	3 00	276 00
Given, John		
Stock of Goods..........500	....	7 00
Gleason, T. and wife		
Real Estate..........800	....	11 20
Glen, D. L.		
Slave..........1		3 00
Glen, Mrs. M. E.		
Slave..........1	....	3 00
Glen, Estate John		
Real Estate..........13,000	182 00	
Slaves..........3	9 00	191 00
Glover, Harriet G.		
Interest on Bonds, &c..........308 00	7 70	
Slaves..........6	18 00	
Dog..........1	2 00	27 70
Glover, Harriet		
Slaves..........2	....	6 00
Glover, Dr. F Y.		
Real Estate..........13,000	182 00	
Slave..........1	3 00	
Carriage..........1	30 00	
Horses..........2	20 00	235 00
Glover, S. L.		
Dog..........1		2 00
Glover, S. L., Trustee		
Slaves..........2		6 00
Glover, Adam B.		
Real Estate..........2,500		35 00
Godber, Mrs. M. S. H.		
Slave..........1		3 00
Goddard, Mrs. E. C.		
Slaves..........7	21 00	
Carriage..........1	20 00	
Horse..........1	10 00	51 00
Godefroy, Eveline		
Real Estate..........6,000	84 00	
Slaves..........4	12 00	96 00
Godet, Ann		
Real Estate..........1,000		14 00
Goldman, L. J		
Real Estate..........1,000	....	14 00

			TAXES.
Goldsmith, Moses			
Real Estate	9,850	137 90	
Slaves	4	12 00	
Horse	1	10 00	
Dogs	2	4 00	163 90
Goldsmith, Moses & Sons			
Stock of Goods	1.500		21 00
Goldsmith, Richard			
Real Estate	14,500	203 00	
Slave	1	3 00	206 00
Goldsmith, Morris, Trustee			
Slaves	3		9 00
Goldstein, J. & A.			
Stock of Goods	2,360		33 04
Goldstein, D.			
Stock of Goods	500		7 00
Goldstein, S.			
Stock of Goods	3.250		45 50
Goldstein, J			
Stock of Goods	500		7 00
Gonfrieville, Harriet			
Real Estate	400		5 60
Goodrich, Mrs. E. J.			
Real Estate	12,200	170 80	
Slaves	6	18 00	188 80
Goodrich, N E.			
Real Estate	5,000	70 00	
Slaves	14	42 00	
Carriage	1	20 00	
Horses	4	40 00	
Dog	1	2 00	174 00
Gordon, A.			
Dog	1		2 00
Gordon, Jane C.			
Real Estate	12,000	168 00	
Slaves	3	9 00	177 00
Gordon's children, John F.			
Real Estate	2,000		28 00
Gordon, James B.			
Interest on Bonds, &c	1,163 75		29 09
Gordon, A. Burgess			
Interest on Bonds, &c	490	12 25	
Horse	1	10 00	
Dog	1	2 00	24 25

			TAXES.
Gordon, John			
Real Estate	1,200	16 80	
Dog	1	2 00	18 80
Gordon, James			
Real Estate	1,400		19 60
Gotjen, John			
Stock of Goods	700		9 80
Goudkop, J.			
Stock of Goods	800		11 20
Gough, Albert E., (minor)			
Slaves	4		12 00
Gourdin, Henry			
Real Estate	12,000	168 00	
Interest on Bonds, &c	1,200	30 00	
Slaves	2	6 00	204 00
Gourdin, Henry, Trustee R. A. Young			
Interest on Bonds, &c	250		6 25
Gourdin, Henry, Trustee E. S. Lee			
Real Estate	5,500		77 00
Gourdin, Henry, Trustee S. O'Hear			
Real Estate	3,900		54 60
Gourdin, Robert N			
Real Estate	10,900	152 60	
Slaves	8	24 00	
Dogs	2	4 00	180 60
Gourdin, R. N., Trustee			
Slaves	7		21 00
Gourdin, Matthiessen & Co.			
Stock of Goods	6,500	91 00	
Interest on Bonds, &c	4,000	100 00	
Commissions	28,000	700 00	891 00
Gourdin, William Alston			
Real Estate	5,000	70 00	
Commissions	3,028	75 70	145 70
Gowan, Peter			
Real Estate	16,000	224 00	
Slaves	6	18 00	242 00
Graber, H. & C Thode			
Stock of Goods	1,000		14 00
Gradick, Charles			
Slave	1		3 00
Grady, James, Trustee of Long's children			
Slave	1		3 00
Graeser, C. A.			
Commissions	4,154		103 85

		TAXES.
Graeser, Trust Estate, Mrs. S. H.		
Slaves...................................2		6 00
Graf, George		
Stock of Goods.....................500		7 00
Graham, John		
Real Estate 4,000		56 00
Graham, Estate Margaret		
Slave...1		3 00
Gralton, Michael		
Real Estate.........................1,400		19 60
Gramann, John H.		
Real Estate.........................1,700		23 80
Grant, Mrs. E. D.		
Slaves..5		15 00
Grant, Charles B.		
Real Estate..........................375		5 25
Grant, Thomas		
Real Estate........................4,900		68 60
Graveley, Cowlam		
Real Estate.......................13,500		189 00
Graveley, Cowlam, in trust		
Real Estate........................6,000	84 00	
Slaves.......................................5	15 00	
Carriage....................................1	20 00	
Shipping................................200	1 50	
Horse.......................................1	10 00	
Dog...1	2 00	132 50
Graveley & Pringle		
Stock of Goods...................36,000		504 00
Graver, John H.		
Real Estate.......................14,000	196 00	
Stock of Goods...................5,000	70 00	
Dogs...3	6 00	272 00
Graves, C. W		
Carriage....................................1	20 00	
Horse.......................................1	10 00	30 00
Graves, C. W., and wife		
Real Estate........................5,000	70 00	
Slaves......................................16	48 00	
Dog..1	2 00	120 00
Graves, D. D.		
Interest on Bonds, &c............362	9 05	
Slaves......................................9	27 00	
Carriage...................................1	20 00	
Horse.......................................1	10 00	
Dogs...2	4 00	70 05

			TAXES.
Gray, John			
Real Estate	2,000		28 00
Gray, James W			
Real Estate	12,000	168 00	
Slaves	3	9 00	177 00
Gray, James W., Trustee			
Slaves	7		21 00
Gray, John B., and B. C. Pressley, Trustees			
Slave	1		3 00
Gray, James W., Master in Equity, Heath vs. Heath			
Slave	1		3 00
Gray, John B., Trustee			
Slaves	8		24 00
Gray, Mrs. M. G.			
Real Estate	2,200	30 80	
Slave	1	3 00	33 80
Gray, Alexander P.			
Income	1,300	32 50	
Horse	1	10 00	42 50
Gray, Mary E.			
Real Estate	5,000	70 00	
Slaves	5	15 00	85 00
Grayson, W P			
Real Estate	10,000	140 00	
Interest on Bonds, &c	1,500	37 50	
Slaves	9	27 00	204 50
Gready, James R., Trustee			
Slaves	2		6 00
Greaton, John			
Real Estate	2,000		28 00
Green, R. M., in trust			
Real Estate	4,000	56 00	
Slave	1	3 00	59 00
Green, Judith			
Slave	1		3 00
Green, Owen			
Real Estate	3,000		42 00
Green, James F			
Shipping	1,500		11 25
Green's children, J F.			
Real Estate	8,500	119 00	
Slaves	4	12 00	
Carriage	1	20 00	
Horses	2	20 00	
Dog	1	2 00	173 00

		TAXES.
Green, Thomas P		
Real Estate..........6,000	84 00	
Slaves..........4	12 00	
Horse..........1	10 00	106 00
Green, Miss E. W		
Real Estate..........3,000	42 00	
Slaves..........4	12 00	54 00
Green, Trapmann & Co.		
Commissions..........10,000		250 00
Greenhill, Estate Miss E. F.		
Slaves..........1		3 00
Greenland, Caroline J.		
Real Estate..........7,000	98 00	
Slaves..........2	6 00	104 00
Greenland, Estate Dr. B R.		
Real Estate..........3,000		42 00
Greenland, Dr. M.		
Slaves..........2	6 00	
Income..........250	6 25	
Dog..........1	2 00	14 25
Greenland, Estate W P		
Real Estate..........8,000		112 00
Greenland, J. S.		
Commissions..........300		7 50
Greenland, Mrs. E. M.		
Real Estate..........5,500	77 00	
Slaves..........4	12 00	89 00
Greer, William		
Real Estate..........8,000	112 00	
Slaves..........34	102 00	
Carriage..........1	20 00	
Horse..........1	10 00	
Dog..........1	2 00	246 00
Greer, John M.		
Real Estate..........8,000	112 00	
Slaves..........3	9 00	
Dogs..........2	4 00	125 00
Greer, J. M. and R. W		
Stock of Goods..........8,000		112 00
Grice, George D.		
Stock of Goods..........8,200		114 80
Griffin, T. H.		
Slaves..........5	15 00	
Commissions..........7,000	175 00	
Horse..........1	10 00	200 00

			TAXES.
Grimke, E. Montague			
Real Estate 7,000	98 00		
Slaves...............6	18 00	116 00	
Grimke, Dr. John			
Real Estate...........6,000	84 00		
Slaves...............2	6 00	90 00	
Grimke, Estate Henry			
Real Estate...........1,400	....	19 60	
Grimke, Mrs. E.			
Slaves...............4		12 00	
Grimke, Mrs. S. D.			
Real Estate...........20,000	280 00		
Interest on Bonds, &c...........2,954	73 85		
Slaves...............21	63 00		
Carriage.............1	30 00		
Horses..............2	20 00	466 85	
Grimball, J. B.			
Slaves...............12	36 00		
Dog.................1	2 00	38 00	
Griner, Ann			
Real Estate...........2,500	35 00		
Slaves..............2	6 00	41 00	
Groning, Estate H.			
Real Estate...........7,500	105 00		
Slaves..............5	15 00	120 00	
Groning, Lewis			
Real Estate...........4,000	56 00		
Dog.................1	2 00	58 00	
Gros, Estate John			
Interest on Bonds, &c..........100		2 50	
Grother, John H.			
Stock of Goods..........250		3 50	
Grovermann, F L.			
Real Estate............400	....	5 60	
Groves, Elizabeth			
Slave...............1	....	3 00	
Grube, J. C.			
Real Estate...........1,500	21 00		
Stock of Goods.........700	9 80	30 80	
Gruber, J A. C.			
Real Estate...........2,000	....	28 00	
Gruber, Elizabeth			
Real Estate...........1,200	....	16 80	

			TAXES.
Gruber, George H.			
Real Estate	6,000	84 00	
Slaves	5	15 00	
Horse	1	10 00	
Dog	1	2 00	111 00
Gruver, William H.			
Slaves	12	36 00	
Carriage	1	20 00	
Horse	1	10 00	
Dog	1	2 00	68 00
Guenebault, Joseph H.			
Real Estate	10,000		140 00
Guenveur, Mrs. E. M.			
Real Estate	1,900		26 60
Guerard, Amelia L.			
Real Estate	10,000	140 00	
Slaves	6	18 00	
Carriage	1	30 00	
Shipping	1,000	7 50	
Horses	2	20 00	215 50
Guerard, J J.			
Slaves	2	6 00	
Dog	1	2 00	8 00
Guignard, James S.			
Slave	1		3 00
Guerry, Grandison			
Slave	1		3 00
Guerry, A. C.			
Real Estate	2,000		28 00
Guy, Estate Joseph			
Real Estate	1,800		25 20
Guy, Theodore B.			
Stock of Goods	1,000		14 00
Guy, Sarah			
Slave	1		3 00
Haas, Estelle			
Stock of Goods	500		7 00
Haas, John and John Ahrens			
Real Estate	6,000		84 00
Habernicht, J. T. L.			
Stock of Goods	500		7 00
Habernicht, Estate John D.			
Real Estate	3,400	47 60	
Interest on Bonds, &c.	124	3 10	50 70

		TAXES.

Hackermann & Castens
Stock of Goods..................400   5 60

Hacker, George S.
Real Estate..................18,400   257 60
Slaves..................6   18 00
Horse..................1   10 00   285 60

Hacker, Francis B.
Real Estate..................1,600   ....   22 40

Haesloop, John H.
Stock of Goods..................600   ....   8 40

Hagermann, Henry
Real Estate..................8,100   113 40
Dog..................1   2 00   115 40

Hagood, John W., Trustee
Slave..................1   3 00

Hahn, H. H.
Real Estate..................4,000   ....   56 00

Haig, Estate George
Slave..................1   3 00

Haig, H. M.
Real Estate..................10,000   ....   140 00

Haig, Ann M.
Real Estate..................4,000   56 00
Slaves..................16   48 00   104 00

Haig, S. M.
Slaves..................20   60 00
Dog..................1   2 00   62 00

Haig, R. M.
Horse..................1   10 00

Haley, J. M.
Real Estate..................500   7 00
Carriages..................2   40 00
Horses..................2   20 00
Dogs..................2   4 00   71 00

Hall, G. N.
Real Estate..................1,500   ....   21 00

Hall, H. T., in trust
Slaves..................2   6 00

Hall, H. T., Trustee of Mrs. F Malga
Slaves..................2   ....   6 00

Hall & Co.
Slave..................1   3 00
Commissions..................20,062   501 55   504 55

Hall, Ann
Real Estate..................4,000   56 00

		TAXES.
Hall, Dr. William		
Real Estate................13,000	182 00	
Slaves................11	33 00	
Dog................1	2 00	217 00
Halsey, Estate E. L.		
Slaves................4	....	12 00
Hamilton, P and wife		
Real Estate................2,500		35 00
Hamilton, Trust Estate D. H. and wife		
Interest on Bonds, &c................1,795	44 88	
Slaves................9	27 00	
Dog................1	2 00	73 88
Hamilton, S. H. D.		
Slave................1	....	3 00
Hamilton, William N.		
Slave................1	....	3 00
Hamilton, John A.		
Slaves................4	12 00	
Dog................1	2 00	14 00
Hamilton, John A., Trustee		
Slaves................2		6 00
Hamilton & Smith		
Stock of Goods................8,000	112 00	
Horse................1	10 00	122 00
Hamlin, Edward		
Real Estate................1,500	....	21 00
Hamlin, James		
Horse................1		10 00
Hamlin, John		
Real Estate................3,000	....	42 00
Hamlin, Mary		
Real Estate................4,000	56 00	
Slaves................8	24 00	
Carriage................1	20 00	
Horse................1	10 00	110 00
Hamlin, Thomas		
Real Estate................2,000	....	28 00
Hamlin, Ann & Mrs. Gadsden		
Real Estate................5,000	....	70 00
Hammond, Elizabeth		
Slaves................8	24 00	
Dog................1	2 00	26 00
Hamner, Mrs. L.		
Slaves................3	....	9 00

		TAXES
Hampton, James		
Slaves.....................................2		6 00
Hanahan, John C.		
Real Estate........................7,300	102 20	
Horse 1	10 00	112 20
Hanahan, Julia J.		
Slaves....................................8	....	24 00
Hanahan, R. S. H.		
Slaves..................................15	45 00	
Dog......................................1	2 00	47 00
Hanahan. R. S. H., Trustee		
Slaves....................................4		12 00
Hanckel, Rev. C.		
Real Estate......................12,000	168 00	
Slaves..................................16	48 00	
Carriage................................1	30 00	
Horses..................................2	20 00	266 00
Hanckel, Allen S.		
Slaves...................................2	6 00	
Dog......................................1	2 00	8 00
Hanckel, John		
Real Estate........................5,500	77 00	
Slaves...................................7	21 00	
Carriage................................1	20 00	
Horses..................................2	20 00	
Dog......................................1	2 00	140 00
Hanckel, Dr. M. S.		
Slaves...................................3	9 00	
Income.................................500	12 50	21 50
Hanckel, Thomas M.		
Slaves..................................10	30 00	
Carriage................................1	30 00	
Horses..................................2	20 00	80 00
Hanckel, Tunno & Nowell		
Interest on Bonds, &c..........200	5 00	
Slaves...................................6	18 00	
Commissions...................3,755	93 88	
Dogs.....................................2	4 00	120 88
Hancock, Estate Henry		
Real Estate........................3,500	....	49 00
Hands, Jane A.		
Slave....................................1		3 00
Happoldt, C. L.		
Real Estate........................3,800	46 20	
Dog......................................1	2 00	48 20

		TAXES.

Happoldt, J. M.
 Interest on Bonds, &c 224 50   5 61
 Slave 1   3 00
 Dog 1   2 00   10 61

Happoldt, J. H.
 Real Estate........................1,200   16 80
 Slave 1   3 00   19 80

Happoldt, Mrs. S. E.
 Real Estate........................6,000   84 00
 Slaves...2   6 00   90 00

Happoldt, Mrs. S. A.
 Real Estate 5,000   70 00
 Slaves 3   9 00   79 00

Harbers, Carolina C.
 Slaves 3   ....   9 00

Harbers, H.
 Stock of Goods......................1,000   14 00

Harbers, C. H.
 Real Estate........................11,100   155 40
 Stock of Goods 300   4 20
 Dog 1   2 00   161 60

Harbers, Estate D. H.
 Real Estate........................2,500   35 00

Harbeson, John
 Stock of Goods....................6,000   84 00

Harbeson, J & M.
 Stock of Goods....................3,000   42 00

Hare, Estate Robert W
 Real Estate........................7,000   98 00

Hare, Calhoun & Co.
 Real Estate......................18,000   ....   252 00

Harenburg, J F
 Stock of Goods.......................300   4 20

Harenburg, H.
 Stock of Goods.......................300   4 20

Harenburg, H., Trustee
 Slaves...2   6 00

Hargrave, John
 Real Estate........................4,600   64 40
 Slave 1   3 00
 Carriage 1   20 00
 Horse... 1   10 00   97 40

Harken, John
 Horse 1   10 00

                                                              TAXES.

Harleston, Edward
  Slaves 4   12 00
Harleston, John, Jr.
  Slaves 3   9 00
  Dog 1   2 00   11 00
Harleston, T. C.
  Slaves 4   .... 12 00
Harleston, John
  Real Estate.........10,000   .... 140 00
Harleston, John M.
  Interest on Bonds, &c.......840 21 00
  Slaves.............6   18 00   39 00
Harleston, Mrs. E. P
  Real Estate.........4,500   63 00
  Slaves.............11   33 00
  Carriage...........1   20 00
  Horse 1   10 00   126 00
Harleston, Miss E.
  Real Estate.........9,000   126 00
  Slaves.............13   39 00
  Dog...............1   2 00   167 00
Harms, C.
  Real Estate.........7,200   100 80
  Horse.............1   10 00   110 80
Harper, Estate Elizabeth
  Slave.............1   3 00
  Dog...............1   2 00   5 00
Harral, William
  Real Estate.........6,000   84 00
  Carriage..........1   20 00
  Horse.............1   10 00   114 00
Harral, Nichols & Co.
  Stock of Goods......30,000   420 00
  Horse.............1   10 00   430 00
Harris, Isaac
  Real Estate.........1,400   19 60
  Stock of Goods......1,500   21 00
  Slaves.............8   24 00   64 60
Harris, Hiram
  Real Estate.........3,500   49 00
Harris, A. J
  Slaves.............3   9 00
Harrison, Joseph W
  Real Estate.........27,200   380 80
  Stock of Goods......5,000   70 00
  Slaves.............5   15 00   465 80

TAXES.

Hart, Samuel, Sr.
 Real Estate..........................2,500 35 00
 Stock of Goods....................5,000 70 00
 Slave.......................................1 3 00 108 00

Hart, S. N.
 Real Estate........................10,000 140 00
 Interest on Bonds, &c..............400 10 00
 Slaves......................................6 18 00
 Dog...1 2 00 170 00

Hart, S. N., in trust for Mary Cohen
 Real Estate..........................6,000 .... 84 00

Hart, S. N., in trust for Caroline E.
 Real Estate..........................3,500   49 00

Hart, S. N & Co.
 Stock of Goods..................40,000 .... 560 00

Hart, S. N. & H. N.
 Real Estate........................17,000 .... 238 00

Hart, Mrs. Rachel N.
 Real Estate........................14,000 196 00
 Slaves......................................2 6 00 202 00

Hart, Henrietta
 Real Estate........................10,000 140 00
 Slave.......................................1 3 00 143 00

Hart, Estate H. N.
 Real Estate..........................6,500 .... 91 00

Harth, William
 Slaves......................................3   9 00

Harth, W I.
 Slaves......................................2 6 00
 Carriage..................................1 30 00
 Horses.....................................2 20 00 56 00

Hartz, John H.
 Real Estate..........................7,000 98 00
 Stock of Goods....................1,000 14 00
 Slaves......................................9 27 00 139 00

Harvey, Estate Isabella
 Real Estate........................18,100 253 40
 Slaves......................................7 21 00 274 40

Hasell, Andrew G.
 Slaves......................................3   9 00

Haseltine & Walton
 Stock of Goods..................15,000 210 00
 Slave.......................................1 3 00
 Carriage..................................1 20 00
 Horses.....................................2 20 00 253 00

			TAXES.
Haseltine, D. B.			
Real Estate	1,500		21 00
Haskell, W E., Trustee			
Real Estate	3,500	49 00	
Slaves	9	27 00	
Carriage	1	20 00	
Horse	1	10 00	106 00
Hastedt, H.			
Real Estate	19,600	274 40	
Stock of Goods	1,000	14 00	
Carriage	1	20 00	
Horse	1	10 00	318 40
Hastie, William S.			
Carriage	1	20 00	
Horse	1	10 00	30 00
Hastie, Calhoun & Co.			
Stock of Goods	27,566	385 92	
Slave	1	3 00	388 92
Hastings, Patrick			
Real Estate	1,000		14 00
Hatch, L. M., self, Trust Estate and Insurance			
Real Estate	13,000	182 00	
Stock of Goods	22,000	308 00	
Slave	1	3 00	
Commissions	2,500	62 50	
Premiums of Insurance	11,881	148 60	704 01
Hatch, William, Trustee			
Slave	1		3 00
Hatch, William			
Real Estate	1,000	14 00	
Slave	1	3 00	17 00
Hatcher, B. J. E.			
Real Estate	7,000	98 00	
Slaves	8	24 00	122 00
Hauck, Estate John H.			
Real Estate	7,600		106 40
Haupt, Eliza			
Real Estate	4,000		56 00
Hautz, Francis			
Stock of Goods	200		2 80
Haviland, Stevenson & Co.			
Stock of Goods	35,000	490 00	
Slaves	2	6 00	496 00
Hawkesworth, William			
Slave	1		3 00

		TAXES.

Hayden, Thomas
 Real Estate 800   11 20

Hayden, Jane
 Real Estate 2,800   39 20
 Slave 1   3 00   42 20

Hayden, A. H.
 Slaves 6   18 00
 Dog 1   2 00   20 00

Hayden & Whilden
 Stock of Goods 50,000   700 00

Hayne, Estate William E.
 Real Estate 5,000   70 00

Hayne, J. W
 Real Estate 16,000   224 00
 Slaves 12   36 00
 Income 5,587   139 68
 Dog 1   2 00   401 68

Hayne, Mary H.
 Real Estate 10,000   140 00
 Interest on Bonds, &c 316   7 90
 Slaves 4   12 00   159 90

Hayne, Miss R. B.
 Interest on Bonds, &c 210   5 25
 Slaves 10   30 00
 Dog 1   2 00   37 25

Hayne, A. P
 Real Estate 9,000   126 00
 Slaves 13   39 00
 Carriage 1   30 00
 Horses 2   20 00
 Dog 1   2 00   217 00

Hayne, Trust Estate, Mrs. R. B. and children
 Real Estate 16,000   224 00
 Interest on Bonds, &c 700   17 50   241 50

Hayne, William A., in trust for E. P and children
 Interest on Bonds, &c 287   7 18
 Slaves 9   27 00   34 18

Hayne, Emily
 Real Estate 8,000   112 00
 Slaves 8   24 00
 Carriage 1   20 00
 Horse 1   10 00   166 00

Hayne, S. S.
 Interest on Bonds, &c 200   5 00
 Slave 1   3 00   8 00

		TAXES.
Hayne, Estate William A.		
Slaves................16		48 00
Hayne, W Alston		
Real Estate............500	7 00	
Slave................1	3 00	10 00
Hayne & Yates		
Real Estate............7,000	98 00	
Stock of Goods............8,000	112 00	
Slave................1	3 00	213 00
Hayes, Leroy W.. Agent of M. Johnston		
Slave................1	....	3 00
Hazelhurst, R., Trustee of E. R. Deas		
Real Estate............5,000	....	70 00
Hazelhurst, Mary and children		
Slaves................13	....	39 00
Heath, Estate Thomas H.		
Real Estate............3,000	42 00	
Slaves................9	27 00	
Dog................1	2 00	71 00
Heath, Eliza		
Real Estate............7,800	109 20	
Slave................1	3 00	112 20
Healy, Patrick		
Stock of Goods............200		2 80
Hedderly, George		
Real Estate............5,000	70 00	
Stock of Goods............600	8 40	78 40
Hedley, Estate J. L.		
Real Estate............15,300	214 20	
Interest on Bonds, &c............490	12 25	
Slaves................5	15 00	241 45
Heesemann, John		
Stock of Goods............975		13 65
Heidt, Mary		
Stock of Goods............200	....	2 80
Heilbron, Estate Mrs. H.		
Real Estate............8,000	....	112 00
Heine, W		
Real Estate............9,000	126 00	
Stock of Goods............300	4 20	
Slaves................4	12 00	
Carriage................1	20 00	
Horse................1	10 00	
Dog................1	2 00	174 20

			TAXES.
Heine, W., Trustee			
Slave	1		3 00
Heins, John			
Stock of Goods	800		11 20
Heins, Trust Estate Caroline L.			
Real Estate	4,000		56 00
Heissenbuttle, C. M.			
Stock of Goods	300		4 20
Hencken, C. F.			
Stock of Goods	800	11 20	
Dog	1	2 00	13 20
Hencken, Henry			
Real Estate	6,000		84 00
Heneberry, Martin			
Real Estate	1,200	....	16 80
Henerey, John T.			
Real Estate	4,200	....	58 80
Henerey, William S.			
Real Estate	13,300	186 20	
Slaves	7	21 00	
Horse	1	10 00	
Dog	1	2 00	219 20
Henerey, Trust Estate M. E.			
Slaves	9		27 00
Henerey, W S., in trust for Whilden			
Real Estate	2,200		30 80
Henry, S. W., Trustee			
Slaves	5		15 00
Henry, E.			
Slave	1	....	3 00
Henry, Estate R. F.			
Real Estate	152,100	2,129 40	
Slaves	13	39 00	2,168 40
Henry, M. C.			
Real Estate	1,000	14 00	
Slave	1	3 00	17 00
Henneke, L.			
Stock of Goods	500		7 00
Hennessey, Michael			
Real Estate	1,700	....	23 80
Hennessey, Thomas			
Real Estate	2,000		28 00
Herbemont, Clara J.			
Slaves	3		9 00

		TAXES.
Herbert, M.		
Stock of Goods..................500	....	7 00
Herckenwrath, Wragg & Co., in liquidation		
Real Estate..................16,000	224 00	
Stock of Goods...............16,000	224 00	
Income..........................15,000	375 00	813 00
Heriott, W B.		
Dividends......................154	3 85	
Shipping 2,500	18 75	
Income 3,600	90 00	112 60
Heriott, B. G.		
Real Estate..................16,500	231 00	
Slaves 6	18 00	
Carriage........................1	20 00	
Commissions 800	20 00	
Horse 1	10 00	299 00
Heriott, B. D.		
Real Estate...................8,000	112 00	
Slaves..........................10	30 00	
Carriage........................1	20 00	
Horse 1	10 00	172 00
Heriott, B. G., and W J Axson, Trustees		
Slaves..........................17		51 00
Heriott, Mrs. C. H.		
Real Estate...................6,500	91 00	
Slave...........................1	3 00	94 00
Heriott, Eliza F		
Real Estate...................2,200	30 80	
Slaves..........................3	9 00	39 80
Heriott, Edwin		
Slaves..........................3	9 00	
Carriage........................1	20 00	
Horse...........................1	10 00	39 00
Heriott, Estate Maria E.		
Real Estate 4,000	56 00	
Slaves..........................8	24 00	80 00
Hernandez, J. W		
Real Estate..................2,500	....	35 00
Hernandez, John		
Real Estate..................3,500	49 00	
Slaves..........................3	9 00	58 00
Hernholm, A.		
Real Estate..................2,000	28 00	
Stock of Goods..................300	4 20	32 20
Herron, J S.		
Real Estate..................5,000	70 00	
Slave 1	3 00	73 00

			TAXES.
Herron, W P., minor			
Real Estate	3,000		42 00
Hertz, E. E., Trustee			
Real Estate	2,000		28 00
Hertz, Dr. T E.			
Carriage	1	20 00	
Income	100	2 50	
Horse	1	10 00	32 50
Hervey, Elizabeth G.			
Slaves	4		12 00
Hervey, George			
Slaves	2		6 00
Hevey, Mrs. F			
Real Estate	2,000		28 00
Hewes, E. E.			
Interest on Bonds, &c	150		3 75
Hewitt, Martha E.			
Real Estate	2,000		28 00
Heyn, J H.			
Real Estate	2,500	35 00	
Stock of Goods	300	4 20	
Dog	1	2 00	41 20
Heyns, Margaret			
Real Estate	800		11 20
Heyward, T. Savage			
Real Estate	14,900	208 60	
Slaves	20	60 00	
Carriage	1	30 00	
Carriage	1	20 00	
Horses	5	50 00	
Dog	1	2 00	370 60
Heyward, T. Savage, Trustee			
Slaves	2		6 00
Heyward, W H.			
Real Estate	20,000	280 00	
Slaves	16	48 00	
Carriage	1	30 00	
Carriage	1	20 00	
Horses	4	40 00	
Dogs	2	4 00	422 00
Heyward, Mrs. A. J			
Real Estate	15,000	210 00	
Interest on Bonds, &c	112	2 88	
Slaves	7	21 00	
Dog	1	2 00	235 80

		TAXES.
Heyward, N		
Real Estate ...2,000		28 00
Heyward, George C.		
Real Estate...7,000	98 00	
Slaves ...14	42 00	
Carriage...1	20 00	
Commissions...4,400	110 00	
Horse...1	10 00	
Dog...1	2 00	282 00
Heyward, Thomas J.		
Interest on Bonds, &c...280		7 00
Heyward, George C., Trustee		
Interest on Bonds. &c...420	10 50	
Slaves...2	6 00	16 50
Heyward, J. B.		
Real Estate...18,000	252 00	
Slaves...22	66 00	
Carriage...1	30 00	
Horses...4	40 00	388 00
Heyward, William		
Slave...1		3 00
Heyward, Daniel		
Real Estate...20,000	280 00	
Slaves...15	45 00	
Carriage...1	30 00	
Horses...2	20 00	375 00
Heyward, Charles		
Real Estate...30,000	420 00	
Slaves...13	39 00	
Carriage...1	30 00	
Carriage...1	20 00	
Shipping...2,000	15 00	
Horses...3	30 00	554 00
Hickey, Charles		
Stock of Goods...1,800	....	25 20
Hicks, H. H.		
Real Estate...300	4 20	
Slaves...2	6 00	10 20
Hiffernan, Dennis		
Real Estate...1,500	....	21 00
Hilken, C.		
Stock of Goods...1,200	16 80	
Dog...1	2 00	18 80
Hill, Eliza C.		
Real Estate...1,000	....	14 00

		TAXES.
Hillegas, Caroline C.		
Real Estate............600		8 40
Hillen, Jacob H.		
Stock of Goods............700	9 80	
Slave............1	3 00	
Dog............1	2 00	14 80
Hilson, Estate John		
Real Estate............2,700	37 80	
Interest on Bonds,&c............183	4 58	
Slaves............4	12 00	54 38
Hilson, W C.		
Real Estate............600		8 40
Hines, J. H.		
Real Estate............1,800	25 20	
Dog............1	2 00	27 20
Hines, P., and M. Crogen		
Real Estate............2,500		35 00
Hinson, Joseph B.		
Slave............1		3 00
Hiott, Martha		
Real Estate............2,000		28 00
Hisch, Frederick		
Real Estate............1,000		14 00
Hitchcock, Dr. Charles M.		
Real Estate............200		1 80
Hobbs, William		
Real Estate............3,500	49 00	
Stock of Goods............200	2 80	51 80
Hockaday, William		
Real Estate............12,000	168 00	
Slaves............2	6 00	
Dogs............2	4 00	178 00
Hockaday, William, Trustee		
Slaves............2		6 00
Hodge, G. P		
Slaves............4		12 00
Hoff, Mrs. M. E.		
Real Estate............3,000	42 00	
Slaves............2	6 00	48 00
Hoffman, H.		
Real Estate............2,000	28 00	
Stock of Goods............800	11 20	
Slaves............5	15 00	54 20
Hogan, Trust Estate Bridgett		
Real Estate............3,000		42 00

			TAXES.

Hogan, Richard
 Real Estate.........................2,500 35 00
 Slaves 5 15 00 50 00
Hogan, Patrick
 Real Estate.........................5,000 70 00
 Slaves...................................5 15 00 85 00
Hogarth, Henry
 Real Estate.........................8,375 117 25
 Slaves.................................23 69 00 186 25
Holbrook, Mrs. H. P., and Miss E. L. Rutledge
 Real Estate.......................15,000 210 00
 Slaves 26 78 00
 Carriage..............................1 30 00
 Horses 2 20 00
 Dog......................................1 2 00 340 00
Holland, Edwin C.
 Real Estate.........................5,000 70 00
 Horse 1 10 00 80 00
Holland, Parker J
 Real Estate.........................6,000 84 00
 Slaves 15 45 00 129 00
Holland, Selina A.
 Slaves 7   21 00
Holley, Mena
 Real Estate.........................1,200 16 80
 Horse..................................1 10 00 26 80
Hollings, B. F
 Real Estate.........................3,500 49 00
 Stock of Goods....................800 11 20
 Dog......................................1 2 00 62 20
Hollings, N.
 Real Estate.........................3,000 42 00
 Stock of Goods....................800 11 20
 Dog 1 2 00 55 20
Holmes, Edmund G.
 Slaves 2 6 00
 Dogs....................................2 4 00 10 00
Holmes, W P
 Commissions.......................1,200 .... 30 00
Holmes, E. E. and others
 Real Estate.........................7,000 98 00
 Slaves 12 36 00
 Dogs....................................2 4 00 138 00
Holmes & Stoney
 Shipping..............................3,200 24 00
 Commissions.......................4,000 100 00 124 00

		TAXES.

Holmes, J. W., Trustee
 Interest on Bonds, &c.............136 3 40
 Slaves..4 12 00 15 40

Holmes, Anna A.
 Real Estate.................2,500 00 35 00
 Interest on Bonds, &c............292 36 7 31
 Slaves......................................16 48 00
 Dog..1 2 00 92 31

Holmes, Rebecca
 Real Estate....................11,500 161 00
 Slaves......................................19 57 00 218 00

Holmes & Co.
 Stock of Goods ....5,000 .... 70 00

Holmes, Rebecca T.
 Slaves..7 21 00

Holmes, F S., Trustee
 Real Estate..........................7,000 98 00
 Slaves.......................................2 6 00 104 00

Holmes, J. G.
 Real Estate........................25,000 350 00
 Slaves.......................................2 6 00 356 00

Holmes, J G., in trust
 Slaves.......................................9 .... 27 00

Holmes, Rebecca T., in trust
 Slaves.......................................3 9 00

Holmes, J E, Trustee
 Interest on Bonds, &c..............490 .... 12 25

Holmes, Estate Mrs. A. M. and Miss Thayer
 Real Estate..........................8,000 112 00
 Slaves......................................17 51 00
 Dog..1 2 00 165 00

Holmes, W H.
 Real Estate........................23,000 322 00
 Slaves.......................................7 21 00 343 00

Holmes, W H., Executor Little
 Slaves.......................................2 .... 6 00

Holmes, Mrs. C. M.
 Interest on Bonds, &c..............625 15 63
 Slaves.....................................11 33 00 48 63

Holmes, Mary E.
 Real Estate..........................4,000 56 00
 Slaves.......................................6 18 00 74 00

Holmes, Edgar H.
 Slaves.......................................2 .... 6 00

			TAXES.
Holmes, Eliza F.			
Real Estate	6,000	84 00	
Interest on Bonds, &c	2,720	68 00	
Slaves	17	51 00	
Carriage	1	30 00	
Horses	2	20 00	
Dog	1	2 00	255 00
Holmes, A. G.			
Slaves	3		9 00
Holmes, W E.			
Slaves	2		6 00
Holmes, Margaret R.			
Slaves	6		18 00
Holmes, John H.			
Real Estate	5,000	70 00	
Slave	1	3 00	73 00
Holmes, George L.			
Horse	1		10 00
Holwell, T. W			
Real Estate	1,200	16 80	
Dog	1	2 00	18 80
Honour, John H.			
Real Estate	8,500	119 00	
Slaves	4	12 00	
Carriage	1	20 00	
Horse	1	10 00	161 00
Honour, Theodore A.			
Real Estate	1,200		16 80
Honour, J Lawrence			
Real Estate	7,500		105 00
Honour, J. H., Jr.			
Real Estate	4,500	63 00	
Slave	1	3 00	66 00
Honour, Susan E.			
Slave	1		3 00
Hood, Eliza			
Stock of Goods	200	2 80	
Slaves	8	24 00	26 80
Hopkins, J Ward			
Dog	1		2 00
Hopkins, Estate James A.			
Real Estate	9,000	126 00	
Slaves	3	9 00	135 00
Hopkins, Hudson & Co.			
Commissions	15,000		375 00

		TAXES.
Hopley, Geo. A. & Co.		
Commissions..................20,000		500 00
Horlbeck, Dr. Elias		
Real Estate..................19,900	278 60	
Interest on Bonds, &c............1,050	26 25	
Slaves.........................18	54 00	
Carriage.......................1	30 00	
Carriage.......................1	20 00	
Income.....................2,000	50 00	
Horses.........................3	30 00	488 85
Horlbeck, Dr. Elias, Trustee		
Slave..........................1		3 00
Horlbeck, Daniel		
Real Estate...................6,700	93 80	
Interest on Bonds, &c............325	8 13	
Slaves..........................2	6 00	
Carriage.......................1	20 00	
Horse..........................1	10 00	137 93
Horlbeck, Daniel, Trustee H. H. and wife		
Real Estate..................25,000	350 00	
Slaves..........................4	12 00	362 00
Horlbeck, Daniel, Executor of J Finley		
Real Estate..................2,300		32 20
Horlbeck, Peter		
Real Estate..................2,500	35 00	
Slave..........................1	3 00	
Dogs...........................2	4 00	42 00
Horlbeck, Edward		
Real Estate..................22,000	308 00	
Slaves.........................7	21 00	
Dog............................1	2 00	331 00
Horlbeck, Henry		
Real Estate..................74,300	1,040 20	
Slaves........................11	33 00	
Carriage.......................1	30 00	
Horses.........................3	30 00	1,133 20
Horlbeck, Henry, Trustee P H. and wife		
Real Estate..................12,000	168 00	
Slave..........................1	3 00	171 00
Horlbeck, Henry, Edward and John		
Slaves.........................5	....	15 00
Horlbeck, Henry, Daniel, Edward and John		
Real Estate..................28,900	404 60	
Slave..........................1	3 00	407 60

			TAXES.
Horlbeck, John			
Real Estate.....................37,500	525 00		
Slaves............................10	30 00		
Carriage..........................1	30 00		
Horses 5	50 00	635 00	
Horlbeck, Louisa M. and Ann G.			
Real Estate.....................12,000	168 00		
Dog................................1	2 00	170 00	
Horlbeck, D., and F D. Richardson and R. Giles			
Slaves...........................6	.....	18 00	
Horlbeck, Dr. W C.			
Slaves...........................10	30 00		
Carriage..........................1	20 00		
Income..........................1,500	37 50		
Horse.............................1	10 00	97 50	
Horry. Estate of E.			
Slaves...........................3	.....	9 00	
Horry, Ann J.			
Interest on Bonds, &c..........700	17 50		
Slaves............................16	48 00	65 50	
Horsey, T. M.			
Real Estate.....................18,500	259 00		
Slaves............................3	9 00		
Carriage..........................1	30 00		
Horses............................2	20 00		
Dog................................1	2 00	320 00	
Horsey, Auten & Co.			
Stock of Goods 12,500	.....	175 00	
Horsey, Mrs. F. R.			
Slave.............................1	.....	3 00	
Horsey, S. G.			
Slave.............................1	.....	3 00	
Horsey, John R., self, and in trust			
Real Estate.....................3,000	42 00		
Slaves............................2	6 00		
Horse.............................1	10 00	58 00	
Hort, Miss S. R.			
Slaves...........................25	.....	75 00	
Horton, T. A. P			
Real Estate.....................14,000	196 00		
Slaves............................6	18 00	214 00	
Horton & Shephard			
Stock of Goods..............6,000		84 00	
Hosegood, George E.			
Real Estate.....................2,800	.....	39 20	

		TAXES.	
Housemeyer, Mrs. E. M.			
Real Estate............2,000	28 00		
Interest on Bonds,&c.........700	17 50		
Slave............1	3 00	48 50	
Houston, W H.			
Real Estate............100,700	1,409 80		
Slaves............23	69 00		
Dog............1	2 00	1,480 80	
Hoves, John			
Horse............1	10 00		
Dog............1	2 00	12 00	
Hovey, Walter			
Stock of Goods............8,000	....	112 00	
Howard, Estate R. F			
Slaves............4	....	12 00	
Howard, Elizabeth W., and children			
Real Estate............4,000	56 00		
Slaves............19	57 00	113 00	
Howard, Estate Harriett Lee			
Slaves............5		15 00	
Howard, Mrs. R. F Lee			
Slaves............2		6 00	
Howard, Estate H. N.			
Real Estate............4,500	....	63 00	
Howard, Stephen L.			
Real Estate............8,400	....	117 60	
Howard, Joseph L.			
Carriage............1	....	20 00	
Howard, Susan J H.			
Slaves............5	....	15 00	
Howe, Malvenia			
Real Estate............4,000		56 0	
Howe, Sarah S.			
Real Estate............2,500	35 00		
Slaves............21	63 00	98 0	
Howell, Adeline M.			
Real Estate............12,000	168 00		
Slaves............13	39 00	207 0	
Howland & Co.,			
Real Estate............8,000	112 00		
Slaves............2	6 00		
Carriage............1	20 00		
Commissions............5,100	127 50		
Horse............1	10 00	275 5	

			TAXES.
Huard, Mrs. C. P			
Real Estate	13,500	189 00	
Slaves	5	15 00	204 00
Hubert, C. N., for self, and as Trustee			
Real Estate	15,000	210 00	
Slaves	7	21 00	
Carriage	1	20 00	
Horse	1	10 00	
Dog	1	2 00	263 00
Hubert, C. N			
Real Estate	8,000	112 00	
Shipping	3,000	22 50	
Income	5,000	125 00	259 50
Huchet, Theodore, in trust			
Real Estate	4,000		56 00
Huchet, Theodore			
Real Estate	9,000		126 00
Huchet, Theodore, in trust for Mrs. Mottett			
Slaves	2		6 00
Hufmann, H. E.			
Stock of Goods	200		2 80
Huger, Dr. W H.			
Real Estate	5,000	70 00	
Slave	1	3 00	
Carriage	1	20 00	
Income	2,000	50 00	143 00
Huger, Daniel E.			
Real Estate	1,200		16 80
Huger, A. M.			
Slaves	7	21 00	
Carriage	1	20 00	
Horses	2	20 00	61 00
Huger, C. K.			
Real Estate	15,000	210 00	
Interest on Bonds, &c	1,352	33 80	
Slave	1	3 00	
Carriage	1	20 00	
Horses	2	20 00	286 80
Huger, A.			
Real Estate	10,000	140 00	
Slaves	8	24 00	
Carriage	1	30 00	
Horses	2	20 00	
Dog	1	2 00	216 00

TAXES.

Huger, Mrs. D. E.
 Real Estate...................13,000 182 00
 Slaves.....................8 24 00
 Carriage...................1 30 00
 Horses....................2 20 00
 Dog......................1 2 00 258 00

Huger, Miss E. P
 Real Estate...................5,000 70 00
 Interest on Bonds, &c............1,458 36 45
 Slaves.....................6 18 00 124 45

Huger, Estate Daniel
 Real Estate...................8,000 112 00
 Interest on Bonds, &c............1,800 46 25
 Slaves....................15 45 00 203 25

Huger, Dr. W H., Trustee for A. H. Dunkin and wife
 Slaves....................4 .... 12 00

Huger, Dr. B.
 Real Estate...................8,000 112 00
 Slaves....................11 33 00
 Carriage...................1 30 00
 Horses....................2 20 00 195 00

Huggins, Thompson & McCoy
 Stock of Goods...............2,000 28 00
 Commissions.................600 15 00 43 00

Huggins, Elizabeth
 Slaves....................2 .... 6 00

Huggins, H.
 Slaves....................4 12 00
 Carriage...................1 30 00
 Horses....................2 20 00 62 00

Hughes, E. T.
 Carriage...................1 20 00
 Horse....................1 10 00 30 00

Hughes, H. A.
 Slave....................1 .... 3 00

Hughes, W N.
 Stock of Goods...............2,094 .... 29 31

Hughes, T. S.
 Stock of Goods................200 .... 2 80

Hughes, Optimus E.
 Real Estate...................5,500 77 00
 Slaves....................8 24 00 101 00

Huguinin, Mrs. A. M., Guardian
 Interest on Bonds, &c.........324 80 8 12
 Slaves....................4 12 00 20 12

		TAXES.

Huguinin, Mrs. A. M.
 Interest on Bonds, &c............4,429 110 73
 Slaves.....................................2   6 00
 Dog..1   2 00 118 73

Hull, A. S. & Co.
 Stock of Goods................1,500 21 00
 Slaves....................................5   15 00 36 00

Hume, Robert
 Real Estate......................10,000 140 00
 Interest on Bonds, &c............2,000 50 00
 Slaves..................................11   33 00
 Carriage................................1   30 00
 Horses...................................2   20 00
 Dog..1   2 00 275 00

Hume, Thomas M.
 Real Estate...................17,000 238 00
 Slaves....................................6   18 00
 Carriage................................1   30 00
 Commissions....................2,000 50 00
 Horses...................................2   20 00
 Dog..1   2 00 358 00

Hume, William, and children
 Real Estate.......................8,700 121 80
 Interest on Bonds, &c............340   8 50
 Slaves....................................6   18 00
 Dog..1   2 00 150 30

Hummel, William
 Real Estate.......................5,500 77 00
 Slaves....................................2   6 00 83 00

Hummel & Schwake
 Stock of Goods................1,400   19 60

Humphrey, Mrs. H. M.
 Real Estate.......................1,400   14 00

Humphrey, Estate John
 Real Estate.......................3,000 42 00
 Slaves....................................6   18 00 60 00

Huncken, George
 Stock of Goods....................800 11 20
 Commissions.......................200   5 00 16 20

Hunt, Ann R.
 Real Estate.......................3,000 42 00
 Slaves....................................3   9 00 51 00

Hunt, Dr. William M.
 Slaves..................................14   .... 42 00

	TAXES.

Hunt, Nathaniel
 Real Estate......................1,000 14 00
 Dog..................................1 2 00 16 00

Hunt, Nathaniel & Co.
 Commissions..................2,500   62 50

Hunter, R.
 Real Estate......................14,800 207 20
 Slave................................1 3 00
 Dog..................................1 2 00 212 20

Hunter, Mrs. John
 Slaves..............................2   6 00

Hunter, Estate John
 Real Estate......................133,200   1,864 80

Hurkamp, John
 Real Estate......................13,000 182 00
 Stock of Goods................3,000 42 00 224 00

Hurst, James M.
 Slave................................1   3 00

Hutchinson, Anna N.
 Slave................................1   3 00

Hutchinson, T Leger
 Real Estate......................7,000 98 00
 Slaves..............................6 18 00
 Dog..................................1 2 00 118 00

Hutson, Estate John
 Real Estate......................800   11 20

Hutson, S. D.
 Real Estate......................3,200   44 80

Hutwalker, William N.
 Real Estate......................1,200   16 80

Hyams, Moses D.
 Real Estate......................77,500 1,085 00
 Slaves..............................8 24 00
 Carriage...........................1 20 00
 Horse...............................1 10 00 1,139 00

Hyams, Pinckney A. & Hamilton
 Stock of Goods................1,365 19 11
 Slave................................1 3 00
 Carriage...........................1 20 00
 Horse...............................1 10 00 52 11

Hyatt, McBurney & Co.
 Real Estate......................18,000 252 00
 Stock of Goods................149,815 2,097 41
 Shipping..........................500 3 75 2,353 16

			TAXES.
Hyde, Simeon			
Slave	1		3 00
Hyde, Gregg & Day			
Stock of Goods	35,000		490 00
Hyer, James S.			
Real Estate	3,900	54 60	
Slave	1	3 00	57 60
Hymes, Rebecca.			
Stock of Goods	500		7 00
Hyndman, T. A.			
Slave	1		3 00
Illing, Augustus			
Stock of Goods	2,000		28 00
Inglesby, William H.			
Real Estate	11,200	156 80	
Interest on Bonds, &c	225	5 63	
Slaves	7	21 00	
Income	848	8 70	
Dog	1	2 00	194 13
Inglesby, J. S.			
Real Estate	17,000	238 00	
Slaves	8	24 00	262 00
Ingraham, Mary R.			
Real Estate	6,500	91 00	
Slaves	13	39 00	130 00
Ingraham, D. N.			
Real Estate	4,700	65 80	
Slave	1	3 00	68 80
Ingraham, William Postell			
Real Estate	18,000	252 00	
Slaves	5	15 00	267 00
Ingraham, J H.			
Real Estate	5,100	71 40	
Slave	1	3 00	
Carriage	1	30 00	
Horses	3	30 00	134 40
Ingraham & Webb			
Income	8,000		200 00
Institute, South Carolina			
Real Estate	50,000	....	700 00
Institution, Charleston Saving			
Real Estate	10,000		140 00
Irvin, Christopher			
Stock of Goods	150	....	2 10

		TAXES.
Isbell, H.		
Stock of Goods..........2,700	....	37 80
Itjen, F.		
Stock of Goods..........1,000		14 00
Itjen, John		
Stock of Goods..........400		5 60
Izard, Allen S.		
Slaves..........2	6 00	
Carriage..........1	30 00	
Horses..........2	20 00	56 00
Jackson, C. F.		
Real Estate..........3,000		42 00
Jackson, C. F & Co.		
Real Estate..........8,500	119 00	
Stock of Goods..........12,000	168 00	287 00
Jackson, Mrs. M. S. S.		
Slave..........1	....	3 00
Jackson, George, Sr.		
Real Estate..........10,000	140 00	
Slaves..........6	18 00	158 00
Jackson, George, Jr.		
Stock of Goods..........1,300	....	18 20
Jackson, Mrs. & Burgess		
Real Estate..........10,000	....	140 00
Jacob, J. S.		
Stock of Goods..........2,000	28 00	
Slave..........1	3 00	31 00
Jacobi, W J.		
Real Estate..........21,600	302 40	
Slave..........1	3 00	305 40
Jacobi, Nathaniel		
Stock of Goods..........1,750	24 50	
Slave..........1	3 00	27 50
Jacobs, F. C.		
Real Estate..........2,500	....	35 00
Jacobs, H. R., Trustee		
Slave..........1		3 00
Jacobs, Myer		
Real Estate..........5,600	78 40	
Slaves..........4	12 00	90 40
Jacobs, Ferdinand		
Slaves..........4	12 00	
Dogs..........2	4 00	16 00
Jacoby, Elizabeth		
Real Estate..........11,200	....	156 80

			TAXES.
Jacoby, S. A.			
Stock of Goods	300		4 20
Jager, Johanna			
Real Estate	4,000	56 00	
Slave	1	3 00	59 00
Jager, John A.			
Real Estate	1,200		16 80
Jager, Henry			
Stock of Goods	1,000		14 00
James, W H.			
Slave	1		3 00
James, Mary Ann			
Real Estate	3,000		42 00
James, Trust Estate Mrs. Robert			
Real Estate	1,500	21 00	
Dog	1	2 00	23 00
Jamieson, Mary			
Real Estate	600		8 40
Jarckey, George H.			
Real Estate	3,500		49 00
Jefferson, George			
Real Estate	1,800		25 20
Jefferson, George & Co.			
Carriage	1	20 00	
Horse	1	10 00	30 00
Jeffords, W G.			
Real Estate	4,000	56 00	
Slave	1	3 00	59 00
Jeffords, John H.			
Slaves	4		12 00
Jeffords, James			
Real Estate	6,000		84 00
Jeffords, Mrs. S. A.			
Slave	1		3 00
Jeffords & Co.			
Stock of Goods	16,000	224 00	
Commissions	9,000	225 00	449 00
Jeffords, R. J.			
Slave	1	3 00	
Dogs	2	4 00	7 00
Jeffords, Elizabeth			
Real Estate	8,500		119 00
Jeffords, T. A.			
Slaves	3		9 00

			TAXES.
Jeffords, Joseph D.			
Slave...............1		3 00	
Jenkins, Catherine C.			
Real Estate............3,500	49 00		
Interest on Bonds, &c........1,694	42 35		
Slaves...............12	36 00	127 35	
Jenkins, C. S.			
Real Estate............1,400	19 60		
Slaves...............2	6 00	25 60	
Jenkins, Miss C. E.			
Slave...............1		3 00	
Jenkins, Estate John			
Slaves...............8	....	24 00	
Jenkins, Elizabeth			
Slaves...............8		24 00	
Jenny, Robert			
Stock of Goods............1,000	14 00		
Slaves...............10	30 00	44 00	
Jennings, John S.			
Slaves...............3		9 00	
Jennings, David			
Real Estate............8,000	112 00		
Slaves...............7	21 00		
Carriage...............1	30 00		
Shipping............4,950	37 13		
Horses...............2	20 00		
Dog...............1	2 00	222 13	
Jennings, Thomlinson & Co.			
Stock of Goods............30,000	420 00		
Shipping............175	1 31	421 31	
Jervey, Thomas D.			
Real Estate............6,500		91 00	
Jervey, Miss G. C.			
Slave...............1		3 00	
Jervey, James P			
Real Estate............6,000	84 00		
Slaves...............4	12 00		
Carriage...............1	20 00		
Income............2,500	62 50		
Horses...............2	20 00	198 50	
Jervey, Theodore D.			
Real Estate............7,000	98 00		
Slaves...............11	33 00		
Carriage...............1	30 00		
Horses...............3	30 00	191 00	

	TAXES.

Jervey, William
    Real Estate..................8,000   112 00
    Interest on Bonds, &c..........420   10 50
    Slaves............................12   36 00
    Carriage...........................1   30 00
    Income.........................2,600   65 00
    Horses.............................2   20 00
    Dog................................1   2 00   275 50

Jervey, William, Trustee under will of F. Cordes
    Real Estate...................12,000   168 00
    Interest on Bonds, &c..........315   7 88   175 88

Jervey, Lewis
    Slave..............................1   3 00
    Dog................................1   2 00   5 00

Jervey, James C.
    Real Estate...................2,500   35 00
    Slave..............................1   3 00   38 00

Jervey, Mrs. E. H.
    Slaves.............................2   6 00

Jervis, Eliza E.
    Real Estate...................1,800   25 20
    Stock of Goods................400   5 60
    Slaves.............................9   27 00   57 80

Jenson, Dr. William
    Stock of Goods................700   9 80
    Dog................................1   2 00   11 80

Jewell vs. Jewell
    Real Estate...................4,000   56 00

Johnson, William
    Real Estate...................6,000   84 00
    Stock of Goods..............1,500   21 00
    Slaves.............................3   9 00
    Carriage...........................1   20 00
    Horse..............................1   10 00
    Dog................................1   2 00   146 00

Johnson, William, Trustee
    Real Estate...................12,000   168 00
    Slaves.............................8   24 00   192 00

Johnson, Horace C.
    Slave..............................1   3 00

Johnson, Estate John
    Real Estate...................3,000   42 00
    Interest on Bonds, &c...........35   88
    Slaves.............................2   6 00   48 88

Johnson, Estate William
    Real Estate...................4,000   ....   56 00

			TAXES.

Johnson, T. N
 Real Estate..........8,000 112 00
 Slave..........1 3 00
 Commissions..........5,500 137 50 252 50

Johnson, Capt. John
 Real Estate..........3,500 49 00

Johnson, Joseph
 Real Estate..........5,000 70 00
 Slaves..........2 6 00
 Dog..........1 2 00 78 00

Johnson, O. E. & A. S.
 Real Estate..........10,000 140 00

Johnson, Oscar E.
 Real Estate..........2,000 28 00
 Slaves..........4 12 00 40 00

Johnsons & Whiting
 Stock of Goods..........7,000 98 00

Johnson, Mary S.
 Real Estate..........7,000 98 00

Johnson, B.
 Real Estate..........3,500 49 00
 Stock of Goods..........1,500 21 00
 Slaves..........4 12 00 82 00

Johnson, John
 Slave..........1 3 00

Johnson, Miss A. W
 Slaves..........10 30 00

Johnson, Augustus S.
 Real Estate..........3,400 47 60

Johnson, Thomas A.
 Real Estate..........2,200 30 80
 Slave..........1 3 00 33 80

Johnson, Louisa B.
 Real Estate..........10,000 140 00
 Slave..........1 3 00 143 00

Johnson, J. W
 Real Estate..........1,500 21 00

Johnson, James H.
 Real Estate..........4,500 63 00
 Slaves..........8 24 00
 Horses..........2 20 00 107 00

Johnston, J M. C.
 Slaves..........11 33 00

Johnston, Charlotte
 Slaves..........12 36 00

			TAXES.
Johnston, C. and A.			
Real Estate	10,000	140 00	
Carriage	1	20 00	
Horse	1	10 00	170 00
Johnston, Crews & Brawley			
Real Estate	25,000	350 00	
Stock of Goods	102,000	1,428 00	
Slave	1	3 00	
Shipping	500	3 75	1,784 75
Johnston, A. S., Trustee M. R. J			
Real Estate	16,000	224 00	
Dividends	133	3 33	
Slaves	2	6 00	
Dog	1	2 00	235 33
Johnston, Anna			
Slaves	4		12 00
Johnston, George A.			
Slave	1		3 00
Jones, L. M.			
Real Estate	7,000	98 00	
Dog	1	2 00	100 00
Jones, Estate William H.			
Real Estate	5,000	70 00	
Slaves	5	15 00	85 00
Jones, Susan L.			
Real Estate	4,000	56 00	
Slaves	5	15 00	71 00
Jones, Sarah B.			
Real Estate	4,000	56 00	
Slave	1	3 00	
Dog	1	2 00	61 00
Jones, Edward C.			
Real Estate	8,500	119 00	
Interest on Bonds, &c	240	6 00	
Slaves	2	6 00	
Carriage	1	20 00	
Dogs	2	4 00	155 00
Jones, Estate William			
Real Estate	5,000	70 00	
Slaves	9	27 00	97 00
Jones, Augustus			
Real Estate	1,700	23 80	
Interest on Bonds, &c	110	2 75	
Slaves	5	15 00	
Dog	1	2 00	43 55

		TAXES.
Jones, F. M.		
Slave..........1		3 00
Jones, A. D.		
Slaves..........4	....	12 00
Jones, E. C. F		
Real Estate..........3,000	....	42 00
Jones, Trust Estate, H. M.		
Real Estate..........1,500	....	21 00
Jones, Margaret and children		
Real Estate..........1,200	....	16 80
Jones, Edward J.		
Real Estate..........5,500	77 00	
Slaves..........9	27 00	104 00
Jones, John H.		
Real Estate..........1,200		16 80
Jones, John H., Trustee		
Slaves..........3	....	9 00
Jones, Robert A.		
Real Estate..........1,000	....	14 00
Jones, Estate Henry		
Real Estate..........2,000		28 00
Jones, Charles L.		
Real Estate..........3,200	....	44 80
Jones, A. D., Trustee		
Slave..........1	....	3 00
Jones & Hanaburg		
Stock of Goods..........22,000	....	308 00
Jordan, Catherine		
Slave..........1		3 00
Jordan, Edward		
Real Estate..........3,500	49 00	
Slaves..........2	6 00	
Dog..........1	2 00	57 00
Jordan, J. F		
Real Estate..........3,200	44 80	
Slaves..........2	6 00	50 80
Joseph, J		
Slave..........1		3 00
Joseph, C. M.		
Real Estate..........3,000		42 00
Joye, Mrs. A. E. and children F S. Joye		
Real Estate..........3,500	....	49 00
Joye, Miss L. H.		
Slaves..........3	....	9 00

			TAXES.
Joye. Mrs. E. G.			
Real Estate	8,500	119 00	
Slaves	8	24 00	143 00
Jugnot, Charles, Estate			
Slaves	3		9 00
Jungbluth, John H.			
Real Estate	7,000	98 00	
Horse	1	10 00	
Dog	1	2 00	110 00
Just, Margaret			
Real Estate	20,000	280 00	
Slaves	12	36 00	
Dog	1	2 00	318 00
Kahrs, Henry			
Real Estate	3,000		42 00
Kalb, J H.			
Real Estate	37,700	527 80	
Slaves	7	21 00	
Carriage	1	20 00	
Horse	1	10 00	578 80
Kanapaux, J Eugene			
Slave	1		3 00
Kanapaux, A. V			
Slave	1		3 00
Kanapaux, F O.			
Slave	1		3 00
Kanapaux, Charles			
Slaves	9	27 00	
Dog	1	2 00	29 00
Kanapaux, J. T.			
Slave	1		3 00
Kanapaux, J T., Trustee E. F K.			
Slaves	7		21 00
Kanapaux, C. E., Trustee of Bolchoz and wife			
Real Estate	1,000		14 00
Kassens, D.			
Real Estate	5,000		70 00
Kaufman, Mrs. A. D.			
Real Estate	28,000	392 00	
Carriage	1	20 00	
Horse	1	10 00	422 00
Kaufman & Brother			
Stock of Goods	700		9 80
Kaul, C.			
Stock of Goods	300		4 20

			TAXES.
Kean, Francis A.			
Slave	1		3 00
Keckley, M. J			
Real Estate	4,500	63 00	
Slaves	5	15 00	78 00
Keefe, Mrs. S. J.			
Stock of Goods	500		7 00
Keeley, Mary G.			
Slaves	2	....	6 00
Keith, Estate C. C.			
Slaves	12	....	36 00
Keith, P Trapier			
Real Estate	12,000	168 00	
Interest on Bonds, &c	1,455	36 38	
Slaves	11	33 00	237 38
Keith, Estate J A.			
Real Estate	5,500	....	77 00
Keith, Susan S.			
Interest on Bonds, &c	1,225	30 63	
Slaves	12	36 00	66 63
Kellers, Dr. E. H.			
Real Estate	2,700	37 80	
Slave	1	3 00	
Carriage	1	15 00	
Income	300	7 50	63 30
Kelly, Wm.			
Real Estate	14,500	203 00	
Slaves	7	21 00	
Dog	1	2 00	226 00
Kelly, John			
Slave	1	....	3 00
Kelly, John			
Slaves	5	....	15 00
Kelly, Louisa and children			
Real Estate	2,000	....	28 00
Kelly, T.			
Real Estate	16,000	224 00	
Stock of Goods	20,000	280 00	504 00
Kelsey, Charlotte C.			
Real Estate	23,000		322 00
Kelsey, Charles			
Real Estate	11,000	....	154 00
Kelton, Otis H.			
Slaves	6	....	18 00

		TAXES.
Kemme, D. H.		
Real Estate.................5,000	70 00	
Stock of Goods...................500	7 00	
Slaves.....................4	12 00	89 00
Kendrick, Rev J. R.		
Interest on Bonds, &c..........280	7 00	
Slaves......................6	18 00	25 00
Kennedy, Mary R.		
Real Estate...............1,200	....	16 80
Kenifick, John		
Real Estate...............3,500	49 00	
Slaves.....................2	6 00	
Dog.......................1	2 00	57 00
Kenifick & Skrine		
Stock of Goods............5,000	70 00	
Shipping....................250	1 88	71 88
Kennedy, Mary A. J		
Real Estate...............9,900	....	138 60
Kennedy, Margaret		
Real Estate...............1,000	....	14 00
Kennedy, Mary A.		
Real Estate...............3,000	42 00	
Slaves.....................6	18 00	60 00
Kennedy, Michael		
Real Estate...............1,600	22 40	
Slave......................1	3 00	25 40
Kennedy, John D.		
Real Estate...............4,000	56 00	
Slave......................1	3 00	
Horse......................1	10 00	69 00
Kennedy, R. A., Trustee		
Slave......................1	....	3 00
Kennedy, James		
Real Estate...............2,500	....	35 00
Kennedy, James		
Slaves.....................2	6 00	
Dog.......................1	2 00	8 00
Kennedy, Estate D.		
Real Estate...............4,000	56 00	
Dog.......................1	2 00	58 00
Kennedy, A. J.		
Slave......................1	....	3 00
Kennedy, Patrick		
Real Estate................750	....	10 50

TAXES.

Kenney, Patrick
 Real Estate..................500   7 00

Kenney, John
 Real Estate................3,000   42 00

Kenney, Thomas
 Slave...........................1   3 00
 Dog..............................1   2 00   5 00

Kenney, James
 Real Estate...............10,600   148 40
 Dog..............................1   2 00   150 40

Kenny, Aeneas
 Dog..............................1   2 00

Kenny, John
 Real Estate................3,500   49 00
 Stock of Goods............500   7 00   56 00

Keogan, John
 Real Estate................1,200   16 80

Keogh, Eliza
 Stock of Goods............300   4 20

Kerr, Miss C.
 Slaves..........................4   12 00

Kerr, T. J
 Real Estate...............33,500   469 00
 Slaves..........................5   15 00
 Carriage........................1   20 00
 Commissions.............3,000   75 00
 Horse...........................1   10 00   589 00

Kerr, Miss M.
 Slaves..........................5   15 00

Kerrison, E. L.
 Real Estate...............14,000   196 00
 Slaves..........................5   15 00   211 00

Kerrison & Leiding
 Real Estate...............24,000   336 00
 Stock of Goods.......105,000   1,470 00   1,806 00

Kerrison, Charles
 Real Estate...............14,000   196 00
 Interest on Bonds, &c...1,295   32 38
 Slaves..........................7   21 00
 Carriage........................1   30 00
 Carriage........................1   20 00
 Horses..........................3   30 00
 Dog..............................1   2 00   331 38

Kiddell, Sarah W
 Real Estate................4,500   63 00

TAXES.

Kiely, William
   Real Estate..........................1,200   16 80

Kiep, John P
   Real Estate...........................9,000   126 00
   Stock of Goods.........................500   7 00   133 00

Kiep, J H.
   Stock of Goods.........................600   8 40

King, Letitia
   Real Estate...........................8,000   112 00
   Slaves....................................4   12 00
   Carriage..................................1   20 00
   Horse.....................................1   10 00
   Dog.......................................1   2 00   156 00

King, Mitchell
   Real Estate.........................101,000   1,414 00
   Interest on Bonds, &c............1,040   26 00
   Slaves...................................24   72 00
   Carriage..................................1   30 00
   Carriage..................................1   20 00
   Horses....................................3   30 00
   Dog.......................................1   2 00   1,594 00

King, Mitchell, Trustee
   Real Estate..........................40,000   560 00

King, Mitchell, Trustee
   Real Estate...........................7,500   105 00
   Interest on Bonds, &c..............875   21 88
   Slave.....................................1   3 00   129 88

King, Mitchell, Trustee, &c.
   Real Estate..........................12,000   168 00

King, Henry C.
   Real Estate...........................4,500   63 00
   Slaves....................................8   24 00
   Dog.......................................1   2 00   89 00

King, Henry C., Trustee
   Slaves....................................8   24 00

King, J G.
   Real Estate...........................9,000   126 00
   Stock of Goods.......................1,500   21 00
   Slave.....................................1   3 00
   Commissions..........................500   12 50   162 50

King, George W
   Shipping............................3,000   22 50
   Commissions.......................1,500   37 50   60 00

King, Archibald
   Real Estate.............................700   9 80
   Stock of Goods.....................4,800   67 20   77 00

			TAXES.
King, John			
Real Estate	8,500	119 00	
Slaves	8	24 00	143 00
King, Sarah A.			
Slave	1		3 00
King, Mrs. E. M.			
Slave	1		3 00
Kingdon, Estate John			
Real Estate	3,000		42 00
Kingman, S.			
Slaves	3		9 00
Kingman, Robert H.			
Slave	1		3 00
Kingman, E. J			
Real Estate	6,835	95 69	
Slave	1	3 00	98 69
Kingman, John			
Real Estate	2,200	30 80	
Slaves	2	6 00	
Carriage	1	20 00	
Horse	1	10 00	66 80
Kinloch, Mrs. M. J			
Slaves	3	9 00	
Dog	1	2 00	11 00
Kinloch, George			
Real Estate	22,000	308 00	
Slaves	10	30 00	
Dog	1	2 00	340 00
Kinloch, George & Son			
Stock of Goods	1,260	17 64	
Slaves	2	6 00	
Horses	2	20 00	43 64
Kinloch, H. W			
Slave	1	3 00	
Carriage	1	20 00	
Horse	1	10 00	
Dogs	2	4 00	37 00
Kinloch, Sarah R.			
Slaves	2		6 00
Kinloch, Dr. R. A.			
Real Estate	9,000	126 00	
Slaves	4	12 00	
Carriage	1	15 00	
Income	1,000	25 00	
Horse	1	10 00	188 00

			TAXES.
Kinloch, Matilda H.			
Slave	1		3 00
Kinsey, George F.			
Real Estate	3,000	42 00	
Slaves	2	6 00	
Carriage	1	20 00	
Horse	1	10 00	
Dog	1	2 00	80 00
Kinsman, H. W			
Stock of Goods	20,000	280 00	
Slaves	6	18 00	
Dog	1	2 00	300 00
Kinsman & Brother			
Stock of Goods	500	7 00	
Slaves	3	9 00	
Horse	1	10 00	
Dog	1	2 00	'28 00
Kirker, Estate James			
Real Estate	2,050	....	28 70
Kirkpatrick, John			
Real Estate	7,000	98 00	
Slaves	3	9 00	107 00
Kirkpatrick, J. & J. D.			
Income	25,000	....	625 00
Kirkpatrick, J. D.			
Slaves	7	....	21 00
Kirkpatrick, Rev. J L.			
Slaves	8	....	24 00
Kirkwood, William			
Real Estate	9,500	133 00	
Slaves	19	57 00	
Carriage	1	20 00	
Horse	1	10 00	220 00
Kirkwood & Knox			
Slaves	8	....	24 00
Kirkwood, W D. H.			
Slave	1	3 00	
Income	1,200	30 00	
Dog	1	2 00	35 00
Klaren, F. W			
Stock of Goods	250	....	3 50
Klein, E.			
Stock of Goods	500	....	7 00
Klencke, C. H.			
Real Estate	3,500	....	49 00

			TAXES.
Klencke, A.			
Real Estate	3,000	42 00	
Stock of Goods	800	11 20	53 20
Klepping, Diedrich			
Interest on Bonds, &c	300	....	7 50
Klinck, John			
Real Estate	5,000	70 00	
Slaves	9	27 00	
Dog	1	2 00	99 00
Klinck & Wickenberg			
Real Estate	30,000	420 00	
Slaves	3	9 00	429 00
Klinck, Wickenberg & Co.			
Stock of Goods	52,500	735 00	
Slave	1	3 00	
Horse	1	10 00	748 00
Klintworth, C.			
Stock of Goods	400		5 60
Klintworth, F.			
Stock of Goods	300		4 20
Knauff, Thomas J			
Real Estate	3,000	42 00	
Slaves	5	15 00	
Horse	1	10 00	67 00
Knauff, Thomas J., Trustee			
Slaves	2		6 00
Knight, James D., Estate			
Slaves	12		36 00
Knowles, Miss E.			
Stock of Goods	600	....	8 40
Knox, J. & W			
Stock of Goods	12,250	....	171 50
Knox, Miss J H.			
Slave	1	....	3 00
Knox, W P			
Real Estate	6,000	84 00	
Slaves	4	12 00	
Dog	1	2 00	98 00
Knox, John F.			
Slave	1		3 00
Knox, Estate Walter			
Real Estate	12,500	175 00	
Slaves	3	9 00	184 00

			TAXES.
Knust, Sarah			
Real Estate	2,000	28 00	
Slaves	2	6 00	34 00
Koennecke, A.			
Real Estate	12,500	175 00	
Slave	1	3 00	
Carriage	1	20 00	
Horse	1	10 00	208 00
Kohlmann, Diedrich			
Real Estate	4,000	56 00	
Stock of Goods	900	12 60	68 60
Kohnke, C. F			
Stock of Goods	1,000		14 00
Koldeway, F.			
Stock of Goods	2,000	28 00	
Dog	1	2 00	30 00
Konig. John H.			
Real Estate	8,000		112 00
Korber, George H.			
Real Estate	2,500		35 00
Kornahrens, C. L.			
Stock of Goods	500		7 00
Kornahrens, John H.			
Real Estate	4,500		63 00
Kornahrens, John L.			
Horse	1		10 00
Kracke, F D. C.			
Real Estate	9,000	126 00	
Stock of Goods	2,000	28 00	
Slaves	2	6 00	
Dog	1	2 00	162 00
Kreete, John			
Real Estate	1,000		14 00
Kressel, F.			
Stock of Goods	200		2 80
Kriete, George			
Stock of Goods	800		11 20
Kruse, Jacob			
Real Estate	8,000	112 00	
Stock of Goods	1,000	14 00	
Dog	1	2 00	128 00
Kuck, H.			
Stock of Goods	900		12 60
Kuck, J.			
Stock of Goods	800		11 20

			TAXES.

Kuck, Henry
- Real Estate................16,100   225 40
- Stock of Goods..............800   11 20
- Slaves.........................3   9 00   245 60

Kugely, Estate John
- Real Estate..................1,500   21 00
- Slaves.........................2   6 00   27 00

Kuhtmann, H. W
- Real Estate..................1,000   ....   14 00

Kunhardt, William
- Real Estate..................2,800   39 20
- Slaves.........................3   9 00
- Dog............................1   2 00   50 20

Laats, Mary M.
- Slaves.........................3   9 00

La Borde, J. P.
- Real Estate..................5,000   70 00
- Slaves.........................11   33 00   103 00

La Bruce, Mrs. C.
- Real Estate..................25,000 00   350 00
- Interest on Bonds, &c........2,597 39   64 93
- Slaves.........................9   27 00
- Carriage.......................1   30 00
- Horses.........................2   20 00   491 93

La Bruce, Selina P and Elizabeth R. Ward
- Slave..........................1   ....   3 00

La Bruce, John
- Slaves.........................3   ....   9 00

Lacassagne, E.
- Real Estate..................12,000   168 00
- Stock of Goods..............1,400   19 60   187 60

Lachicotte, P A.
- Shipping.....................600   ....   4 50

Lacoste, Charles A.
- Slave..........................1   ....   3 00

La Coste, Adel
- Slaves.........................7   21 00

Ladson, W H.
- Slaves.........................4   ....   12 00

Ladson, J H.
- Slaves.........................2   6 00
- Carriage.......................1   30 00
- Horses.........................2   20 00   56 00

Ladson, J. H., Trustee W C. Bee and children
- Slaves.........................4   ....   12 00

			TAXES.
Lafar, Rev. D. X.			
Real Estate	8,000 00	112 00	
Interest on Bonds, &c.	481 60	12 04	
Slaves	4	12 00	136 04
Lafar, Mrs. S. E.			
Slave	1		3 00
Lafar, W H.			
Slaves	3	9 00	
Dog	1	2 00	11 00
Lafar, Estate J J.			
Slave	1		3 00
Lafitte, John B.			
Real Estate	1,000		14 00
Lafitte, E.			
Slave	1		3 00
Lafitte, E. & Co.			
Slaves	3	9 00	
Shipping	8,000	60 00	
Income	4,600	115 00	184 00
Lafitte, Mrs. A. M.			
Slaves	4		12 00
Laidler, Wm.			
Real Estate	9,000	126 00	
Slaves	2	6 00	
Dog	1	2 00	134 00
Laidler, W., Trustee Gitsinger			
Slaves	2		6 00
Lalane, Peter B.			
Stock of Goods	2,500	35 00	
Slaves	7	21 00	
Dog	1	2 00	58 00
Lalaue, John A.			
Stock of Goods	1,000		14 00
Lamb, Mary S.			
Real Estate	12,000	168 00	
Slaves	5	15 00	
Carriage	1	30 00	
Horses	2	20 00	
Dog	1	2 00	235 00
Lamb, George B.			
Real Estate	6,550		91 70
Lambert & Brother			
Real Estate	18,000		182 00
Lambert & Howell			
Stock of Goods	18,000		252 00

			TAXES.
Lamble, Joseph			
Real Estate	5,700		79 80
Lampe, F			
Stock of Goods	1,000	14 00	
Slave	1	3 00	
Carriage	1	20 00	
Dog	1	2 00	39 00
Lance, F.			
Slaves	4		12 00
Lance, F and children			
Slaves	5		15 00
Lance, Sarah L.			
Slave	1		3 00
Landreth, David			
Real Estate	14,000		196 00
Landreth, D. & Co.			
Stock of Goods	3,800		53 20
Lange, John H.			
Real Estate	6,000	84 00	
Stock of Goods	300	4 20	88 20
Langley, Jane T.			
Real Estate	2,500		35 00
Lanigan, Michael			
Real Estate	1,000		14 00
Lanigan, Daniel			
Real Estate	1,450		20 30
Lanneau, Mrs. B.			
Real Estate	6,000	84 00	
Slave	1	3 00	87 00
Lanneau, Wm. S.			
Horse	1		10 00
Lanneau, Fleetwood			
Real Estate	16,500	231 00	
Slaves	7	21 00	
Horses	2	20 00	272 00
Lanneau & Whilden			
Stock of Goods	29,500		413 00
Lapenne, E. A.			
Real Estate	900		12 60
Lapenne, Elizabeth			
Real Estate	4,000		56 00
Laqueux, Harriet, Trust Estate			
Slave	1		3 00

		TAXES.
Larranaga, V Antonio de		
Real Estate............12,000	168 00	
Slaves............3	9 00	177 00
Lassen, H.		
Stock of Goods............1,000	....	14 00
Laurens, John		
Real Estate............5,500	77 00	
Slaves............10	30 00	
Carriage............1	20 00	
Horse............1	10 00	137 00
Laurens, K. S.		
Slaves............3	....	9 00
Laurens, Estate R. C.		
Slaves............3	....	9 00
Laurens, Estate Margaret H.		
Slaves............4	....	12 00
Laurens, Mrs. A.		
Slaves............2	....	6 00
Laval, Wm.		
Real Estate............22,000	308 00	
Slaves............4	12 00	
Dog............1	2 00	322 00
Laval, W J		
Real Estate............7,000	98 00	
Slaves............5	15 00	113 00
Lawrence, Samuel P		
Stock of Goods............1,000	....	14 00
Lawrence, Sarah C.		
Slaves............2	....	6 00
Lawrence, Trust Estate S. C.		
Slave............1	....	3 00
Lawton, Wm., Jr.		
Slaves............2	6 00	
Commissions............1,500	37 50	
Horse............1	10 00	53 50
Lawton, William M.		
Real Estate............18,500	259 00	
Slaves............13	39 00	
Carriage............1	30 00	
Shipping............2,200	16 50	
Commissions............6,000	150 00	
Horses............3	30 00	
Dog............1	2 00	526 50
Lawton, A. J		
Real Estate............4,500		63 00

			TAXES.
Lazarus, B. D.			
Real Estate..................26,000	364 00		
Interest on Bonds, &c...........500	12 50		
Slaves 4	12 00		
Horse 1	10 00	398 50	
Lazarus, B. D. and J.			
Real Estate..................10,000		140 00	
Lazarus, B. D., Executor			
Real Estate..................7,000	98 00		
Slaves.........................2	6 00	104 00	
Lazarus, B. D., Trustee			
Real Estate..................2,000	....	28 00	
Lazarus, Joshua			
Real Estate..................57,700	807 80		
Slaves.........................13	39 00		
Dog............................1	2 00	848 80	
Lazarus, G.			
Real Estate..................6,500	91 00		
Slaves.........................2	6 00	97 00	
Lazarus, Misses E. and A. and Mrs. B. Phillips			
Real Estate..................3,800	....	53 20	
Lazarus, Misses E. and A.			
Real Estate..................22,000		308 00	
Lazarus, Joshua E. P			
Commissions..................1,500	....	37 50	
Lazarus, Michael			
Slaves.........................2	....	6 00	
Lazarus, Trust Estate R.			
Slaves.........................4	....	12 00	
Lea's children, W P			
Slaves.........................2		6 00	
Lea, Charles E.			
Slaves.........................2		6 00	
Lea, Mrs. S. J.			
Real Estate..................7,000	98 00		
Slave..........................1	3 00	101 00	
Lea, John C.			
Real Estate..................2,500	....	35 00	
Leader, Mary			
Slave..........................1	....	3 00	
Leahey, John			
Real Estate..................2,000	....	28 00	

			TAXES.
Leaumont, Victoria de			
Real Estate	1,200	16 80	
Slave	1	3 00	
Dog	1	2 00	21 80
Lebby, W			
Real Estate	15,000	210 00	
Interest on Bonds,&c	651	16 28	
Slaves	2	6 00	
Carriage	1	20 00	
Horse	1	10 00	
Dog	1	2 00	264 28
Lebby, Dr. Robert			
Real Estate	7,500	105 00	
Slave	1	3 00	
Carriage	1	20 00	
Income	2,500	62 50	
Horses	2	20 00	210 50
Lebby, Captain Henry S.			
Slaves	2	....	6 00
Lebby, Trust Estate, Mrs. E. E.			
Slaves	5	....	15 00
Lebby, Ann E.			
Slave	1	....	3 00
Le Bleux, Louis F.			
Real Estate	5,000	70 00	
Dog	1	2 00	72 00
Le Bleux, Mrs. A. L.			
Slaves	4	....	12 00
Le Buffe, F.			
Stock of Goods	500	....	7 00
Leckie, David			
Dog	1	....	2 00
Lee, Estate William T.			
Real Estate	5,000	....	70 00
Lee, A. M., Trustee			
Real Estate	11,500	161 00	
Slaves	7	21 00	
Carriage	1	20 00	
Horse	1	10 00	212 00
Lee, P H.			
Real Estate	2,500	....	35 00
Lee, Joseph T.			
Interest on Bonds, &c	100	2 50	
Slave	1	3 00	5 50

		TAXES.
Lee, Mary E. D.		
Slaves...............3		9 00
Lee, Sarah		
Slaves...............8		24 00
Lee, Francis W		
Horse...............1		10 00
Lee, Hudson		
Real Estate...............2,500	35 00	
Slaves...............7	21 00	
Income...............800	20 00	76 00
Lee, Francis D.		
Real Estate...............6,000	84 00	
Slave...............1	3 00	
Income...............1,200	30 00	117 00
Lee, B. M.		
Real Estate...............8,000	112 00	
Slaves...............7	21 00	133 00
Lee, Kezia		
Slaves...............5		15 00
Lee, Thomas S.		
Slave...............1		3 00
Legaré, James		
Real Estate...............5,000	70 00	
Slaves...............16	48 00	
Carriage...............1	30 00	
Horses...............2	20 00	168 00
Legaré, Abigail T.		
Interest on Bonds, &c...............250	6 25	
Slaves...............6	18 00	24 25
Legaré, A. T. and J. L.		
Real Estate...............5,000		70 00
Legaré, Mary J.		
Interest on Bonds, &c...............1,200	30 00	
Slaves...............4	12 00	42 00
Legaré, James, Jr.		
Slave...............1		3 00
Legaré, Colcock & Co.		
Commissions...............11,000		275 00
Legaré, J. C. W., Estate		
Real Estate...............7,000	98 00	
Slaves...............10	30 00	128 00
Legaré, Eliza C.		
Interest on Bonds, &c...............153	3 83	
Slave...............1	3 00	6 83

		TAXES.
Legaré, Solomon		
Real Estate..................20,000	280 00	
Slaves..................23	69 00	
Carriage..................1	30 00	
Horses..................2	20 00	
Dog..................1	2 00	401 00
Legaré, Mrs. and Miss Seabrook		
Real Estate..................20,000	280 00	
Slaves..................11	33 00	
Carriage..................1	30 00	
Horses..................2	20 00	363 00
Legrix, Rosine		
Slaves..................3		9 00
Lehre, Estate Thomas		
Slaves..................5		15 00
Lehre, Jane C.		
Slaves..................5	15 00	
Dog..................1	2 00	17 00
Leich, Isabella C.		
Real Estate..................3,700	51 80	
Slaves..................5	15 00	66 80
Leiding, Hermann		
Slaves..................3		9 00
Leindstedt, Charles H.		
Stock in Trade..................400	....	5 60
Leitch, Jane		
Real Estate..................1,600		22 40
Leitch, W Y		
Real Estate..................5,000	70 00	
Slaves..................2	6 00	
Dog..................1	2 00	78 00
Leman, E. P		
Income..................2,000	....	50 00
Leman, E. P., Trustee		
Real Estate..................4,000	56 00	
Slave..................1	3 00	59 00
Leman, W W		
Stock of Goods..................13,000	182 00	
Slaves..................10	30 00	212 00
Leman, Louisa		
Real Estate..................4,500	....	63 00
Lengnick, Albert		
Stock of Goods..................12,000	168 00	
Slaves..................6	18 00	186 00

	TAXES.

Leprince, A.		
Real Estate..........6,500		91 00
Lesesne, Henry D.		
Real Estate..........13,000 00	182 00	
Interest on Bonds, &c..........799 77	19 99	
Slaves..........16	48 00	
Carriage..........1	20 00	
Income..........3,937	98 43	
Horse..........1	10 00	378 42
Lesesne, H. D. and others		
Slave..........1	....	3 00
Lesesne, Anna C.		
Interest on Bonds, &c..........876	21 90	
Slaves..........16	48 00	
Carriage..........1	20 00	
Horse..........1	10 00	99 90
Lesesne, Miss Anna C.		
Interest on Bonds, &c..........42	1 05	
Slave..........1	3 00	4 05
Lesesne, Daniel		
Real Estate..........12,000	168 00	
Slaves..........18	54 00	
Carriage..........1	30 00	
Carriage..........1	20 00	
Horses..........3	30 00	302 00
Lesesne, Ann E.		
Slave..........1	....	3 00
Lesesne, Trust Estate Juliana		
Slaves..........14	....	42 00
Levin, Mary		
Real Estate..........6,000	84 00	
Slaves..........4	12 00	96 00
Levy, Mrs. R. M.		
Interest on Bonds, &c..........44 94	1 12	
Slave..........1	3 00	4 12
Levy, Moses		
Real Estate..........5,300	74 20	
Carriage..........1	20 00	
Horses..........2	20 00	
Dog..........1	2 00	116 20
Levy, Moses and T. Boag, Trustees		
Slave..........1	....	3 00
Levy, Eliza, in trust		
Real Estate..........8,500	119 00	
Slaves..........17	51 00	170 00

			TAXES.
Levy, Trust Estate Abigail			
Real Estate	4,000		56 00
Levy, Charles F., Trustee			
Real Estate	16,000		224 00
Levy, O. R., Trustee			
Real Estate	1,800		25 20
Levy, Estate M. C.			
Real Estate	57,500		805 00
Levy, Jane			
Real Estate	12,000	168 00	
Slaves	3	9 00	177 00
Levy, Theresa			
Real Estate	7,000		98 00
Lewis, Estate Henry			
Real Estate	1,800		25 20
Lewis, John W			
Real Estate	4,000	56 00	
Slaves	9	27 00	83 00
Lewith, E. J.			
Stock of Goods	600		8 40
Limbaker, Selina			
Slave	1		3 00
Limehouse, R. J.			
Real Estate	9,000		126 00
Lindsay, Sarah			
Slaves	9		27 00
Lindsay, J. L.			
Income	2,000		50 00
Lindsay, Mrs. H. M.			
Slave	1		3 00
Lindsay, John T.			
Real Estate	6,000	84 00	
Carriage	1	30 00	
Horses	2	20 00	134 00
Lindsteadt, George H.			
Stock of Goods	400		5 60
Lindsteadt, A.			
Real Estate	3,500	49 00	
Stock of Goods	1,200	16 80	
Slave	1	3 00	68 80
Ling, Jane			
Real Estate	11,500	161 00	
Slaves	5	15 00	176 00

		TAXES.

Ling, Margaret
 Real Estate..................1,500 21 00
 Slaves 4 12 00 33 00

Ling, Joanna M.
 Slaves................................2   6 00

Lining, Henrietta P
 Interest on Bonds, &c.........176 4 40
 Slaves................................6 18 00 22 40

Lining, Dr. Thomas
 Slave 1   3 00

Lining, Charles
 Slaves................................4 12 00
 Dog 1 2 00 14 00

Linn, John
 Stock of Goods................300   4 20

Linser, Mary M.
 Real Estate..................6,000 84 00
 Slaves................................8 24 00
 Carriage............................1 20 00
 Horse 1 10 00 138 00

Little, W T.
 Real Estate..................1,200   16 80

Livinsohn, Jacob
 Stock of Goods................200   2 80

Livingston, John A.
 Slave 1   3 00

Livingstons, (minors)
 Slaves................................9   27 00

Lloyd, E. W
 Real Estate..................2,300 32 20
 Stock of Goods...........10,000 140 00
 Slaves................................3 9 00
 Carriage............................1 20 00
 Horse................................1 10 00 211 20

Lloyd, William
 Real Estate..................1,500   21 00

Lloyd, Daniel
 Real Estate.....................300   4 20

Locke, E. H.
 Real Estate................12,500 175 00
 Slaves................................3 9 00 184 00

Locke, Estate George B.
 Real Estate................14,500 203 00
 Slaves................................4 12 00 215 00

			TAXES.
Locke, E. H., and Brother			
Stock of Goods	10,000		140 00
Locke, George A.			
Real Estate	15,500	217 00	
Stock of Goods	1,000	14 00	
Slaves	4	12 00	
Carriage	1	20 00	
Shipping	1,000	7 50	
Horse	1	10 00	280 50
Locke, Palmer P			
Slave	1	3 00	
Dog	1	2 00	5 00
Locke, G. B. and G. A.			
Real Estate	1,200		16 80
Locke, Benjamin C.			
Stock of Goods	1,000		14 00
Lockwood, Dr. S. L.			
Slaves	3	9 00	
Carriage	1	20 00	
Income	500	12 50	
Horses	2	20 00	
Dog	1	2 00	63 50
Lockwood, Thomas P.			
Real Estate	5,500	77 00	
Income	1,200	30 00	
Horse	1	10 00	117 00
Lockwood, J A.			
Real Estate	7,000	98 00	
Slaves	5	15 00	113 00
Lockwood, C. D. L., and others			
Slaves	8		24 00
Lockwood, Paul L.			
Slave	1		3 00
Lockwood, J A., Trustee			
Slave	1		3 00
Lockwood, Mrs. C. D. L.			
Real Estate	5,500	77 00	
Slaves	5	15 00	
Dog	1	2 00	94 00
Lockwood, Regina A.			
Slaves	3		9 00
Lockwood & Johnson			
Real Estate	8,000	112 00	
Slaves	2	6 00	
Dog	1	2 00	120 00

		TAXES.

Lodge, St. Andrew's, No. 10
 Real Estate..................2,000 .... 28 00
Logan, Mrs. S. W A.
 Slaves ....2 .... 6 00
Logan, Dr. Samuel
 Carriage..........................1   20 00
 Income............................600   15 00
 Horse...............................1   10 00   45 00
Logan, G. W & children
 Slaves ....12 .... 36 00
Logan, Miss H. E. M.
 Interest on Bonds, &c..............349   8 73
 Slave 1   3 00   11 73
Logemann, G.
 Stock of Goods..................400   5 60
Long, John H.
 Slaves ....4 .... 12 00
Loper, H. G.
 Slaves...............................8   24 00
 Dog 1   2 00   26 00
Loper, H. G., Trustee
 Slave ....1 .... 3 00
Lopez, David, Trustee
 Real Estate..................7,500   105 00
 Slaves...............................7   21 00   126 00
Lopez, Administrator of M.
 Real Estate..................3,500   49 00
 Slaves 7   21 00   70 00
Lopez, D. Jr., Trustee
 Slaves 5   15 00
 Horse...............................1   10 00   25 00
Lord, Louisa C.
 Real Estate..................9,000   126 00
 Slaves...............................8   24 00
 Carriage..........................1   20 00
 Horse...............................1   10 00   180 00
Lord, Samuel
 Interest on Bonds, &c..............550   13 75
 Commissions..................250   6 25   20 00
Lord, Samuel, Trustee
 Slave ....1 .... 3 00
Lord, Catherine and children
 Real Estate..................3,300 .... 46 20
Lord, Miss E.
 Slaves ....2 .... 6 00

		TAXES.
Lord, John		
Slave...................................1		3 00
Lord, Mrs. M.		
Slave...................................1		3 00
Lord, Ann E.		
Slaves..................................5	....	15 00
Loryea, Aaron		
Stock of Goods............ 7,500	105 00	
Slaves................................2	6 00	111 00
Loryea, Esther		
Real Estate........................3,500		49 00
Love, Charles		
Real Estate........................6,500	91 00	
Slaves ...'............................2	6 00	
Dog..................................1	2 00	99 00
Love & Weinges		
Real Estate........................9,000	126 00	
Stock of Goods...................3,000	42 00	168 00
Lovegreen, Mrs. S. H.		
Real Estate........................19,000	266 00	
Slaves..............................11	33 00	299 00
Lovell, A. F.		
Real Estate........................1,100		15 40
Lovell, S. E.		
Real Estate........................1,100		15 40
Lowndes, Henry D.		
Interest on Bonds, &c............1,000	25 00	
Slaves................................2	6 00	
Carriage............................1	20 00	
Horse................................1	10 00	61 00
Lowndes, Estate T. P		
Slaves................................2	....	6 00
Lowndes, Mrs. M. M.		
Slaves................................5	....	15 00
Lowndes, M. L.		
Real Estate........................15,000	210 00	
Interest on Bonds, &c............1,470	36 75	
Slaves................................6	18 00	264 75
Lowndes, Estate James		
Slaves................................2	....	6 00
Lowndes, Estate Catharine		
Real Estate........................7,500	....	105 00

                                                                    TAXES.

Lowndes, Miss S. J.
    Interest on Bonds, &c............1,034   25 85
    Slave...................... 1   3 00
    Dog..1   2 00   30 85

Lowndes, Mrs. A. D.
    Interest on Bonds, &c............2,185   54 63
    Slaves.......................................8   24 00
    Carriage....................................1   30 00
    Horses......................................2   20 00
    Dog..1   2 00   130 63

Lowndes, Charles T.
    Real Estate........................20,000   280 00
    Interest on Bonds, &c..............140   3 50
    Slaves.....................................16   48 00
    Carriage....................................1   30 00
    Carriage....................................1   15 00
    Horses......................................3   30 00
    Dogs..2   4 00   410 50

Lowndes, C. T. and William Stuart
    Shipping............................5,000   37 50

Lowndes, C. T., Trustee
    Slaves......................................2   ....   6 00

Lowry, Thomas
    Slave.......................................1   3 00

Loyal, Louisa C.
    Real Estate..........................4,000   ....   56 00

Lubs, H. D.
    Stock of Goods.......................500   7 00

Lubs, C. F.
    Stock of Goods.......................600   ....   8 40

Lucas, William
    Real Estate........................27,000   378 00
    Slaves.....................................14   42 00
    Carriage....................................1   30 00
    Carriage....................................1   20 00
    Horses......................................3   30 00   500 00

Lucas, R. H.
    Real Estate........................15,000   210 00
    Slaves.....................................12   36 00
    Carriage....................................1   30 00
    Horses......................................2   20 00
    Dog..1   2 00   298 00

Lucas, Estate Thomas B.
    Real Estate......................101,325   1,418 55
    Slaves...................................160   480 00   1,898 52

                                                                TAXES.

Lucas, Eleanor B.
 Real Estate..........................2,000 28 00
 Slaves.......................................4 12 00
 Carriage...................................1 30 00
 Horses 2 20 00 90 00

Lucas, Edward S.
 Real Estate..........................20,000 280 00
 Slaves.......................................9 27 00
 Carriage...................................1 30 00
 Carriage...................................1 15 00
 Horses 3 30 00
 Dog...1 2 00 384 00

Lucas, J. & B.
 Real Estate..........................35,600 498 40
 Slaves.....................................10 30 00
 Carriage...................................1 20 00
 Horse 1 10 00
 Dog...1 2 00 560 40

Lucas, Julius
 Carriage...................................1 20 00
 Horse 1 10 00
 Dog...1 2 00 32 00

Lucas, J. J.
 Real Estate..............................400   5 60

Lucas & Strohecker
 Stock of Goods ....20,000 .... 280 00

Luhrs, M.
 Real Estate............................6,910 96 74
 Stock of Goods........................700 9 80 106 54

Luken, Anna
 Real Estate............................5,000 .... 70 00

Lutjen, L.
 Stock of Goods........................300   4 20

Loyall, H. L.
 Real Estate............................1,000 14 00
 Slaves.......................................5 15 00 29 00

Lynch, Right Rev. Dr.
 Real Estate...........................15,000 210 00
 Slaves.....................................10 30 00 240 00

Lynch, Thomas
 Real Estate............................1,500 .... 21 00

Lynch, Thomas B.
 Interest on Bonds, &c..............208 5 20
 Slaves.......................................4 12 00
 Annuity 200 5 00 22 20

		TAXES.
Lynch, James G.		
Real Estate..................1,200	....	16 80
Lyon, Estate Mordecai		
Real Estate..................10,000	140 00	
Slave......................1	3 00	143 00
Macaulay, E. M.		
Real Estate..................5,500	....	77 00
Macaulay, Allen		
Real Estate..................2,500	....	35 00
Macbeth, Charles		
Real Estate..................13,000	182 00	
Slaves......................10	30 00	
Carriage......................1	30 00	
Carriage......................1	20 00	
Horses......................5	50 00	
Dogs......................2	4 00	316 00
Macbeth, Robert		
Real Estate..................8,500	119 00	
Slaves......................24	72 00	
Carriage......................1	30 00	
Carriage......................1	20 00	
Horses......................3	30 00	271 00
Macbeth, Charles J.		
Carriage......................1	20 00	
Income..................1,550	38 75	
Dog......................1	2 00	60 75
Macbeth, Charles, Trustee James and wife		
Real Estate..................12,000	....	168 00
Macbeth, James		
Slave......................1	3 00	
Carriage......................1	20 00	
Horse......................1	10 00	
Dog......................1	2 00	35 00
Macbeth, James, Trustee A. E. Bradley		
Real Estate..................3,000	....	42 00
Macbeth, James, Guardian H. S. Trenholm		
Slave......................1	....	3 00
Macbeth, James, Guardian S. E. Macbeth		
Real Estate..................6,000	84 00	
Slaves......................10	30 00	114 00
Macbeth, James, Guardian M. L. Macbeth		
Slave......................1	....	3 00
Mackay, W A.		
Shipping..................600	....	4 50
Mackay, E. R.		
Slaves......................2	....	6 00

			TAXES.
Mackay, A. G.			
Real Estate	4,000	56 00	
Slaves	3	9 00	65 00
Mackenzie, John			
Slave	1	3 00	
Dog	1	2 00	5 00
Mackintosh, Estate Margaret			
Real Estate	1,500	....	21 00
Macdonald, Daniel			
Real Estate	16,000	....	224 00
Macmillan, W B.			
Real Estate	600	....	8 40
Madden, Judith			
Slave	1	....	3 00
Maguire, Michael			
Real Estate	4,000	....	56 00
Maguire, D.			
Real Estate	5,000	70 00	
Stock of Goods	500	7 00	77 00
Maguire, Estate James			
Real Estate	1,500	....	21 00
Magrath, W J. and Edward, Trustees			
Real Estate	30,000	420 00	
Interest on Bonds, &c	270	6 75	
Slaves	9	27 00	
Carriage	1	20 00	
Horse	1	10 00	483 75
Magrath, Edward			
Income	1,500	....	37 50
Magwood, S. J			
Real Estate	7,000	98 00	
Slaves	5	15 00	
Carriage	1	20 00	
Horse	1	10 00	
Dog	1	2 00	145 00
Magwood, Estate Charles A.			
Real Estate	12,200	170 80	
Slaves	5	15 00	185 80
Maher, Thomas			
Real Estate	1,500	21 00	
Slave	1	3 00	
Dog	1	2 00	26 00
Mahony, John, Jr.,			
Real Estate	3,000	....	42 00

174

		TAXES.
Mahony, John		
Real Estate 200	....	2 80
Mahony, Trust Estate John, Sr., and children		
Real Estate 1,500	....	21 00
Main, W C.		
Real Estate 2,000	28 00	
Interest on Bonds, &c 275	4 38	
Slaves 6	18 00	50 38
Main, A. R.		
Real Estate 7,000	98 00	
Slaves 7	21 00	119 00
Malga, Victor		
Slaves 2		6 00
Malone, Thomas W		
Real Estate 35,100	491 40	
Interest on Bonds, &c 161	4 03	
Slaves 16	48 00	
Horse 1	10 00	
Dog 1	2 00	555 43
Malone, Michael		
Real Estate 1,000		14 00
Malone, Mrs. Philip		
Slaves 4		12 00
Man, Ralph		
Real Estate 2,000		28 00
Man, Elizabeth		
Real Estate 2,500	35 00	
Dog 1	2 00	37 00
Man, Elizabeth, Trustee of R. Man's children		
Real Estate 2,000	....	28 00
Man, Mary		
Real Estate 1,000		14 00
Manigault, H. M.		
Real Estate 7,000	98 00	
Slaves 7	21 00	
Carriage 1	20 00	
Horse 1	10 00	
Dog 1	2 00	151 00
Manigault, the Misses		
Interest on Bonds, &c 987	24 68	
Slaves 11	33 00	
Dogs 2	4 00	61 68
Manigault, Estate M. J		
Real Estate 12,000		168 00

			TAXES.
Manigault, Edward			
Interest on Bonds, &c.	700	17 50	
Slaves	2	6 00	
Carriage	1	20 00	
Horse	1	10 00	53 50
Manigault, E. H.			
Real Estate	25,000	350 00	
Slaves	6	18 00	
Carriage	1	30 00	
Carriage	1	20 00	
Horses	4	40 00	
Dog	1	2 00	460 00
Manigault, Estate G.			
Real Estate	16,000		224 00
Manigault, Gabriel			
Slaves	3	9 00	
Carriage	1	30 00	
Horses	2	20 00	59 00
Manson, Mrs. E. V			
Real Estate	10,000		140 00
Manson, Mrs. E. V., Trustee			
Real Estate	1,800	25 20	
Slaves	2	6 00	31 20
Manson, Eleanor V., Guardian			
Real Estate	2,500	35 00	
Slaves	2	6 00	41 00
Mantone, E., Agent			
Stock of Goods	3,000		42 00
Mantone, B.			
Stock of Goods	800		11 20
Marchant, P J.			
Real Estate,	600		8 40
Margraff, H.			
Slave	1		3 00
Marion, John			
Real Estate	10,000	140 00	
Stock of Goods	1,000	14 00	
Slaves	9	27 00	181 00
Marion, John, Trustee			
Slave	1		3 00
Marion, Ann			
Slave	1		3 00
Marjenhoff, E. H.			
Real Estate	10,000	140 00	
Stock of Goods	3,000	42 00	182 00

		TAXES.

Markley, Hester
 Slaves........2   6 00

Marks, Alexander
 Real Estate........5,000   70 00

Marschar, William
 Stock of Goods........3,500   49 00
 Carriage........1   20 00   69 00

Marsh, James
 Real Estate........77,200   1,080 80
 Slaves........32   96 00
 Carriage........1   30 00
 Horses........2   20 00   1,226 80

Marsh, Estate James
 Real Estate........12,500   175 00

Marsh, Elizabeth
 Real Estate........9,000   126 00
 Slave........1   3 00   129 00

Marsh, Ann H.
 Real Estate........3,500   49 00
 Slaves........9   27 00   76 00

Marsh, James G.
 Slaves,........2   6 00
 Dog........1   2 00   8 00

Marshall, Mary Jane, and Susan Beatty
 Real Estate........1,500   21 00

Marshall & Burge
 Stock of Goods........31,000   434 00

Marshall, E. W
 Real Estate........4,000   56 00
 Slaves........2   6 00   62 00

Marshall, John T.
 Real Estate........40,500   567 00
 Slaves........20   60 00
 Carriage........1   20 00
 Horse........1   10 00
 Dog........1   2 00   659 00

Marshall, Estate Mary S.
 Real Estate........10,000   140 00

Marshall, M. C.
 Slaves........20   60 00

Marshall, Alexander W
 Slaves........9   27 00
 Horse........1   10 00
 Dog........1   2 00   39 00

		TAXES.
Marshall, Sarah Ann		
Slaves 10		30 00
Marshall, R. M,		
Commissions.........................3,800	....	95 00
Marshall, R. M., Trustee		
Real Estate........................3,100	....	43 40
Marshall, Estate Thomas C.		
Real Estate........................1,000	....	14 00
Marshall, S. A. and others		
Real Estate........................1,000	....	14 00
Marshall, Estate Eleanor		
Real Estate........................2,000	....	28 00
Marshall, John		
Real Estate......................67,000	938 00	
Slaves 10	30 00	
Carriage..........................1	20 00	
Horses 2	20 00	
Dog................................1	2 00	1010 00
Marshall, S. R.		
Slaves 2	6 00	
Dog................................1	2 00	8 00
Martin, Lewis V		
Real Estate........................4,000	56 00	
Slave 1	3 00	
Carriage 1	20 00	
Horse 1	10 00	89 00
Martin, the heirs of J P		
Real Estate........................5,000		70 00
Martin, Mrs. M. S.		
Real Estate......................18,400	257 60	
Slaves............................7	21 00	
Carriage..........................1	30 00	
Horses 2	20 00	
Dog................................1	2 00	330 60
Martin, Trust Estate Mary D.		
Real Estate........................2,000		28 00
Martin, W S.		
Real Estate........................3,500	49 00	
Dogs..............................2	4 00	53 00
Martin, Estate Lewis V		
Real Estate........................5,200	....	72 80
Martin, George M.		
Real Estate........................3,000	42 00	
Slaves 5	15 00	57 00

12

		TAXES
Martin, William M.		
Real Estate..........10,000	140 00	
Slaves..........10	30 00	
Horse..........1	10 00	
Dog..........1	2 00	182 00
Martin, William M. & J C.		
Real Estate..........10,000	140 00	
Income..........5,000	125 00	265 00
Martin, John C.		
Slave..........1	3 00	
Dog..........1	2 00	5 00
Martin, William E.		
Real Estate..........6,000	84 00	
Slaves..........9	27 00	
Income..........3,979 84	99 48	
Dog..........1	2 00	212 48
Martin, Trust Estate Marion and James		
Slaves..........4		12 00
Martin, Estate James		
Real Estate..........7,000		98 00
Martin, Francis R.		
Slave..........1	....	3 00
Martindale, C. O.		
Slaves..........3	....	9 00
Marshburn, James H.		
Real Estate..........6,500	91 00	
Slaves..........7	21 00	120 00
Mason, Thomas		
Stock of Goods..........200	....	2 80
Massot, H.		
Real Estate..........3,000	42 00	
Slaves..........3	9 00	
Horse..........1	10 00	
Dog..........1	2 00	63 00
Matheson, Elizabeth		
Real Estate..........4,500	63 00	
Slaves..........11	33 00	96 00
Matheson, M. P.		
Slaves..........8	24 00	
Dog..........1	2 00	26 00
Matheson, P M., Trustee		
Slave..........1		3 00
Mathews, Eliza M.		
Slave..........1		3 00

		TAXES.
Mathews, John Raven		
Real Estate................16,000	224 00	
Slaves.........4	12 00	
Dog.........1	2 00	238 00
Mathews, J E., Trustee		
Real Estate.........7,000	....	98 00
Mathews, Mrs. A.		
Interest on Bonds, &c.........2,000	50 00	
Slaves.........6	18 00	68 00
Mathews, Edward		
Interest on Bonds, &c.........200	5 00	
Slave.........1	3 00	8 00
Mathews, Sarah		
Slave.........1	3 00	
Carriage.........1	20 00	
Horse.........1	10 00	33 00
Mathews, Jane		
Interest on Bonds, &c.........532	13 30	
Slaves.........3	9 00	22 30
Mathews' children, James		
Real Estate.........21,800	305 20	
Slaves.........8	24 00	
Horse.........1	10 00	
Dog.........1	2 00	341 20
Mathews, Mrs. M. A.		
Interest on Bonds, &c.........700	17 50	
Slaves.........36	108 00	125 50
Mattie, Joseph		
Stock of Goods.........100	....	1 40
Matthiessen, William		
Real Estate.........18,600	260 40	
Slaves.........7	21 00	
Carriage.........1	20 00	
Horse.........1	10 00	
Dog.........1	2 00	313 40
Matthiessen, O'Hara & Co.		
Stock of Goods.........25,000	....	350 00
Matthiesson, Frederick C.		
Real Estate.........10,000	140 00	
Interest on Bonds, &c.........1,200	30 00	
Dogs.........2	4 00	174 00
Matthiesson, F. C., Trustee		
Interest on Bonds, &c.........582	....	14 55
Maule, Mary R.		
Slaves.........6	....	18 00

			TAXES
Maule, C.			
Stock of Goods	500	7 00	
Slave	1	3 00	
Dog	1	2 00	12 00
May, Mary			
Real Estate	8,000	112 00	
Slaves	5	15 00	127 00
May, James W			
Real Estate	3,500	49 00	
Slave	1	3 00	52 00
Mayrant, Mrs. S. H.			
Real Estate	3,000		42 00
Mazyck, N. B.			
Slaves	2	6 00	
Income	1,192	29 80	35 80
Mazyck & Howard			
Commissions	5,096		127 40
Mazyck, William			
Real Estate	9,000		126 00
Mazyck, Miss A. M. H.			
Slave	1		3 00
Mazyck, Alexander H.			
Income	500		12 50
Mazyck, Catherine			
Slaves	7		21 00
Mazyck, Trust Estate Mrs. E. M.			
Slaves	2		6 00
Mazyck, Alexander			
Real Estate	2,500	35 00	
Slave	1	3 00	38 00
Mazyck, P P			
Real Estate	12,000	168 00	
Slaves	18	54 00	
Carriage	1	30 00	
Horses	3	30 00	
Dog	1	2 00	284 00
Mazyck, W St. John			
Real Estate	8,000	112 00	
Slaves	10	30 00	
Carriage	1	20 00	
Horse	1	10 00	
Dog	1	2 00	174 00
Mazyck, J. W			
Slaves	9	27 00	
Horse	1	10 00	37 00

TAXES

Mazyck, Estate R. W
   Real Estate............6,000   84 00
   Interest on Bonds,&c......210   5 25
   Slaves.........................5   15 00   104 25

Mazyck, William
   Real Estate............12,000   168 00
   Slaves...................12   36 00
   Carriage..................1   30 00
   Horses....................3   30 00
   Dog.......................1   2 00   266 00

Mazyck, Edward
   Slave.....................1   ....   3 00

Meagher, Ellen
   Stock of Goods.......... 300   4 20

Meeker, Samuel
   Real Estate............12,000   ....   168 00

Mehan, John
   Real Estate..............500   7 00

Mehrtens, C. L.
   Stock of Goods..........300   4 20
   Dog.......................1   2 00   6 20

Mehrtens, Joseph
   Stock of Goods..........300   4 20

Mehrtens & Oppenheim
   Stock of Goods.........8,000   ....   112 00

Mehrtens, Mrs. C.
   Real Estate............2,500   35 00
   Stock of Goods..........400   5 60   40 60

Mehrtens & Renken
   Slaves....................4   12 00
   Carriage..................1   20 00
   Dog.......................1   2 00   34 00

Meldau, G. F.
   Real Estate............12,000   168 00
   Stock of Goods........2,500   35 00
   Slave.....................1   3 00
   Carriage..................1   20 00
   Horse.....................1   10 00
   Dog.......................1   2 00   238 00

Melfi, F.
   Stock of Goods..........200   2 80

Mellichamp, Mary Jane and Sarah Ann
   Slaves....................4   ....   12 00

			TAXES.
Melvin, James			
Real Estate	3,000	42 00	
Slave	1	3 00	45 00
Memminger, C. G.			
Real Estate	18,000	252 00	
Interest on Bonds, &c	7,322	183 05	
Slaves	8	24 00	
Carriage	1	30 00	
Carriage	1	20 00	
Income	8,700	217 50	
Horses	4	40 00	
Dogs	2	4 00	770 55
Mencke, John P			
Real Estate	2,500	35 00	
Interest on Bonds, &c	360	9 00	44 00
Mendel & Son, Jacob			
Stock of Goods	300		4 20
Menken, D.			
Stock of Goods	200	2 80	
Slaves	7	21 00	23 80
Menlove & Davidson			
Commissions	3,500		87 50
Mensing, C			
Stock of Goods	600		8 40
Merkhardt, J. P			
Real Estate	1,200	16 80	
Slave	1	3 00	19 80
Mey, F. C.			
Real Estate	7,000	98 00	
Commissions	1,000	25 00	123 00
Meyer, O.			
Stock of Goods	200		2 80
Meyer, Morris			
Real Estate	4,000	56 00	
Stock of Goods	3,500	49 00	
Slaves	4	12 00	117 00
Meyer, Martin			
Stock of Goods	300		4 20
Meyer, John			
Slaves	3		9 00
Meyer, Henry			
Real Estate	2,500	35 00	
Slaves	5	15 00	
Dog	1	2 00	52 00

			TAXES.
Meyer, J. C.			
Slave.....................1	3 00		
Dog.........................1	2 00	5 00	
Meyer, J E.			
Stock of Goods............350	....	4 90	
Meyer, B. H.			
Stock of Goods............800	....	11 20	
Meyer, C. L., Trustee			
Slaves...........................6	....	18 00	
Meyers, Amelia			
Stock of Goods............400	....	5 60	
Meyerhoff, B.			
Stock of Goods............500	....	7 00	
Meynardie, James H.			
Slaves...........................3	....	9 00	
Michel, Dr. William			
Real Estate...............8,500	119 00		
Interest on Bonds, &c........91	2 28		
Slaves.............................21	63 00	184 28	
Michel, Dr. Middleton			
Carriage..............................1	20 00		
Income.........................2,000	50 00		
Horses................................2	20 00	90 00	
Michel, Anna			
Slaves................................14	42 00		
Horse..................................1	10 00	52 00	
Michel, Catherine J.			
Real Estate..................3,800	53 20		
Slave..................................1	3 00		
Dog....................................1	2 00	58 20	
Michel, Estate John			
Real Estate.................22,500	315 00		
Slaves................................27	81 00		
Carriage..............................1	15 00		
Horse..................................1	10 00		
Dogs....................................2	4 00	425 00	
Michel, Dr. R. Fraser			
Carriage..............................1	15 00		
Horse..................................1	10 00	25 00	
Michel, Estate Mrs. A. M.			
Slaves..................................6	....	18 00	
Michel, Estate Francis			
Real Estate...................6,000	84 00		
Slaves................................13	39 00	123 00	

TAXES.

Middleton, Thomas
 Real Estate..........9,000 126 00
 Slaves..........10 30 00
 Dog..........1 2 00 158 00

Middleton & Co.
 Commissions..........7,000 175 00

Middleton, O. H.
 Real Estate..........18,000 252 00
 Interest on Bonds, &c..........600 15 00
 Slaves..........21 63 00
 Carriage..........1 30 00
 Carriage..........1 20 00
 Shipping..........12,000 90 00
 Horses..........4 40 00
 Dog..........1 2 00 512 00

Middleton, W I.
 Slaves..........3 .... 9 00

Middleton, W I., Trustee
 Slaves..........3 .... 9 00

Middleton, N R.
 Real Estate..........9,000 126 00
 Slaves..........14 42 00 168 00

Middleton, Williams
 Real Estate..........31,000 434 00
 Slaves..........14 42 00
 Carriage..........1 30 00
 Shipping..........1,000 7 50
 Horses..........2 20 00
 Dog..........1 2 00 535 50

Middleton, R. J.
 Slaves..........4 .... 12 00

Middleton, H. A.
 Real Estate..........17,500 245 00
 Interest on Bonds, &c..........1,540 38 50
 Slaves..........18 54 00
 Carriage..........1 30 00
 Horses..........3 30 00
 Dog..........1 2 00 399 50

Middleton, Mrs. S. M.
 Slaves..........4 12 00

Middleton, Thomas, Trustee
 Slave..........1 .... 3 00

Mikell, Ephraim
 Slave..........1 3 00

		TAXES.

Mikell, J. Jenkins
    Real Estate..........................20,000   280 00
    Slave.................................1   3 00
    Carriage..............................1   30 00
    Horses................................2   20 00
    Dog...................................1   2 00   335 00

Miler, Daniel
    Slaves................................4   12 00
    Dogs..................................2   4 00   16 00

Miles, Edward R.
    Interest on Bonds, &c...............105   2 63
    Horse.................................1   10 00
    Dog...................................1   2 00   14 63

Miles, Mrs. S. B.
    Interest on Bonds, &c...............446   11 15
    Slaves................................5   15 00   26 15

Miles, C. Richardson
    Slaves................................2   6 00
    Income............................2,700   67 50
    Dog...................................1   2 00   75 50

Miles, William Porcher
    Real Estate.......................1,800   ....   25 20

Miles, Eliza S.
    Slaves...............................21   ....   63 00

Miles, Susan
    Slave.................................1   3 00

Miles, J. A.
    Interest on Bonds, &c...............255   6 38
    Slaves................................4   12 00
    Dogs..................................2   4 00   22 38

Miles, Ann W
    Slave.................................1   3 00

Millar, R. S.
    Real Estate..........................57,000   798 00
    Slaves...............................19   57 60
    Carriage..............................1   20 00
    Horses................................2   20 00
    Dog...................................1   2 00   897 00

Millar, Caroline J
    Slaves................................3   ....   9 00

Miller, Estate Wm.
    Real Estate.......................3,000   42 00

Miller, Wm. C.
    Real Estate.......................1,500   ....   21 00

		TAXES.

Miller, A. E.
 Real Estate 7,000   98 00
 Stock of Goods 200   2 80
 Slaves 7   21 00   121 80

Miller, Samuel Stent
 Real Estate.................... 1,200   ....   16 80

Miller, Estate R. A.
 Real Estate.................... 36,000   504 00

Miller, J Claudius
 Real Estate.................... 3,500   ....   49 00

Miller, Zadoc
 Real Estate 3,000   42 00
 Stock of Goods 7,100   99 40
 Slaves 3   9 00   150 40

Miller, Estate Jacob
 Real Estate 2,500   35 00

Miller, F. C.
 Dog 1   2 00

Miller, F C., in trust
 Real Estate 2,000   ....   28 00

Miller, Wm.
 Slave 1   ....   3 00

Miller, John C.
 Commissions 74   1 85
 Dog 1   2 00   3 85

Miller, John C., Guardian
 Real Estate 300   4 20

Miller, Ann J.
 Real Estate 4,000   56 00
 Slaves 25   75 00   131 00

Miller, Mrs. C. L.
 Real Estate 6,000   84 00
 Slaves 7   21 00   105 00

Miller, S. H. H.
 Slave 1   3 00

Milligan, Jane and Margaret
 Real Estate 8,000   112 00
 Slave 1   3 00
 Dogs 2   4 00   119 00

Milliken, Thomas
 Slaves 7   21 00
 Carriage 1   30 00
 Horses 2   20 00   71 00

Milliken, E. P
 Slave 1   ....   3 00

		TAXES.	
Milliken, E. P., Assignee			
Real Estate................3,000		42 00	
Milliken. Jas. H.			
Slave...............1		3 00	
Mills, Otis			
Real Estate...............137,000	1,918 00		
Slaves................10	30 00		
Carriage................1	30 00		
Horses................2	20 00	1,998 00	
Mills, Otis & Co.			
Real Estate...............248,000	3,472 00		
Slaves................18	54 00	3,526 00	
Mills, Beach & Co.			
Real Estate...............7,000	98 00		
Stock of Goods...............1,300	18 20		
Slaves................13	39 00	155 20	
Mills, S. S., Trustee			
Real Estate...............3,500		49 00	
Mills, Otis and others			
Slave................1		3 00	
Mills' children, Eliza			
Real Estate................800		11 20	
Milne, Mrs. E. C. S.			
Real Estate...............15,000	210 00		
Interest on Bonds, &c................630	15 75		
Slaves................9	27 00		
Carriage................1	30 00		
Horses................2	20 00	302 75	
Milnor, John G.			
Real Estate...............39,500	553 00		
Slaves................4	12 00		
Carriage................1	20 00		
Horse................1	10 00	595 00	
Milnor, John G. & Co.			
Stock of Goods...............25,000	350 00		
Commissions................500	12 50	362 50	
Minnis, Robert			
Stock of Goods................200	2 80		
Horse................1	10 00		
Dog................1	2 00	14 80	
Minott, Wm. B.			
Slave................1	3 00		
Commissions...............1,000	25 00	28 00	
Minott, Susan J.			
Slaves................2		6 00	

		TAXES.

Minott, Estate Susan C.
 Slaves ...5   15 00

Minott, Miss T. C.
 Slave...1   3 00

Mintz, A. J.
 Real Estate ...200   2 80

Miscally, D. W
 Real Estate...1,000   14 00

Missroon, H. & Co.
 Real Estate...2,000   28 00
 Shipping...7,500   56 25
 Commissions...6,500   162 50   246 75

Missroon, H., Trustee
 Real Estate...22,000   308 00
 Slaves...2   6 00
 Carriage...1   20 00
 Horse...1   10 00   344 00

Mitchell, Edward
 Slave...1   3 00

Mitchell, Edward, Trustee
 Real Estate...3,000   42 00

Mitchell, Estate Eliza M.
 Slaves...7   21 00

Mitchell, Alexander R.
 Real Estate...15,200   212 80
 Slaves...12   36 00
 Carriage...1   20 00
 Income...500   12 50
 Horse...1   10 00   291 30

Mitchell, A. R., Trustee M. S. Hopkins
 Slaves...2   6 00

Mitchell, A. R. and T. S. Gourdin
 Real Estate...5,000   70 00

Mitchell, A. R. & Co.
 Real Estate...19,500   273 00

Mitchell, C. T.
 Real Estate...14,000   196 00
 Slave...1   3 00
 Shipping...200   1 50
 Dog...1   2 00   202 50

Mitchell, C. T. & Co.
 Stock of Goods...1,200   16 80
 Income...16,000   400 00   416 80

Mitchell, H. W
 Dogs...2   4 00

			TAXES.
Mitchell, T. A.			
Slaves	7	21 00	
Carriage	1	20 00	41 00
Mitchell, Estate A. D. V			
Real Estate	8,000		112 00
Mitchell, R. C.			
Real Estate	1,300		18 20
Mitchell, Estate James			
Real Estate	1,800	25 20	
Dog	1	2 00	27 20
Mitchell, Miss M.			
Real Estate	6,000	84 00	
Stock of Goods	500	7 00	
Slave	1	3 00	94 00
Mitchell, Julian			
Slaves	3	9 00	
Carriage	1	20 00	
Horse	1	10 00	39 00
Mitchell, Charlotte			
Real Estate	7,000	98 00	
Slaves	10	30 00	
Carriage	1	20 00	
Horse	1	10 00	158 00
Mitchell, Nelson			
Real Estate	5,000	70 00	
Slaves	4	12 00	
Income	8,788	219 70	301 70
Mitchell, J. D.			
Real Estate	10,000	140 00	
Carriage	1	20 00	
Horse	1	10 00	170 00
Mitchell, J. S.			
Real Estate	5,000	70 00	
Slaves	10	30 00	
Carriage	1	15 00	
Income	2,000	50 00	
Horses	2	20 00	185 00
Mitchell, W R., (minor)			
Slaves	4		12 00
Mixer, D.			
Real Estate	3,000	42 00	
Slaves	6	18 00	60 00
Moffett, Anna			
Real Estate	6,000	84 00	
Slaves	8	24 00	
Dog	1	2 00	110 00

			TAXES.
Moffett, George			
Carriage...................1	20 00		
Horse........................1	10 00		
Dog..........................1	2 00	32 00	
Moise, Louisa A.			
Real Estate.............8,000	112 00		
Interest on Bonds, &c......349	8 73	120 73	
Moise, Abraham			
Real Estate..........12,800 00	179 20		
Income.................335 98	8 39	187 59	
Moise, Abraham, Trustee			
Slave.........................1		3 00	
Moise, Penina			
Interest on Bonds, &c........50	1 25		
Slave.........................1	3 00	4 25	
Moise, Estate Isaac			
Real Estate............14,000	196 00		
Interest on Bonds, &c......1,190	29 75	225 75	
Moise, Mrs. H. L.			
Real Estate.............9,000	126 00		
Slaves......................4	12 00	138 00	
Moise, Charles H.			
Real Estate.............4,000	56 00		
Dog..........................1	2 00	58 00	
Moise, Thomas J. and C. H.			
Stock of Goods.........20,000	....	280 00	
Moise, Cecelia			
Interest on Bonds, &c........400	....	10 00	
Molle, J. W			
Carriage...................1	15 00		
Income.................2,000	50 00		
Horse.......................1	10 00	75 00	
Molony, John			
Real Estate.............9,000	126 00		
Stock of Goods..........1,000	14 00	140 00	
Molony, J J			
Stock of Goods..........4,000		56 00	
Monefeldt, Estate M. H.			
Interest on Bonds, &c......675	16 88		
Slave.........................1	3 00	19 88	
Monpoey, Estate Honore			
Real Estate.............4,000	56 00		
Slave.........................1	3 00		
Horse.......................1	10 00	69 00	

		TAXES.
Monses, John		
Stock of Goods 500		7 00
Montgomery, Lydia		
Real Estate............4,000	....	56 00
Montgomery, A.		
Real Estate............4,500	63 00	
Slaves 2	6 00	69 00
Mood, Rev. John		
Real Estate............8,500	119 00	
Stock of Goods............8,000	112 00	231 00
Mood, Dr. J R.		
Slaves............9	27 00	
Carriage............1	20 00	
Income............2,300	57 50	
Horse............1	10 00	114 50
Mood, W G.		
Slaves 3	....	9 00
Mood, C. R., in trust		
Real Estate............1,700	....	23 80
Moodie, Mrs. R. A.		
Real Estate............7,000	98 00	
Slave 1	3 00	101 00
Moore, R. D.		
Real Estate............2,000	28 00	
Slaves............6	18 00	
Income 1,500	37 50	83 50
Moore. Dr. Samuel P		
Slave............1	....	3 00
Moore, Trust Estate Virginia		
Slaves............6	....	18 00
Moore, Frances		
Interest on Bonds, &c............595	14 88	
Slaves............3	9 00	23 88
Moore, Jacob F		
Slave............1	....	3 00
Moore, George W		
Real Estate............3,000	42 00	
Slaves............3	9 00	51 00
Moorhead, James		
Real Estate............16,000	224 00	
Stock of Goods 2,500	35 00	
Slaves 4	12 00	
Dog............1	2 00	273 00
Moorhead, Sarah Ann		
Real Estate............1,500	....	21 00

		TAXES.

Moran, John
 Real Estate..........................3,000 42 00
 Slaves 2   6 00 48 00

Moran, Miles
 Real Estate..........................2,000   28 00

Moran, W
 Slaves 4 12 00
 Carriage 1 20 00 32 00

Moran, Estate William
 Real Estate..........................1,800   25 20

Mordecai, Benjamin
 Real Estate..........................52,200 730 80
 Slaves.................................10 30 00
 Carriage 1 20 00
 Commissions........................1,500 37 50
 Horse 1 10 00 828 30

Mordecai, Thomas W., Trustee L. C. M. and children
 Real Estate..........................26,600 372 40
 Slave...................................1   3 00 375 40

Mordecai, Misses Hetty and Harriet
 Slaves 2   6 00

Mordecai, M. C.
 Real Estate..........................48,500 679 00
 Interest on Bonds, &c..............376 9 40
 Slaves 11 33 00
 Shipping 12,500 93 75
 Dogs 2   4 00 819 15

Mordecai & Co.
 Stock of Goods.....................4,500 63 00
 Shipping 18,000 135 00
 Commissions........................8,000 200 00 398 00

Moreland, Andrew
 Real Estate.........................10,000 140 00
 Slaves..................................8 24 00
 Carriage 1 30 00
 Horses 2 20 00 214 00

Moreland, E. M.
 Slaves ....2 .... 6 00

Morello, J B.
 Real Estate..........................6,000 84 00
 Stock of Goods.....................1,000 14 00
 Dog......................................1   2 00 100 00

Morey, Montaner Y
 Real Estate..........................6,500 .... 91 00

                                                                    TAXES.
Morgan, J. B.
   Real Estate............................4,400   61 60
   Slaves...................................12   36 00
   Dog......................................1   2 00   99 60
Morgan, Mary
   Slaves 5   ....   15 00
Morillo, R.
   Stock of Goods 100   ....   1 40
Moroso, A.
   Real Estate............................8,000   112 00
   Stock of Goods 750   10 50
   Slave....................................1   3 00   125 50
Morris, Mary J
   Real Estate............................8,000   112 00
   Interest on Bonds, &c............1,500   37 50
   Slaves...................................6   18 00
   Dog......................................1   2 00   169 50
Morris, Trust Estate E. & L.
   Interest on Bonds, &c.............241   ....   6 03
Morris, Lewis
   Slaves...................................5   ....   15 00
Morrison, Jane
   Slave....................................1   ....   3 00
Morrison, Samuel
   Real Estate............................2,000   ....   28 00
Mortimer, Thomas H. and Sarah M.
   Real Estate............................5,500   77 00
   Slaves..................................28   84 00
   Carriage.................................1   20 00
   Horse....................................1   10 00
   Dog......................................1   2 00   193 00
Mortimer, Samuel H.
   Carriage.................................1   20 00
   Horse....................................1   10 00
   Dog......................................1   2 00   32 00
Mortimer, Trust Estate Jackson & children
   Real Estate............................1,500   21 00
Morton, W R.
   Stock of Goods...................20,000   280 00
Morse, Anson H.
   Real Estate.............................600   ....   8 40
Moses, A. J.
   Real Estate..........................32,110   449 54
   Slaves...................................2   6 00
   Carriage.................................1   20 00   475 54

		TAXES	
Moses, Mary			
Real Estate..................16,200	226 80		
Slaves..................6	18 00	244 80	
Moses, Miss H. A.			
Slaves..................2		6 00	
Moses, Rebecca J.			
Real Estate..................5,000	70 00		
Slaves..................21	63 00	133 00	
Moses, L. J.			
Real Estate..................5,000	70 00		
Slaves..................15	45 00	115 00	
Moses, L. J., in trust for Mrs. Goldsmith			
Real Estate..................2,000	....	28 00	
Motte, Trust Estate J. W and children			
Real Estate..................5,000	70 00		
Slave..................1	3 00	73 00	
Mottet, E., in trust for Mrs. Huchet			
Slaves..................5		15 00	
Mottet, E., in trust for Mrs. Roger			
Slave..................1		3 00	
Mottet, Huchet & Co.			
Stock of Goods..................4,000	56 00		
Slave..................1	3 00		
Shipping..................8,000	60 00		
Commissions..................20,000	500 00	619 00	
Moultrie, Dr. James			
Real Estate..................13,000	182 00		
Interest on Bonds, &c..................2,450	61 25		
Slaves..................20	60 00		
Carriage..................1	30 00		
Carriage..................1	20 00		
Horses..................3	30 00	383 25	
Moultrie, Margaret and sisters			
Real Estate..................6,000	84 00		
Interest on Bonds, &c..................948	23 70		
Slaves..................13	39 00	146 70	
Moultrie, Cornelia			
Slave..................1		3 00	
Moultrie, Dr. W L.			
Slaves..................7	21 00		
Carriage..................1	30 00		
Horses..................2	20 00	71 00	
Mousseau, Trust Estate Henrietta			
Real Estate..................1,500	....	21 00	

			TAXES
Mouzon, L. H.			
Interest on Bonds, &c.	170	4 25	
Slaves	5	15 00	
Carriage	1	20 00	
Income	1,000	25 00	
Horse	1	10 00	74 25
Mouzon, L. H., Trustee of Van Winkle			
Slaves	4		12 00
Mouzon, S. C.			
Horse	1		10 00
Mouzon, Rev. W P			
Interest on Bonds, &c.	46	1 15	
Slaves	3	9 00	
Dogs	2	4 00	14 15
Mowry, S., Jr.			
Real Estate	39,000	546 00	
Dividends	950	23 75	
Slaves	7	21 00	
Carriage	1	30 00	
Horses	2	20 00	
Dogs	2	4 00	644 75
Mowry, S. & L. & Co.			
Stock of Goods	5,000	70 00	
Dividends	260	6 50	
Commissions	16,500	412 50	489 00
Mowry, Elisha C.			
Real Estate	11,700	163 80	
Interest on Bonds, &c.	50	1 25	
Dividends	75	1 88	
Income	1,500	37 50	204 43
Muckenfuss, H. W			
Real Estate	16,000	224 00	
Slaves	2	6 00	230 00
Muckenfuss, H. W., in trust			
Real Estate	2,000	28 00	
Slaves	6	18 00	46 00
Muckenfuss, B. S. D.			
Real Estate	10,500	147 00	
Slaves	8	24 00	
Carriage	1	20 00	
Horse	1	10 00	
Dog	1	2 00	203 00
Muckenfuss, B. S. D., Trustee			
Slaves	9		27 00
Muckenfuss, Catherine D.			
Slaves	2	....	6 00

			TAX
Muir, Jane, Agnes and Anna			
Slaves	3		9
Muirhead, R. M.			
Real Estate	6,500		91
Mulkai, Patrick			
Dogs	2		4
Muller, J. H.			
Stock of Goods	300		4
Muller, M.			
Stock of Goods	300		4
Muller, Frederick			
Slaves	2		6
Mulligan, A. B.			
Stock of Goods	8,816		123 4
Mullings, Henry A.			
Real Estate	3,000	42 00	
Slave	1	3 00	45 (
Mullings, Robert E.			
Horse	1		10 0
Mullings, William			
Real Estate	2,000		28 0
Mullings, Estate John			
Real Estate	12,000	168 00	
Slaves	6	18 00	186 0
Munro, Estate Margaret			
Real Estate	13,000	182 00	
Slaves	6	18 00	200 0
Munro, G. C. & W J.			
Commissions	1,010		25 2
Munzenmair, Charles A.			
Real Estate	1,500		21 0
Murcheson, J. D.			
Commissions	801		20 0
Murden, Malvina			
Slaves	5		15 0
Murden, Victoria			
Slaves	2		6 0
Murdock, James			
Real Estate	13,000		182 0
Mure, Robert			
Real Estate	7,000	98 00	
Slaves	2	6 00	
Shipping	7,000	52 50	
Income	6,000	150 00	
Dog	1	2 00	308 50

			TAXES.
Mure, Robert, Trustee			
Real Estate	400		5 60
Murphy, Francis			
Stock of Goods	4,000	56 00	
Slaves	5	15 00	
Horse	1	10 00	
Dog	1	2 00	83 00
Murphy, W H., and F. Grizzell			
Real Estate	1,800	....	25 20
Murphy, Eliza			
Real Estate	2,200	30 80	
Slave	1	3 00	33 80
Murray, Estate W C.			
Real Estate	12,000	....	168 00
Murray, Joseph			
Real Estate	3,000	42 00	
Slave	1	3 00	45 00
Murray, John H.			
Real Estate	2,500	....	35 00
Murray, B.			
Stock of Goods	500	....	7 00
Murray, Estate John D.			
Real Estate	1,500	....	21 00
Murrell, Susan			
Real Estate	4,000	56 00	
Slaves	29	87 00	143 00
Murrell, James H.			
Real Estate	4,500	63 00	
Slaves	2	6 00	69 00
Myers, S. D. & H.			
Slaves	18	54 00	
Carriage	1	20 00	
Horse	1	10 00	84 00
Myers, Estate Mary			
Real Estate	1,500	....	21 00
Myers, E. H.			
Real Estate	7,000	98 00	
Slaves	5	15 00	
Dog	1	2 00	115 00
Myers, Mary E.			
Slave	1	....	3 00
Myers, L. J.			
Slave	1		3 00
Myers, Trust Estate Mrs. L. J			
Real Estate	4,500		63 00

		TAXES.
Myers, Christopher		
Real Estate...............4,000	56 00	
Slave...............1	3 00	59 00
McAdam, John		
Real Estate...............700		9 80
McAllister, Charles		
Real Estate...............15,200	212 80	
Stock of Goods...............5,000	70 00	
Slaves...............3	9 00	
Carriage...............1	20 00	
Horse...............1	10 00	
Dog...............1	2 00	323 80
McAnally, Elizabeth S.		
Real Estate...............3,500	49 00	
Dog...............1	2 00	51 00
McAndrew, James		
Stock of Goods...............400	5 60	
Slaves...............2	6 00	11 60
McBride, M.		
Real Estate...............10,000	140 00	
Carriage...............1	20 00	
Commissions...............500	12 50	
Horse...............1	10 00	182 50
McBride, Philip A.		
Real Estate...............16,800	235 20	
Slaves...............2	6 00	241 20
McBride, P., in trust		
Real Estate...............1,500	....	21 00
McBurney, William		
Real Estate...............7,000	98 00	
Slaves...............7	21 00	
Carriage...............1	30 00	
Horses...............2	20 00	169 00
McCaa, William L.		
Slaves...............9	27 00	
Carriage...............1	20 00	
Income...............1,910	47 75	
Horses...............2	20 00	114 75
McCabe, James		
Slaves...............5	15 00	
Horse...............1	10 00	
Dog...............1	2 00	27 00
McCall, B.		
Commissions...............1,000		25 00
McCall, B. and wife		
Real Estate...............4,200	....	58 80

			TAXES.
McCall, J P			
Real Estate..................2,800	39 20		
Slaves........................11	33 00	72 20	
McCall. Mary			
Real Estate..................9,500	133 00		
Interest on Bonds, &c........670	16 75		
Slaves........................15	45 00	194 75	
McCall, Mrs. M. and Miss E. P. Ravenel			
Slaves........................3	9 00		
Carriage......................1	30 00		
Horses........................2	20 00	59 00	
McCary, James			
Real Estate..................17,400	....	243 60	
McCarter, James J.			
Real Estate..................10,000	140 00		
Slaves........................3	9 00		
Dog...........................1	2 00	151 00	
McCarter & Dawson			
Stock of Goods...............25,000	....	350 00	
McCarter, James J., Trustee			
Slave.........................1	....	3 00	
McCarthy, D. L.			
Real Estate..................14,000	196 00		
Stock of Goods...............1,500	21 00		
Slaves........................2	6 00	223 00	
McCay. Jane Frances and Mary			
Real Estate..................1,000		14 00	
McClure, W J.			
Real Estate..................3,000	42 00		
Slave.........................1	3 00	45 00	
McConkey, James			
Real Estate..................7,000	98 00		
Stock of Goods...............500	7 00		
Slave.........................1	3 00	108 00	
McCormick, H. L. P			
Slaves........................3	9 00		
Shipping.....................10,000	75 00		
Commissions..................1,500	37 50	121 50	
McCormick, Jane			
Real Estate..................9,000	126 00		
Slaves........................10	30 00		
Dog...........................1	2 00	158 00	
McCrady, Edward			
Slaves........................2	....	6 00	

			TAXES.
McCrady & Son			
Income	6,800		215 00
McCrady, Jane			
Real Estate	3,000	42 00	
Interest on Bonds, &c	146	3 65	45 65
McCready, W T., Trustee Lansdell			
Slaves	6		18 00
McDonald, W H.			
Real Estate	4,500	63 00	
Slaves	7	21 00	84 00
McDonald, Margaret			
Real Estate	7,500	105 00	
Slave	1	3 00	108 00
McDonald, D.			
Slave	1		3 00
McDonnell, Thomas			
Real Estate	2,750		38 50
McDougal, David			
Real Estate	3,000		42 00
McDougal, Charlotte			
Slaves	4		12 00
McDowall, Andrew			
Real Estate	14,500	203 00	
Stock of Goods	15,850	221 90	
Carriage	1	30 00	
Horses	2	20 00	474 90
McDowell, Robert H.			
Real Estate	11,500	161 00	
Stock of Goods	5,000	70 00	
Slave	1	3 00	234 00
McDowell, W B.			
Slaves	3		9 00
McDowell, John T.			
Real Estate	5,000		70 00
McDowell's children, W			
Real Estate	3,000		42 00
McElhenney, Susan R.			
Interest on Bonds, &c	770	19 25	
Slaves	4	12 00	31 25
McElmoyle, Mrs. E. M.			
Real Estate	10,300	144 20	
Slaves	7	21 00	165 20
McElroy, John			
Real Estate	1,700		23 80

		TAXES.
McElroy, James		
Carriage....1		20 00
McEvoy, Michael		
Real Estate....2,000		28 00
McFeely, Trust Estate H., and children		
Real Estate....3,500	49 00	
Slaves....11	33 00	82 00
McFeeters, Mary Ann		
Real Estate....5,000	70 00	
Dog....1	2 00	72 00
McGary, F P		
Real Estate....3,000	42 00	
Stock of Goods....200	2 80	44 80
McGillivray, Misses M. and E. B.		
Real Estate....2,500	35 00	
Slaves....6	18 00	
Dog....1	2 00	55 00
McGinn, James		
Real Estate....10,000		140 00
McGorty, Michael		
Real Estate....8,500	119 00	
Slaves....5	15 00	134 00
McGrath, John		
Real Estate....400		5 60
McGrath, David		
Real Estate....1,800		25 20
McHugh, Mary Q.		
Real Estate....33,000		462 00
McHugh, Maria T.		
Real Estate....15,500	217 00	
Slaves....3	9 00	226 00
McHugh, Francis, Q.		
Real Estate....15,000	210 00	
Interest on Bonds, &c....390	9 75	
Slaves....3	9 00	228 78
McInerhney, Timothy		
Real Estate....1,200	....	16 80
McInnes, Benjamin		
Real Estate....13,800	193 20	
Slaves....11	33 00	
Dog....1	2 00	228 20
McIntosh, William		
Real Estate....1,000	....	14 00
McIntosh, W R.		
Slaves....3		9 00

			TAXES.
McIntosh, Louisa			
Real Estate	2,500		35 00
McIntyre, Julia C.			
Real Estate	2,000	28 00	
Slaves	2	6 00	34 00
McIntyre, Mary N., in trust			
Real Estate	15,200	212 80	
Slaves	2	6 00	218 80
McKay, D. L.			
Real Estate	8,000	112 00	
Slaves	3	9 00	121 00
McKee, Abel			
Real Estate	1,000		14 00
McKee, John			
Real Estate	4,000		56 00
McKee, Estate John			
Real Estate	16,500	231 00	
Slave	1	3 00	234 00
McKeegan, John			
Real Estate	22,500	315 00	
Slaves	9	27 00	
Carriage	1	20 00	
Horse	1	10 00	372 00
McKenna, Estate James			
Real Estate	2,700		37 80
McKenzie, Miss S.			
Slave	1		3 00
McKenzie, Archibald			
Real Estate	35,000	490 00	
Slaves	15	45 00	
Carriage	1	20 00	
Horse	1	10 00	
Dogs	2	4 00	569 00
McKenzie, Archibald & Co.			
Stock of Goods	13,000		182 00
McKenzie, Archibald, in trust			
Slaves	3	....	9 00
McKenzie, Archibald. Executor of Preston			
Real Estate	5,000	70 00	
Slaves	5	15 00	85 00
McKenzie, A., Trustee			
Slaves	8		24 00
McKenzie, Estate Richard			
Real Estate	10,000	....	140 00

		TAXES.
McKewn, W B.		
Slaves 5		15 00
McKewn, W T.		
Slave 1		3 00
McKewn, Estate Euphy		
Slave 1		3 00
McKewn, J. C.		
Slaves 6		18 00
McKewn, Barnard		
Stock of Goods........1,350	....	18 90
McKinlay, Peter		
Real Estate........3,000	42 00	
Dog 1	2 00	44 00
McLaren, James		
Carriage 1	20 00	
Horse 1	10 00	30 00
McLaren, Estate J.		
Real Estate........6,000 00	84 00	
Interest on Bonds, &c........5,014 92	125 37	
Slaves................4	12 00	221 37
McLaren, Mrs S.		
Slaves................9	27 00	
Carriage................1	20 00	
Horse 1	10 00	57 00
McLean, Margaret		
Slave................1		3 00
McLean, William		
Real Estate........5,000	70 00	
Slaves................5	15 00	
Carriage................1	20 00	
Horse 1	10 00	
Dog................1	2 00	117 00
McLeish, James		
Real Estate........3,600		50 40
McLeish, Archibald		
Real Estate........8,500	119 00	
Slaves 4	12 00	
Horse 1	10 00	141 00
McLeod & Bell		
Commissions........1,800	....	45 00
McLeod, H. A., Trustee		
Real Estate........3,000	42 00	
Slave 1	3 00	45 00
McLoy, Alexander		
Stock of Goods........5,000	....	70 00

                                                                        TAXES.

McMakin, Mary
 Real Estate..........................8,400 117 60
 Slaves 6 18 00 135 60
McMakin, James
 Slaves.......................................2   6 00
McManmon, M.
 Real Estate..........................3,000 42 00
 Slaves 3 9 00
 Horse.......................................1 10 00 61 00
McManus, T. F.
 Stock of Goods 300   4 20
McMaster, Martha
 Stock of Goods.....................2,000 28 00
 Slaves.......................................4 12 00 40 00
McMillan, Margaret E.
 Slaves.....................................13 .... 39 00
McMillan, James W
 Real Estate...........................3,000 .... 42 00
McMillan, John
 Real Estate.. .. ..8,000 .... 112 00
McMillan, W F.
 Slaves.......................................2 6 00
 Commissions......................2,000 50 00 56 00
McNally, Trust Estate Bernard
 Real Estate..........................1,200 .... 16 80
McNeal, Mary
 Real Estate..........................3,300 46 20
 Slaves.......................................2 6 00 52 20
McNellage, Lydia
 Slaves.......................................8 .... 24 00
McNellage, John
 Real Estate........................36,000 504 00
 Slaves.......................................6 18 00
 Carriage...................................1 20 00
 Horse.......................................1 10 00
 Dog..1 2 00 554 00
McOwen, Sarah
 Real Estate..........................4,000 56 00
 Slaves......................................3 9 00 65 00
McPherson, Estate
 Real Estate........................10,000 140 00
 Slaves.....................................36 108 00
 Carriage...................................1 30 00
 Horses......................................2 20 00 298 00

		TAXES.
McPherson, Catherine		
Real Estate............4,000	56 00	
Slave........1	3 00	59 00
McPherson, M. A.		
Slave........1	....	3 00
McPherson, John		
Real Estate............12,500	175 00	
Slaves........4	12 00	
Horses........2	20 00	207 00
McPherson, Estate Susan		
Real Estate............2,000		28 00
McQueen, W C.		
Slave........1	3 00	
Dog........1	2 00	5 00
McSwiney & Brother		
Slaves........2	6 00	
Horse........1	10 00	16 00
McTureous, B. Warren		
Real Estate............3,000	42 00	
Slaves........4	12 00	
Horse........1	10 00	64 00
McTureous, E.		
Slaves........3	....	9 00
McTureous, Estate E. W		
Real Estate............3,000	....	42 00
Nabb, Sarah		
Real Estate............4,500		63 00
Nagle, John		
Real Estate............1,000	....	14 00
Napier, Thomas		
Real Estate............48,000	672 00	
Slave........1	3 00	
Carriage........1	30 00	
Horses........2	20 00	725 00
Naser, Trust Estate Ann		
Real Estate............3,000	42 00	
Slave........1	3 00	45 00
Nathans, Estate N		
Real Estate............77,200	1,080 80	
Slaves........9	27 00	1,107 80
Nathans, M. H.		
Real Estate............9,000	126 00	
Stock of Goods............6,800	95 20	
Slave........1	3 00	224 20

			TAXES.
Nathans, M. H.			
Real Estate	3,500	49 00	
Slaves	3	9 00	
Dog	1	2 00	60 00
Nayel, Vincent			
Real Estate	7,000	....	98 00
Nayler, William			
Real Estate	11,000	154 00	
Carriage	1	20 00	
Horse	1	10 00	
Dog	1	2 00	186 00
Nayler, Smith & Co.			
Stock of Goods	84,913	....	1,188 78
Nayler, Mrs. H. G.			
Real Estate	5,000	70 00	
Slaves	29	87 00	157 00
Nell, Ursula S. & Mary A.			
Slaves	6	....	18 00
Nelson, C.			
Real Estate	3,000	....	42 00
Nelson, W			
Real Estate	2,000	28 00	
Slave	1	3 00	31 00
Neufville, Harriet E, Executrix B. S. N.			
Real Estate	8,000	....	112 00
Neufville, Elizabeth			
Real Estate	1,300	....	18 20
Neumann, Trust Estate M.			
Real Estate	6,000	84 00	
Stock of Goods	3,000	42 00	
Slave	1	3 00	129 00
Neumann, Philip			
Carriage	1	....	20 00
Newton, Susan C.			
Real Estate	6,000	84 00	
Slaves	4	12 00	96 00
Neyle, Mrs. M. J.			
*Real Estate	10,000	140 00	
Slaves	7	21 00	161 00
Nichols, Henry			
Slaves	5	....	15 00
Nichols, James H.			
Slaves	5	....	15 00

TAXES.

Nickerson, G. W
    Real Estate.........................3,000   42 00
    Slave 1   3 00   45 00

Nihaus, F.
    Real Estate........................5,000   70 00
    Stock of Goods.....................500   7 00   77 00

Nipson, Thomas S.
    Stock of Goods...................2,000   28 00

Nipson, Francis
    Real Estate........................2,440   34 16
    Slave 1   3 00
    Commissions 30   75
    Horse 1   10 00   47 91

Nipson, Francis, Trustee
    Slaves 6   18 00

Noelken, C.
    Stock of Goods.....................400   ....   5 60

Nohrden, Carsten
    Real Estate........................9,800   137 20
    Stock of Goods.....................800   11 20
    Slaves 3   9 00   157 40

Noland, John C. C.
    Real Estate........................4,000   56 00
    Slave 1   3 00   59 00

Nolen, Estate James
    Real Estate........................3,000   42 00

Norman, Charles, and wife
    Real Estate........................2,000   ....   28 00

Norman, Estate Henry
    Real Estate........................4,500   63 00

Norris, W H.
    Real Estate........................1,800   ....   25 20

North. Dr. Edward
    Real Estate......................13,150   184 10
    Slaves 20   60 00
    Carriage 1   30 00
    Carriage 1   20 00
    Income...........................4,000   100 00
    Horses 3   30 00
    Dogs 2   4 00   428 10

North, Dr. Edward, Trustee
    Slaves 3   9 00

North, Dr. E., and P J Porcher, Trustees
    Slaves 11   ....   33 00

		TAXES.
North, R. L.		
Slaves 6	18 00	
Carriages 2	40 00	
Horses 2	20 00	78 00
Northrop, Emily		
Slaves 2		6 00
Northrop, Anna		
Slave 1		3 00
Northrop, C. B., Trustee		
Slaves 21		63 00
Northrop & Allemong		
Income 6,310	....	157 75
Northrop, L. B.		
Real Estate 700	9 80	
Slaves 36	108 00	
Carriage 1	20 00	137 80
Norton, Jabez		
Slaves 3	9 00	
Horse 1	10 00	
Dog 1	2 00	21 00
Nowell, L. C.		
Dogs 2		4 00
Nowell, John L.		
Interest on Bonds, &c 147	3 68	
Slaves 16	48 00	
Carriage 1	30 00	
Horses 2	20 00	
Dog 1	2 00	103 68
Nowell, John L., Trustee		
Slave 1	....	3 00
Nowell, E. W., Administrator of Wigfall		
Slaves 3	....	9 00
Nunan, George		
Real Estate 6,500	91 00	
Slave 1	3 00	94 00
Oakes, Z. B.		
Real Estate 72,500	1,015 00	
Slaves 16	48 00	
Carriages 2	40 00	
Income 5,000	125 00	
Horses 2	20 00	
Dog 1	2 00	1,250 00
Oakes, Z. B., in trust		
Real Estate 2,000	28 00	
Slaves 3	9 00	37 00

			TAXES.
Oakley, Robert S.			
Real Estate	6,500	91 00	
Slave	1	3 00	94 00
Oakley, W C.			
Income	100		2 50
Oberhausser, J			
Stock of Goods	500	7 00	
Slave	1	3 00	10 00
O'Brien, Luke			
Real Estate	2,000		28 00
O'Brien, T.			
Horse	1		10 00
O'Brien, M. J.			
Slaves	2		6 00
O'Brien, David			
Slave	1		3 00
O'Brien, Patrick			
Real Estate	3,000		42 00
O'Brien, Thomas			
Real Estate	13,000	182 00	
Interest on Bonds, &c	678	16 95	
Slaves	10	30 00	228 95
O'Brien, E.			
Real Estate	2,500	35 00	
Slaves	4	12 00	47 00
O'Bryan, Lewis			
Slaves	2		6 00
O'Callahan, Dennis			
Real Estate	8,300		116 20
O'Callahan, Estate Charles			
Real Estate	4,500		63 00
O'Connell, P.			
Real Estate	2,500	35 00	
Carriage	1	20 00	
Horse	1	10 00	65 00
O'Connor, M. P			
Real Estate	30,500	427 00	
Slave	1	3 00	
Income	1,200	30 00	460 00
O'Connor, Trust Estate Elizabeth			
Real Estate	2,000		28 00
O'Connor, Mary			
Slave	1		3 00

		TAXES.
O'Donnell, Patrick		
Real Estate.........28,500	399 00	
Slaves 11	33 00	432 00
Oelund, Peter		
Real Estate.........1,000		14 00
Oetjen, Henry		
Real Estate.........26,800		375 20
Oetjen, Henry, Trustee		
Slaves............3		9 00
Ogemann, John C.		
Real Estate.........15,000	210 00	
Stock of Goods.........2,500	35 00	
Slaves 4	12 00	257 00
Ogier, Dr. T. L.		
Real Estate.........14,000	196 00	
Slaves 9	27 00	
Carriage............1	30 00	
Carriage............1	15 00	
Income.........8,000	200 00	
Horses............3	30 00	498 00
Ogilvie, Mathew		
Stock of Goods.........13,000	182 00	
Slaves 5	15 00	
Carriage............1	20 00	
Horse............1	10 00	
Dog............1	2 00	229 00
Ogilvie, Trust Estate M. M.		
Real Estate.........5,000	....	70 00
O'Hara, W P		
Interest on Bonds, &c.........400	....	10 00
O'Hara, W P., in trust		
Slaves............3		9 00
O'Hara, Mary L.		
Slaves............7		21 00
O'Hara, Martha		
Interest on Bonds, &c.........280	7 00	
Slaves............5	15 00	22 00
O'Hear, James		
Real Estate.........10,400	145 60	
Slaves............8	24 00	
Carriage............1	30 00	
Commissions.........5,851	146 28	
Horses............3	30 00	
Dogs............5	10 00	385 88

TAXES.

O'Hear, Dr. J. S.
    Real Estate..........10,000   140 00
    Slaves..........11   33 00
    Carriage..........1   30 00
    Horses..........2   20 00
    Dog..........1   2 00   225 00

Ohlandt, D. W
    Stock of Goods..........350   4 90

Ohlandt, John H.
    Stock of Goods..........300   4 20

Oland, Catherine
    Real Estate..........5,000   ....   70 00

Oldenburg, E. H.
    Stock of Goods..........1,200   16 80
    Dog..........1   2 00   18 80

Olney, G. W
    Real Estate..........20,000   280 00
    Stock of Goods..........3,000   42 00
    Slaves..........7   21 00
    Carriage..........1   20 00
    Horse..........1   10 00
    Dog..........1   2 00   375 00

Olney, G. W., Trustee
    Slaves..........5   ....   15 00

Olsen, Charles M.
    Real Estate..........1,800   25 20
    Dog..........1   2 00   27 20

Olsen, Trust Estate H. Julia
    Real Estate..........9,000   126 00
    Slaves..........5   15 00   141 00

O'Mara, John
    Real Estate..........8,500   119 00
    Stock of Goods..........1,500   21 00   140 00

O'Neale, James
    Real Estate..........4,500   63 00
    Slaves..........5   15 00   78 00

O'Neale & Crawford
    Slaves..........2   6 00
    Commissions..........11,000   275 00   281 00

O'Neill, Dennis & Son
    Stock of Goods..........400   ....   5 60

O'Neill, P.
    Real Estate..........10,000   140 00

		TAXES
O'Neill, Bernard		
Real Estate.....................19,000	266 00	
Stock of Goods...................8,000	112 00	
Slaves.................................7	21 00	
Carriage..............................1	20 00	
Horse..................................1	10 00	429 00
O'Neill, John F		
Real Estate.....................23,500	329 00	
Stock of Goods.................8,000	112 00	
Slaves.................................4	12 00	
Carriage..............................1	20 00	
Horse..................................1	10 00	
Dog....................................1	2 00	485 00
O'Neill, John F., Administrator of A. Magee		
Real Estate.......................6,000	84 00	
Slave..................................1	3 00	87 00
O'Neill, Hugh		
Real Estate.......................6,000	84 00	
Slaves.................................2	6 00	
Dog....................................1	2 00	92 00
O'Neill, Patrick		
Real Estate.......................6,800	95 20	
Slaves................................19	57 00	
Carriage..............................1	20 00	
Horse..................................1	10 00	182 20
O'Neill, P		
Real Estate.....................29,200	408 80	
Slaves.................................9	27 00	
Carriage..............................1	20 00	
Horses................................2	20 00	475 80
O'Neill, Executor of Hutson		
Real Estate.......................1,200	....	16 80
O'Neill, Executor of Crohan		
Real Estate.......................1,200	....	16 80
O'Neill, P., Trustee A. Drake		
Real Estate.....................12,000		168 00
O'Neill, Margaret A.		
Real Estate.....................18,500	259 00	
Interest on Bonds, &c............173	4 33	
Slaves.................................3	9 00	
Horse..................................1	10 00	
Dogs...................................2	4 00	286 33
O'Neill, Trustee of M. and I. Hogan		
Real Estate.......................4,000		56 00
O'Neill, P., Trustee		
Slaves.................................4	....	12 00

			TAXES
Oppenheim, J. H. & Brother			
Real Estate	8,000		112 00
Oppenheim Brothers			
Stock of Goods	5,000	70 00	
Carriage	1	20 00	90 00
Oppenheim, Joseph H.			
Real Estate	3,000	42 00	
Slaves	3	9 00	
Carriage	1	20 00	
Dog	1	2 00	73 00
Oppenheim, C.			
Real Estate	23,000	322 00	
Slaves	8	24 00	346 00
Oppenheim, C., Executrix			
Real Estate	8,000	112 00	
Slaves	8	24 00	136 00
Orcutt, L.			
Stock of Goods	2,000		28 00
O'Rourke, F			
Real Estate	600		8 40
Ostendorff, J. M.			
Real Estate	8,000		112 00
Osterholtz, J. D.			
Real Estate	5,500	77 00	
Stock of Goods	400	5 60	
Dog	1	2 00	84 60
O'Sullivan, Thomas F.			
Real Estate	1,500	21 00	
Slave	1	3 00	24 00
Otgen, J. C.			
Stock of Goods	600	8 40	
Horse	1	10 00	
Dog	1	2 00	20 40
Otgen, John C.			
Real Estate	1,200	16 80	
Slaves	2	6 00	22 80
Otten, Estate Cord			
Real Estate	4,000	56 00	
Slave	1	3 00	59 00
Otten, H.			
Stock of Goods	800	11 20	
Dog	1	2 00	13 20
Otten, Henrich			
Stock of Goods	800	11 20	
Dog	1	2 00	13 20

		TAXES.
Otten, Catherine, Agent		
Stock of Goods 1,000		14 00
Otten, J. B.		
Stock of Goods...............1,000	14 00	
Dog...............................1	2 00	16 00
Ottolengui, Sarah		
Real Estate...............13,500		189 00
Ottolengui, Jacob		
Real Estate...............2,000	28 00	
Slaves...............5	15 00	
Commissions...............500	12 50	
Dog...............1	2 00	57 50
Ottolengui, Israel		
Real Estate...............2,500	35 00	
Slaves...............2	6 00	
Dog...............1	2 00	43 00
Ottolengui, Israel and Daniel		
Real Estate...............28,500	....	399 00
O'Wen, Leslie		
Real Estate...............700		9 80
Owens, Alexander		
Real Estate...............25,600	358 40	
Slaves...............13	39 00	
Horses...............4	40 00	437 40
Oxlade, Thomas C.		
Real Estate...............5,000		70 00
Paine, Margaret B.		
Real Estate...............3,400	47 60	
Interest on Bonds, &c...............35	88 00	48 60
Paine, Estate Thomas		
Real Estate...............15,900	222 60	
Interest on Bonds, &c...............100	2 50	
Slaves...............10	30 00	
Carriage...............1	20 00	
Horse...............1	10 00	285 10
Palma, Nareno		
Slaves...............4	....	12 00
Palma, Clementina		
Slaves...............4	....	12 00
Palmer, W J.		
Slaves...............2	....	6 00
Panknin, C. H.		
Real Estate...............28,000	392 00	
Stock of Goods...............8,000	112 00	
Carriage...............1	20 00	
Horse...............1	10 00	534 00

		TAXES.
Panzerbieter, H.		
Stock of Goods....................1,400		19 60
Parker, Thomas		
Real Estate......................12,000	168 00	
Slaves 3	9 00	
Carriage..............................1	30 00	
Horses.................................2	20 00	
Dogs 2	4 00	231 00
Parker, Elizabeth and George		
Slaves 5		15 00
Parker, Mrs. A. G.		
Stock of Goods..................2,000	28 00	
Carriage..............................1	20 00	
Horse..................................1	10 00	
Dog 1	2 00	60 00
Parker, Susan J.		
Interest on Bonds, &c 404	10 10	
Slaves..................................2	6 00	16 10
Parker, J J		
Slaves 3		9 00
Parker, J. J		
Slaves 4		12 00
Parker, Francis J., Trustee of Gaillard		
Real Estate......................6,500	91 00	
Interest on Bonds, &c.............784	19 60	
Slaves..................................4	12 00	122 60
Parker. J. J., agent of Bowrie		
Real Estate......................4,500		63 00
Parker, Mrs. E. H., and children		
Real Estate......................5,000	70 00	
Slaves 5	15 00	85 00
Parker, Wm. McK.		
Slaves 19	57 00	
Horses 3	30 00	87 00
Parker, Edward L.		
Slave 1		3 00
Parker, Francis S.		
Real Estate......................14,000	196 00	
Slaves 17	51 00	
Carriage..............................1	30 00	
Horses.................................4	40 00	
Dog 1	2 00	319 00
Parker, Sarah S.		
Interest on Bonds, &c............1,260	31 50	
Slaves..................................2	6 00	37 50

		TAXES.
Parker, Mrs. A. M.		
Slaves 2		6 00
Parker, Sarah E.		
Interest on Bonds, &c............200	5 00	
Slaves 8	24 00	29 00
Parker, Rachel V		
Real Estate.................5,000	70 00	
Slaves 5	15 00	85 00
Parker, Mary		
Interest on Bonds, &c............200	5 00	
Slaves 10	30 00	35 00
Parker, Robert D.		
Real Estate.................9,000	126 00	
Slaves 21	63 00	
Carriage..........................1	20 00	
Horse 1	10 00	
Dog 1	2 00	221 00
Parker, Sarah E., in trust		
Slaves 2		6 00
Parrott, Estate George		
Real Estate................17,000	....	238 00
Parry, Harriet E.		
Real Estate.................3,200	44 80	
Slave 1	3 00	47 80
Passailaigue, Mrs. E.		
Real Estate.................1,500	21 00	
Slaves 6	18 00	39 00
Paterson, Sarah C.		
Real Estate.................4,500	63 00	
Slaves 11	33 00	96 00
Patrenovicth, Philip		
Real Estate.................3,200	....	44 80
Patrick, J B.		
Real Estate................12,500	175 00	
Slaves............................3	9 00	
Carriage 1	30 00	
Income...........................3,500	87 50	
Horses 2	20 00	321 50
Patrick, Julia C.		
Slaves 6		18 00
Patrick & McMillan		
Real Estate.................2,000	28 00	
Dog 1	2 00	30 00
Patterson, F. & Co.		
Stock of Goods..............500	....	7 00

			TAXES.
Patterson & Stock			
Shipping	10,000	75 00	
Commissions	4,000	100 00	175 00
Patterson, J L., Agent			
Slaves	2	6 00	
Dog	1	2 00	8 00
Patterson, F J. C.			
Slaves	6	....	24 00
Patterson, J. L., Trustee			
Slaves	2	....	6 00
Patterson, F J. C., Trustee			
Slaves	2	....	6 00
Patterson, Sarah W			
Real Estate	15,800	....	221 20
Pattini, Joseph			
Real Estate	2,500	35 00	
Stock of Goods	1,000	14 00	
Slaves	18	54 00	103 00
Pattini, B.			
Stock of Goods	500		7 00
Patton, Estate William			
Real Estate	53,500	749 00	
Slaves	10	30 00	
Carriage	1	30 00	
Horses	2	20 00	829 00
Paty, James			
Real Estate	3,500	49 00	
Slave	1	3 00	52 00
Paul, Dunbar			
Real Estate	27,000	378 00	
Slaves	7	21 00	
Carriage	1	20 00	
Horse	1	10 00	
Dogs	2	4 00	433 00
Paul, D., & Co.			
Stock of Goods	26,000	364 00	
Dog	1	2 00	366 00
Pauls, H.			
Stock of Goods	400		5 60
Pauls, G. H.			
Real Estate	3,000	42 00	
Stock of Goods	400	5 60	47 60
Paxton, W Y.			
Stock of Goods	8,000	....	112 00

		TAXES.
Payne, Jane L.		
Slave 1		3 00
Payne, Estate J. S.		
Real Estate........................10,500		147 00
Payne, Rebecca		
Slaves....................................4		12 00
Payne, Julia H.		
Slaves....................................4	12 00	
Carriage...............................1	20 00	
Horse 1	10 00	42 00
Peake, Henry T.		
Real Estate..........................4,500	63 00	
Slaves....................................9	27 00	
Carriage...............................1	20 00	
Horses...................................2	20 00	130 00
Pearce. William T.		
Slave 1		3 00
Peixotto, Grace		
Real Estate........................15,000	210 00	
Slaves....................................7	21 00	231 00
Pelerin, Madam S.		
Stock of Goods....................1,000	14 00	
Slaves....................................2	6 00	
Dog.......................................1	2 00	22 00
Pelerin, A.		
Stock of Goods.......................200		2 80
Pelzer, Dr. A. P		
Real Estate..........................7,000	98 00	
Slaves....................................5	15 00	
Carriage...............................1	30 00	
Income................................3,000	75 00	
Horses...................................2	20 00	
Dog.......................................1	2 00	240 00
Pelzer, George S.		
Slave.....................................1	3 00	
Carriage...............................1	20 00	
Income................................2,000	50 00	
Horse 1	10 00	83 00
Pelzer, Francis J.		
Real Estate........................13,000	182 00	
Slaves..................................19	57 00	
Carriage...............................1	20 00	
Horses...................................2	20 00	
Dog.......................................1	2 00	281 00
Pelzer, Francis J., Trustee		
Real Estate..........................2,400	....	33 60

			TAXES.
Pennal, Estate Robert			
Real Estate	33,500	469 00	
Slaves	3	9 00	478 00
Pennal, Mary			
Real Estate	15,000	210 00	
Carriage	1	20 00	
Horse	1	10 00	240 00
Peoples, William			
Real Estate	1,200	....	16 80
Pepper, A. M.			
Slaves	9	....	27 00
Perkins, Margaret A.			
Slave	1	....	3 00
Peronneau, Misses E. A. and A. B.			
Real Estate	250	3 50	
Interest on Bonds, &c	543	13 58	
Slaves	17	51 00	68 08
Perrier, Adelle			
Slave	1		3 00
Perry, Maria A.			
Slave	1		3 00
Perry, Mary S.			
Slave	1		3 00
Perry, A. S. J., Trustee M. H. Perry			
Real Estate	11,000	154 00	
Slaves	3	9 00	163 00
Perry, A. S. J.			
Slaves	12	36 00	
Carriage	1	30 00	
Horses	2	20 00	
Dogs	2	4 00	90 00
Perry, Mrs. M. A. R.			
Slaves	3		9 00
Perry, Julia			
Slaves	7		21 00
Perry, Miss C. M.			
Slaves	13	....	39 00
Peterman, J. H.			
Real Estate	3,000	42 00	
Stock of Goods	500	7 00	
Carriage	1	20 00	
Dog	1	2 00	71 00
Peterman, M.			
Stock of Goods	425		5 94

		TAXES.

Peterman, Mrs. F.
    Real Estate..........................7,000   98 00
    Stock of Goods....................800   11 20
    Dog...................................1   2 00   111 20

Peters, Henrich
    Interest on Bonds, &c..............725   18 13

Peters, Mrs. C. C.
    Slaves..............................3   9 00

Peters, H. T.
    Slaves..............................2   6 00

Peters, Jane W
    Slaves..............................2   6 00

Pettigrew, J Johnston
    Real Estate.....................5,000 00   70 00
    Interest on Bonds, &c.......2,318 86   57 97
    Horse................................1   10 00
    Dog..................................1   2 00   139 97

Pettigrew, Dr. William
    Income.............................500   12 50
    Dog..................................1   2 00   14 50

Pettigrew, Dr. William, in trust
    Real Estate......................4,500   63 00
    Carriage............................1   20 00   83 00

Petigru, James L.
    Real Estate....................20,550   287 70
    Interest on Bonds, &c..........240   6 00
    Slaves..............................17   51 00
    Carriage............................1   30 0C
    Horses..............................2   20 00
    Dogs................................2   4 00   398 70

Petigru & King
    Income....................14,721 40   368 03

Petigru, Mrs. M. A.
    Real Estate....................10,000   140 00
    Interest on Bonds, &c..........154   3 85
    Slaves..............................9   27 00
    Carriage............................1   30 00
    Horse...............................1   2 20
    Dog.................................1   2 00   222 85

Petit, N. F.
    Real Estate....................18,500   259 00
    Slaves..............................2   6 00
    Dog.................................1   2 00   267 00

Petit, N. F., in trust
    Real Estate....................10,500   147 00

		TAXES.
Petit, Edmund W		
Dog.................1		2 00
Petit, L. F		
Real Estate.........10,000	140 00	
Stock of Goods.......1,000	14 00	
Slaves.................9	27 00	
Dog....................1	2 00	183 00
Peurifoy, A. M.		
Real Estate.........3,200		44 80
Peurifoy, A., Guardian		
Slave..................1		3 00
Peurifoy, A., Trustee		
Stock of Goods.........50	70	
Slaves.................5	15 00	15 70
Pezant, Louis		
Slaves.................2		6 00
Pezant, Estate John L.		
Slaves................11		33 00
Pezant, Bonne Sophia		
Real Estate.........2,000	28 00	
Dog....................1	2 00	30 00
Phelps, Seth		
Real Estate.........1,200	16 80	
Slave..................1	3 00	19 80
Philbrick, John, Agent		
Stock of Goods......5,000		70 00
Phillips, Dr. St. John		
Real Estate.........7,000	98 00	
Slaves................20	60 00	
Carriage..............1	30 00	
Carriage..............1	20 00	
Income.............1,000	25 00	
Horses.................3	30 00	
Dog....................1	2 00	265 00
Phillips, Otis		
Real Estate........16,000	224 00	
Stock of Goods........700	9 80	
Slaves.................2	6 00	
Carriage..............1	30 00	
Income...............500	12 50	
Horses.................2	20 00	302 30
Phillips, Estate John M.		
Real Estate.........5,000	70 00	
Slaves.................8	24 00	94 00

                                                                    TAXES.
Phillips, John
    Real Estate..........................14,500   203 00
    Interest on Bonds, &c............1,560   39 00
    Slaves..6   18 00
    Carriage....................................1   20 00
    Shipping 1,000   7 50
    Income.................................6,000   150 00
    Horse 1   10 00   447 50
Phillips, John E.
    Slaves 4   12 00
Phillips, L. M.
    Real Estate.............................1,500   21 00
Phillips, Eleazar
    Real Estate.............................2,000   28 00
    Slave...1   3 00   31 00
Phin, A. C.
    Real Estate.............................5,000   70 00
    Slave...1   3 00
    Dog..1   2 00   75 00
Phin & Dorn
    Stock of Goods 4,000   56 00
Phinney, Mrs. R. C.
    Slave...1   3 00
Picault, Carolina
    Stock of Goods 1,000   14 00
    Slaves..2   6 00   20 00
Pickett, Rev. John R.
    Real Estate.............................4,800   67 20
Pierce, Phineas
    Real Estate.............................8,000   112 00
    Interest on Bonds, &c................800   20 00
    Slaves..3   9 00   141 00
Pierson & Jennings
    Real Estate...........................12,000   168 00
Pierson, Smith & Co.
    Stock of Goods 22,000   308 00
Pinckney, Mrs. Lucia
    Real Estate.............................6,200   86 80
    Slaves 19   57 00
    Carriage....................................1   30 00
    Horses.......................................2   20 00   193 80
Pinckney, M. S. and children
    Real Estate.............................9,500   133 00
    Slaves..5   15 00   148 00

TAXES.

Pinckney, B. G.
 Real Estate 5,000 70 00
 Slaves 5 15 00
 Carriage 1 20 00
 Income........................3,700 92 50
 Horse 1 10 00 207 50

Pinckney, R. Q.
 Slaves 3 9 00
 Carriage........................1 30 00
 Horses........................2 20 00 59 00

Pinckney, R. Q., Jr.
 Carriage 1 20 00
 Commissions........................1,500 37 50 57 50

Pinckney, Miss H.
 Real Estate........................148,000 2,072 00
 Slaves........................12 36 00
 Carriage........................1 30 00
 Horses........................2 20 00 2,158 00

Pinckney, H. L.
 Real Estate........................2,500 35 00
 Slaves........................8 24 00
 Dog........................1 2 00 61 00

Pinckney, H. L. & P Porcher
 Slaves ....5 .... 15 00

Pinckney, Charles
 Horse........................1 .... 10 00

Pinckney, Charles, Trustee
 Slaves........................2 .... 6 00

Pinckney, Rev. C. C.
 Real Estate........................10,000 140 00
 Interest on Bonds, &c........................1,408 35 20
 Slaves 9 27 00
 Carriage........................1 20 00
 Horse........................1 10 00 232 20

Pinckney, Eliza
 Real Estate........................16,000 224 00
 Slaves 2 6 00 230 00

Pinckney, H. L., Jr.
 Real Estate........................6,000 84 00
 Slaves........................6 18 00
 Carriage........................1 20 00
 Horse........................1 10 00 132 00

Pinkerssohn, P
 Stock of Goods........................1,000 .... 14 00

Plane, Wm. A.
 Real Estate........................5,000 .... 70 00

		TAXES.
Plane, Thomas		
Real Estate.................4,000	....	56 00
Plenge, C.		
Real Estate.................8,000	112 00	
Stock of Goods.............500	7 00	119 00
Plessmann, George W		
Slave.........................1		3 00
Ploger, F H.		
Stock of Goods.............800	11 20	
Dog............................1	2 00	13 20
Pogson, Trust Estate Milward		
Real Estate.................4,500	63 00	
Slaves.........................9	27 00	
Carriage.......................1	20 00	
Horse..........................1	10 00	120 00
Pointell, C.		
Slave..........................1		3 00
Poincignon, E.		
Real Estate...............106,000	1,484 00	
Interest on Bonds, &c........500	12 50	
Slaves........................15	45 00	1,541 50
Poincignon, E., Trustee		
Slave..........................1		3 00
Police, Francis		
Real Estate................20,400	285 60	
Slaves.........................3	9 00	
Dog............................1	2 00	296 60
Pooser, Mrs. E. C.		
Real Estate..................300	4 20	
Slave..........................1	3 00	7 20
Pooser, E. W		
Real Estate.................3,300	46 20	
Slave..........................1	3 00	49 20
Pope, J J., Jr.		
Real Estate.................8,000	112 00	
Slaves........................10	30 00	
Income.....................1,877	46 93	
Dog............................1	2 00	190 93
Pope, Dr. Franklin, Trustee		
Slaves........................11	....	33 00
Popen, Andreas		
Real Estate.................1,000	....	14 00

			TAXES.
Poppenheim, John F.			
Real Estate	14,000	196 00	
Slaves	14	42 00	
Carriage	1	20 00	
Horse	1	10 00	268 00
Porcher, Philip J.			
Real Estate	10,200	142 80	
Slaves	24	72 00	
Carriage	1	30 00	
Horses	2	20 00	
Dog	1	2 00	266 80
Porcher, P J. & Baya			
Commissions	3,500		87 50
Porcher, Mrs. Catherine			
Real Estate	8,000		112 00
Porcher, F A.			
Slaves	13		39 00
Porcher, M. L.			
Slaves	2		6 00
Porcher, F. Y.			
Real Estate	13,700	191 80	
Slaves	13	39 00	
Carriage	1	30 00	
Carriage	1	20 00	
Income	1,000	25 00	
Horses	2	20 00	325 80
Porcher, Estate Isaac			
Interest on Bonds, &c	900	22 50	
Slaves	13	39 00	61 50
Porcher, Catharine			
Slaves	5		15 00
Porcher, Selina M.			
Real Estate	6,000	84 00	
Slaves	7	21 00	
Carriage	1	30 00	
Horses	2	20 00	155 00
Porcher, Dr. Peter			
Real Estate	9,000	126 00	
Slaves	15	45 00	
Carriage	1	20 00	
Income	1,500	37 50	
Horse	1	10 00	
Dogs	4	8 00	246 50
Porcher, Mrs. E. L.			
Interest on Bonds, &c	350	8 75	
Horse	1	10 00	18 75

15

TAXES

Porcher, F. J
 Real Estate..........15,000 210 00
 Slaves.........8 24 00
 Carriage.........1 20 00
 Shipping.........250 1 88
 Income.........9,000 225 00
 Horses.........2 20 00
 Dogs.........2 4 00 504 8
Porcher, Harriet
 Interest on Bonds, &c.........420 10 50
 Slaves.........2 6 00 16 5
Porcher, Maria L.
 Slaves.........2 6 0
Porcher, F. Y., for A. Cripps
 Slaves.........3 9 0
Porcher, Philip E., Trustee Egleston
 Real Estate.........5,500 77 00
 Slaves.........11 33 00
 Carriage.........1 30 00
 Horses.........2 20 00 160 0
Porcher, Dr. F. Peyre
 Interest on Bonds, &c.........140 3 50
 Slaves.........5 15 00
 Carriage.........1 20 00
 Income.........1,200 30 00
 Horse.........1 10 00 78 5
Porcher, Dr. F. Y., Trustee
 Slaves.........3 9 0
Porteous, John F.
 Slaves.........7 21 0
Porter, N. M.
 Real Estate.........47,000 658 00
 Slaves.........4 12 00
 Carriage.........1 20 00
 Shipping.........6,000 45 00
 Horses.........4 40 00
 Dogs.........2 4 00 779 0
Porter, N. M. & Co.
 Stock of Goods.........18,000 252 0
Porter, Trust Estate W L. and A. and children
 Real Estate.........6,000 84 00
 Interest on Bonds, &c.........75 1 88
 Slaves.........2 6 00 91 8
Porter, J. H.
 Horse.........1 10 0

                                                            TAXES.

Porter, William D.
    Real Estate................8,000   112 00
    Slaves..........................7   21 00
    Carriage........................1   20 00
    Horses..........................2   20 00
    Dog.............................1   2 00   175 00
Porter, Rev. A. Toomer
    Real Estate................4,000   56 00
    Interest on Bonds, &c......500   12 50
    Slaves..........................9   27 00   95 50
Postell, Estate Sarah
    Real Estate................1,500   ....   21 00
Postell, Estate J. G.
    Slaves..........................5   15 00
Potter, L. T., in trust
    Real Estate................2,000   28 00
    Slaves..........................2   6 00
    Carriage........................1   20 00
    Horse...........................1   10 00   64 00
Potts, Mary
    Interest on Bonds, &c......760   19 00
    Slaves..........................2   6 00
    Annuity.......................300   7 50   32 50
Poujaud, Mrs. C. M.
    Real Estate................3,000   42 00
    Slaves..........................4   12 00
    Carriage........................1   20 00
    Horse...........................1   10 00
    Dog.............................1   2 00   86 00
Poujaud & Salas, and Augustus Poujaud, Trustee
    Shipping...................7,000   52 50
    Commissions..............16,550 413 75 466 25
Poujaud, Augustus, Trustee
    Slaves..........................4   ....   12 00
Powers, James and Thomas
    Real Estate................2,900   ....   40 60
Powers, Pierce
    Slave...........................1   3 00
Poyas, W R.
    Slave...........................1   ....   3 00
Poyas, John E., Trustee
    Real Estate................6,000   84 00
    Slaves..........................3   9 00   93 00
Poyas, James, Trustee
    Slave...........................1   ....   3 00

			TAX
Poyas, James			
Real Estate	10,000	140 00	
Slaves	17	51 00	
Carriage	1	30 00	
Horses	2	20 00	
Dog	1	2 00	243
Poyas, Mrs. Providence			
Real Estate	7,200	100 80	
Interest on Bonds, &c	126	3 15	
Slaves	9	27 00	130
Poznanski, G.			
Real Estate	10,000		140
Pregnall, H.			
Horse	1	10 00	
Dog	1	2 00	12
Pregnall, E. J			
Slaves	2		6
Prendergast, Edward			
Real Estate	9,000	126 00	
Stock of Goods	600	8 40	
Interest on Bonds, &c	500	12 50	
Slave	1	3 00	149
Prentiss, Rev. W O.			
Interest on Bonds, &c	175	4 38	
Slaves	21	63 00	
Carriage	1	30 00	
Horses	3	30 00	127
Press, Ship Cotton			
Real Estate	15,000		210
Pressley, B. C.			
Real Estate	25,800	361 20	
Slaves	5	15 00	
Income	2,000	50 00	426
Pressley, B. C., Trustee			
Real Estate	16,750		234
Preston, Ann			
Real Estate	6,000	84 00	
Slave	1	3 00	
Horse	1	10 00	97
Preston & Fitzpatrick			
Income	2,500		62
Prevost, Joseph			
Real Estate	109,500	1,533 00	
Slaves	21	63 00	
Carriage	1	30 00	
Carriage	1	20 00	
Horses	3	30 00	1,676

			TAXES.
Price, Mary E.			
Slaves	2	6 00	
Dog	1	2 00	8 00
Price, Philip S., and wife			
Real Estate	3,000	42 00	
Slaves	2	6 00	48 00
Price, Philip S.			
Real Estate	4,500	63 00	
Slave	1	3 00	66 00
Priggé, Claus			
Real Estate	8,500	119 00	
Slave	1	3 00	122 00
Prince, Mary			
Slaves	4	....	12 00
Prince, Mary E.			
Slave	1	....	3 00
Prince, George			
Stock of Goods	3,000	42 00	
Slaves	4	12 00	54 00
Prince, Sarah			
Real Estate	6,000	84 00	
Slaves	10	30 00	
Dog	1	2 00	116 00
Pringle, Motte A.			
Slaves	2	6 00	
Commissions	2,277	56 93	62 93
Pringle, Motte A., in trust			
Slave	1		3 00
Pringle, William Bull			
Real Estate	18,000	252 00	
Interest on Bonds, &c	490	12 25	
Slaves	34	102 00	
Carriage	1	30 00	
Carriage	1	20 00	
Horses	4	40 00	456 25
Pringle, R. A. & Co.			
Stock of Goods	18,000	....	252 00
Pringle, Robert A.			
Real Estate	5,000	70 00	
Slaves	2	6 00	76 00
Pringle, S. M.			
Real Estate	9,000	126 00	
Slaves	9	27 00	153 00

			TAXES.
Pringle, Mrs. R. M.			
Interest on Bonds, &c	200	5 00	
Slaves	8	24 00	29 00
Pringle, Robert			
Real Estate	5,000	70 00	
Slaves	5	15 00	
Shipping	10,000	75 00	160 00
Pringle, William Allston			
Real Estate	5,000	70 00	
Interest on Bonds, &c	1,500	37 50	
Slaves	9	27 00	
Income	800	20 00	
Dog	1	2 00	156 50
Pringle, James R.			
Real Estate	12,000	168 00	
Slaves	15	45 00	
Carriage	1	30 00	
Horses	3	30 00	
Dogs	2	4 00	277 00
Pringle, J. St. J.			
Slave	1	....	3 00
Pringle, Miss E. F.			
Real Estate	10,000	140 00	
Interest on Bonds, &c	1,750	43 75	
Slaves	10	30 00	
Carriage	1	30 00	
Horses	2	20 00	263 75
Prioleau, Dr. Thomas G.			
Real Estate	5,000	70 00	
Slaves	12	36 00	
Carriage	1	30 00	
Income	3,000	75 00	
Horse	1	10 00	
Dog	1	2 00	223 00
Prioleau, E. M.			
Slaves	6	....	18 00
Prioleau, Martha			
Real Estate	24,500	343 00	
Slaves	4	12 00	
Carriage	1	30 00	
Horses	2	20 00	405 00
Prioleau, F. C.			
Real Estate	4,000	56 00	
Slaves	3	9 00	65 00
Prioleau, F. C., Agent			
Slaves	11	....	33 00

			TAXES.
Prior, John			
Slaves	5		15 00
Pritchard, William			
Real Estate	7,000	98 00	
Dog	1	2 00	100 00
Pritchard, Trustee Elizabeth			
Slaves	3	....	9 00
Pritchard, Dr. C. C.			
Real Estate	10,000	140 00	
Slave	1	3 00	
Carriage	1	20 00	
Income	1,000	25 00	
Horse	1	10 00	198 00
Pritchard, Catherine			
Real Estate	2,500	....	35 00
Pritchard, Elizabeth			
Slaves	2	....	6 00
Pritchard, Trust Estate L. C., and children			
Real Estate	8,000	....	112 00
Pritchard, Catherine E.			
Slaves	3	....	9 00
Proctor, William			
Real Estate	3,500	49 00	
Dog	1	2 00	51 00
Puckhaber, F.			
Stock of Goods	1,000	14 00	
Dog	1	2 00	16 00
Purcell, Mrs. C.			
Slaves	3	....	9 00
Purcell, Dr. James			
Slaves	6		18 00
Purcell, Miss M. C.			
Slaves	4	....	12 00
Purcell, Estate E. H.			
Slave	1		3 00
Purcell, Joseph			
Slaves	4	....	12 00
Purse, Maria H.			
Slave	1		3 00
Purse, Martha E.			
Real Estate	1,500		
Slaves	2	6 00	27 00
Purse, Eliza A.			
Slaves	7		21 00

			TAXES.
Purse, Isaiah N			
Real Estate	1,900	26 60	
Slaves	3	9 00	
Dog	1	2 00	37 60
Purse, W H.			
Slave	1		3 00
Purvis, Mrs. A.			
Slave	1		3 00
Pyatt, Mrs. M. H.			
Real Estate	18,000	252 00	
Slaves	16	48 00	
Carriage	1	30 00	
Horses	3	30 00	
Dog	1	2 00	362 00
Pyatt, John F.			
Slaves	5	15 00	
Carriage	1	30 00	
Horses	3	30 00	75 00
Pyatt, Joseph B.			
Slaves	3		9 00
Quackenbush, T. L.			
Real Estate	12,500	175 00	
Stock of Goods	2,000	28 00	
Slaves	8	24 00	227 00
Quash, Francis D.			
Slaves	7	21 00	
Carriage	1	20 00	
Horse	1	10 00	
Dog	1	2 00	53 00
Quash, Constantia			
Interest on Bonds, &c	665	16 63	
Slaves	14	42 00	58 63
Quash, Mrs. H. H.			
Interest on Bonds, &c	466	11 65	
Slaves	5	15 00	26 65
Quinnan, Estate B.			
Real Estate	5,000		70 00
Quinnan, A. E.			
Slaves	2		6 00
Quinby, Laurence			
Real Estate	1,200		16 80
Rabb, Jacob			
Real Estate	6,500	91 00	
Slaves	3	9 00	100 00

			TAXES.
Rabuske, Trust Estate, Mrs. M.			
Real Estate....................1,000			14 00
Radcliffe, Mrs. M.			
Slaves............................2			6 00
Rahal, P			
Real Estate....................3,000		....	42 00
Rahal, James			
Real Estate....................2,200			30 80
Raine, James H.			
Slaves............................8			24 00
Ramsey, David			
Real Estate....................3,725	52 15		
Slaves............................3	9 00		
Income....................2,177 99	54 44		
Horse............................1	10 00		125 59
Ramsey, David, Attorney of Cromwell			
Real Estate....................3,000	42 00		
Slave............................1	3 00		45 00
Ramsey, David, Attorney of Ramsey			
Real Estate....................6,000			84 00
Ramsey, David, Attorney Roper			
Real Estate....................18,000	252 00		
Interest on Bonds,&c.......2,000	50 00		
Slaves............................4	12 00		314 00
Ramsey, David, Attorney of Ward			
Real Estate....................3,000	....		42 00
Ramsey, W M.			
Dog............................1	....		2 00
Ramsey, Miss M. G.			
Slaves............................19	57 00		
Carriage............................1	30 00		
Horses............................2	20 00		
Dog............................1	2 00		109 00
Ramspeck, Charlotte R.			
Slave............................1			3 00
Ransdale, John			
Real Estate....................2,500	35 00		
Slave............................1	3 00		38 00
Raoul, Dr. A.			
Slaves............................12	36 00		
Carriage............................1	30 00		
Carriage............................1	20 00		
Income....................2,000	50 00		
Horses............................3	30 00		166 00

		TAXES.
Ravenel, John		
Real Estate.........................25,000	350 00	
Interest on Bonds, &c............3,470	86 75	
Slaves 3	9 00	
Shipping............................10,000	75 00	
Dog..1	2 00	522 75
Ravenel, James		
Slaves...2	6 00	
Dogs 2	4 00	10 00
Ravenel, Elizabeth C.		
Real Estate.........................24,000	336 00	
Interest on Bonds, &c...............700	17 50	
Slaves 8	24 00	
Carriage 1	30 00	
Horses...2	20 00	427 50
Ravenel, Daniel		
Real Estate.........................12,000	168 00	
Slaves 4	12 00	180 00
Ravenel, Daniel and John, Trustees, &c.		
Real Estate.........................12,000	....	168 00
Ravenel, Dr. W C.		
Real Estate...........................7,000	98 00	
Slaves 5	15 00	
Carriage 1	20 00	
Income 1,200	30 00	
Horse 1	10 00	
Dog...1	2 00	175 00
Ravenel, William T., Trustee		
Slave 1	....	3 00
Ravenel, Miss E. P		
Interest on Bonds, &c...............933	....	23 33
Ravenel, William		
Real Estate.........................54,500	763 00	
Interest on Bonds, &c..............300	7 50	
Slaves 12	36 00	
Carriage 1	30 00	
Carriage 1	20 00	
Horses...5	50 00	906 50
Ravenel, William, Trustee		
Slaves 5		15 00
Ravenel & Co.		
Shipping.............................50,000	375 00	
Income 15,000	375 00	750 00
Ravenel, J. & S. P		
Stock of Goods..................12,700	177 80	
Commissions.......................5,252	131 30	309 10

			TAXES.
Ravenel, A. F.			
Interest on Bonds, &c.........25		63	
Carriage........................1		20 00	
Horse............................1		10 00	30 63
Ravenel, A. F., in trust			
Slave.............................1		....	3 00
Ravenel, A. F., Trustee			
Interest on Bonds, &c.........810		20 25	
Slaves............................9		27 00	47 25
Ravenel, Huger & Milliken			
Stock of Goods...............28,000		....	392 00
Ravenel, F. G.			
Interest on Bonds, &c......... 25		63	
Slave.............................1		3 00	
Carriage........................1		20 00	
Horse 1		10 00	33 63
Ravenel, Edmond			
Real Estate...............21,500		301 00	
Slave.............................1		3 00	304 00
Raworth, G. F., Committee of Jones			
Slaves............................8		....	24 00
Raymond, Mrs. Mary			
Real Estate...............12,000		168 00	
Slaves...........................11		33 00	
Carriage........................1		30 00	
Horses...........................2		20 00	251 00
Raymond, Joint Estate Mary and H. H.			
Real Estate...............10,500		147 00	
Interest on Bonds, &c.........147		3 50	
Dog..............................1		2 00	152 50
Raymond, Trust Estate H. H. and wife			
Slaves............................4		....	12 00
Read, Estate J. H.			
Real Estate...............23,000		....	322 00
Read, J. Harleston			
Real Estate...............21,000		....	294 00
Read, W W & J. R.			
Real Estate.................7,000		98 00	
Stock of Goods.............4,700		65 80	163 80
Read, B. H.			
Slaves...........................17		51 00	
Carriage........................1		30 00	
Horses...........................2		20 00	101 00
Rebb, Estate Lewis			
Real Estate...............12,035		....	168 49

		TAXES.
Rebb, Mrs. M. C.		
Slave 1	....	3 00
Redfern, Elizabeth		
Real Estate.....1,000	14 00	
Slaves.....6	18 00	32 00
Reed, J. P., in trust		
Real Estate.....6,000	84 00	
Stock of Goods.....1,500	21 00	
Slaves.....2	6 00	111 00
Reeder, Oswell		
Real Estate.....6,000	84 00	
Slaves.....10	30 00	
Horse.....1	10 00	124 00
Reeder & De Saussure		
Shipping.....250	1 88	
Commissions.....15,002	375 05	376 93
Reeder, Estate L. M.		
Real Estate.....12,500	175 00	
Slaves.....3	9 00	184 00
Reese, Jane E.		
Real Estate.....12,000	168 00	
Slaves.....13	39 00	207 00
Reeves, Mrs. A. D.		
Real Estate.....3,500	....	49 00
Reid, George B.		
Real Estate.....6,000	84 00	
Slaves.....4	12 00	
Dog.....1	2 00	98 00
Reid, Ann		
Slave.....1		3 00
Reid, Caroline		
Real Estate.....2,000		28 00
Reid, Andrew		
Stock of Goods.....250	3 50	
Slave.....1	3 00	
Carriage.....1	20 00	
Income.....500	12 50	39 00
Reid, George		
Carriage.....1	20 00	
Horse.....1	10 00	
Dog.....1	2 00	32 00
Reidheimer, J P		
Real Estate.....1,500	21 00	
Slave.....1	3 00	24 00

			TAXES.
Reigné, A. P			
Real Estate	3,000	42 00	
Slave	1	3 00	45 00
Reilly, Mary Ann			
Slave	1		3 00
Reils, B.			
Real Estate	5,400	75 60	
Stock of Goods	500	7 00	82 60
Reils, J P			
Stock of Goods	300		4 20
Reils, Jacob			
Stock of Goods	500		7 00
Rein, John			
Real Estate	1,800	25 20	
Horse	1	10 00	35 20
Reinhardt, H. D. & Co.			
Horse	1		10 00
Reippe, W			
Stock of Goods	500		7 00
Relyea, C. J.			
Real Estate	3,000	42 00	
Slave	1	3 00	45 00
Remley, Paul			
Real Estate	5,000	70 00	
Slaves	4	12 00	82 00
Remley, M. E.			
Real Estate	4,300		60 20
Remousin, Estate Mary			
Real Estate	2,800		39 20
René, Gracia			
Real Estate	2,000		28 00
Renneker, John H.			
Real Estate	10,500	147 00	
Slaves	3	9 00	
Horse	1	10 00	
Dog	1	2 00	168 00
Renneker & Glover			
Real Estate	1,600	22 40	
Stock of Goods	7,000	98 00	
Slave	1	3 00	123 40
Reynolds, R. F			
Real Estate	5,500	77 00	
Carriage	1	20 00	
Horse	1	10 00	107 00

		TAXES.
Reynolds, Miss Sarah P.		
Slaves 13		39 00
Reynolds, George N		
Real Estate............44,000	616 00	
Slaves............2	6 00	
Carriage............1	20 00	
Horse 1	10 00	652 00
Reynolds, George N., Jr.		
Real Estate............21,500	301 00	
Stock of Goods............10,000	140 00	
Slaves............11	33 00	474 00
Reynolds & Smith		
Carriage............1	20 00	
Carriage............1	15 00	35 00
Rhett, R. B.		
Real Estate............12,000	168 00	
Slaves............8	24 00	
Carriage............1	30 00	
Horses............2	20 00	
Dog............1	2 00	244 00
Rhett, B. S.		
Real Estate............10,000	140 00	
Slaves 13	39 00	
Carriage............1	30 00	
Horses 3	30 00	239 00
Rhett, William		
Slaves............4	12 00	
Income............500	12 50	24 50
Rhett, James M., Trustee		
Real Estate............5,000		70 00
Rhett & Robson		
Real Estate............6,000	84 00	
Stock of Goods............4,000	56 00	
Commissions............4,468	111 70	251 70
Rhodé, H.		
Stock of Goods............800	....	11 20
Rhodes, Sarah A.		
Real Estate............400		5 60
Rice, R. B.		
Slaves............5	....	15 00
Rice, Alexander G.		
Real Estate............5,000	....	70 00
Rice, Sims & Barksdale		
Commissions............10,750		268 75

                                                                    TAXES.
Rich, L.
    Stock of Goods........................500 .... 7 00
Rich, George C.
    Real Estate............................350 4 90
Rich, Miss A. M. K.
    Real Estate..........................1,500 .... 21 00
Richards, Frederick
    Real Estate........................12,000 168 00
    Slaves..................................13 39 00
    Carriage................................1 20 00
    Horses..................................2 20 00
    Dog.....................................1 2 00 249 00
Richards, George R.
    Real Estate........................13,500 189 00
    Slaves..................................12 36 00
    Carriage................................1 20 00
    Horse...................................1 10 00
    Dog.....................................1 2 00 257 00
Richardson, J. C. E.
    Real Estate.........................2,800 39 20
    Slaves..................................2 6 00
    Dog.....................................1 2 00 47 20
Richardson, C. Y. & Brother
    Stock of Goods......................4,000 .... 56 00
Richtous, John
    Slaves..................................4 12 00
Rickels, John H.
    Stock of Goods........................300 4 20
Rickels, E. F.
    Stock of Goods........................400 .... 5 60
Riecke, Estate George
    Real Estate.........................4,000 56 00
Riggs, John S.
    Real Estate........................60,500 847 00
    Slaves..................................23 69 00
    Carriage................................1 20 00
    Commissions.......................8,707 217 68
    Horses..................................3 30 00 1,183 68
Riker, David
    Real Estate........................12,200 170 80
    Slaves...................................3 9 00
    Carriage................................1 20 00
    Horse...................................1 10 00 209 80
Riley, William
    Real Estate...........................800 .... 11 20

		TAXES.

Rimrodt, Louis
    Horse.............................1   10 00

Ring, A. M. E.
    Slaves............................7   21 00

Rinker, Charles F.
    Real Estate...............2,000   28 00
    Annuity........................35   88   28 88

Riols, B.
    Slaves............................3   9 00

Ritter, John F
    Real Estate...............2,000   28 00

Rivers, W Horace
    Slaves............................9   ....   27 00

Rivers, Estate John
    Slaves............................5   ....   15 00

Rivers, John E.
    Slaves............................7   21 00
    Income.......................800   20 00   41 00

Rivers, Miss C. M.
    Slave.............................1   3 00

Rivers, W M.
    Stock of Goods..........3,000   42 00

Rivers, Susan A.
    Interest on Bonds, &c.......500   12 50
    Slave.............................1   3 00   15 50

Rivers, Mary H.
    Slaves............................2   6 00

Roach, E.
    Slaves............................2   6 00

Roach, Estate Edward
    Real Estate...............6,000   84 00
    Slaves............................2   6 00   90 00

Roach, Mary C.
    Real Estate...............4,500   63 00
    Slaves............................4   12 00   75 00

Robb, Estate James
    Real Estate..............66,000 924 00
    Slaves...........................37 111 00
    Carriage.........................1   20 00
    Horse............................1   10 00 1,065 00

Robb, William
    Real Estate..............15,000 210 00
    Carriage.........................1   20 00
    Horse............................1   10 00
    Dog..............................1   2 00   242 00

			TAXES.
Robb, James			
Real Estate	3,500		49 00
Robb, W & J			
Real Estate	62,450	874 30	
Slaves	17	51 00	
Shipping	1,500	11 25	
Horses	2	20 00	956 55
Robbins, A.			
Real Estate	8,000	112 00	
Stock of Goods	1,500	21 00	
Slaves	6	18 00	151 00
Robbins, A., Trustee			
Slave	1		3 00
Roberts, Emma C.			
Real Estate	2,000		28 00
Roberts, John F.			
Real Estate	5,000	70 00	
Dog	1	2 00	72 00
Roberts, Agnes M.			
Real Estate	4,000	56 00	
Slaves	4	12 00	68 00
Robertson, Dr. F. M.			
Real Estate	9,000	126 00	
Slaves	8	24 00	
Carriage	1	20 00	
Income	2,000	50 00	
Horse	1	10 00	230 00
Robertson, Trust Estate Mrs. C. W			
Slaves	3		9 00
Robertson, Trust Estate Mrs. H. M.			
Slave	1		3 00
Robertson, Mrs. S. B. and Mrs. Rowan			
Interest on Bonds, &c	366	9 15	
Slaves	15	45 00	54 15
Robertson, George			
Real Estate	800	11 20	
Slave	1	3 00	
Carriage	1	30 00	
Commissions	5,000	125 00	
Horses	3	30 00	
Dogs	2	4 00	203 20
Robertson, George and Mary			
Real Estate	18,000	252 00	
Slaves	15	48 00	300 00

		TAXES	
Robertson, Alexander			
Real Estate	8,000 00	112 00	
Interest on Bonds, &c.	473 00	11 82	
Dividends	56 95	1 42	
Slaves	21	63 00	
Carriage	1	30 00	
Carriage	1	20 00	
Horses	2	20 00	
Dog	1	2 00	260 24
Robertson, Blacklock & Co.			
Commissions	23,000	....	575 00
Robertson, Ellen			
Real Estate	6,000	....	84 00
Robertson, Miss A. R.			
Real Estate	3,000	....	42 00
Robertson, Mrs. A.			
Real Estate	4,000	56 00	
Slaves	2	6 00	62 00
Robertson, Estate John			
Real Estate	600	....	8 40
Robertson, Mrs. Mary			
Slaves	3	....	9 00
Rober, C.			
Stock of Goods	300	4 20	
Dog	1	2 00	6 20
Robinson, S. T.			
Real Estate	20,000	280 00	
Slaves	17	51 00	
Carriage	1	30 00	
Carriage	1	20 00	
Horses	3	30 00	411 00
Robinson, S. T., Executor			
Real Estate	7,000	....	98 00
Robinson, S. T., Administrator, &c.			
Interest on Bonds, &c.	70	1 75	
Slaves	8	24 00	25 75
Robinson, S. T., Trustee of Simons			
Interest on Bonds, &c.	1,123	28 08	
Slaves	2	6 00	
Carriage	1	20 00	
Horse	1	10 00	
Dog	1	2 00	66 08
Robinson, in trust for John and L. G. Robinson			
Interest on Bonds, &c.	70	....	1 75
Robinson, J. A.			
Real Estate	5,500	....	77 00

			TAXES.
Robinson, Mrs. E. M. and children			
Slaves	16		48 00
Robinson, W D.			
Slaves	2		6 00
Robinson, S. A.			
Real Estate	4,000	56 00	
Slave	1	3 00	59 00
Robinson, S. A., Trustee			
Slave	1		3 00
Robinson, James K.			
Real Estate	15,000	210 00	
Interest on Bonds, &c	3,000	75 00	
Slaves	15	45 00	
Carriage	1	30 00	
Horses	3	30 00	
Dogs	4	8 00	398 00
Robinson, Ann			
Slaves	3		9 00
Robinson, Mrs. E. M.			
Slaves	12		36 00
Robinson, W J			
Real Estate	2,000	28 00	
Slaves	4	12 00	
Horse	1	10 00	50 00
Robinson, W J., Trustee			
Slaves	2		6 00
Robinson, James K., in trust			
Real Estate	3,000		42 00
Robio, Amelia			
Slaves	2		6 00
Robson, S. A.			
Slave	1		3 00
Robson, J. N.			
Slave	1	3 00	
Interest on Bonds, &c	70	1 75	
Carriage	1	20 00	
Horse	1	10 00	34 75
Roddin, B.			
Slaves	4		12 00
Rodgers, Thomas L.			
Real Estate	8,775	122 85	
Slaves	11	33 00	
Commissions	205	5 13	160 98
Rodgers, E. H. & Co.			
Commissions	22,000		550 00

			TAXES.
Rodgers, E. H.			
Real Estate............18,000	252	00	
Slaves............14	42	00	
Carriage............1	20	00	
Horses............3	30	00	
Dog............1	2	00	346 00
Rodgers, P. D.			
Real Estate............7,000	....		9 80
Rodrigues, B. A.			
Real Estate............35,500	497	00	
Slaves............10	30	00	
Carriage............1	30	00	
Income............500	12	50	
Horses............2	20	00	589 50
Roeblitz, William A.			
Stock of Goods............300	4	20	
Dog............1	2	00	6 20
Roessler, F.			
Real Estate............4,000	56	00	
Dog............1	2	00	58 00
Rogers, M. E.			
Real Estate............1,200	16	80	
Slaves............4	12	00	28 80
Rogers, Juliet S.			
Slaves............16	48	00	
Carriage............1	20	00	
Horse............1	10	00	78 00
Rolando, F G.			
Real Estate............16,700	233	80	
Slaves............10	30	00	263 80
Rolando, F G., in trust			
Real Estate............3,500	....		49 00
Ronan, H.			
Real Estate............2,000	....		28 00
Ronan, Wm.			
Stock of Goods............300	....		4 20
Roosevelt, H. L.			
Slave............1	....		3 00
Roper, Richard			
Real Estate............10,000	140	00	
Interest on Bonds, &c............759	18	98	
Slaves............13	39	00	
Carriage............1	30	00	
Commissions............5,851	146	28	
Horses............3	30	00	
Dog............1	2	00	406 26

		TAXES.
Roper, B. D.		
Real Estate............8,000	112 00	
Slaves 5	15 00	
Carriage......1	20 00	
Horse......1	10 00	
Dog......1	2 00	159 00
Rose, Arthur G.		
Real Estate............20,000	280 00	
Interest on Bonds, &c......1,000	25 00	
Dividends......500	12 50	
Slaves......9	27 00	
Carriage......1	30 00	
Shipping......3,000	22 50	
Horses......2	20 00	417 00
Rose, James		
Slaves......15	45 00	
Carriage......1	30 00	
Carriage......1	20 00	
Horses......3	30 00	125 00
Rose, Misses A. and M.		
Real Estate............12,000	168 00	
Slaves......8	24 00	
Carriage......1	30 00	
Horses......2	20 00	242 00
Rose, John A.		
Real Estate............1,500	21 00	
Dog......1	2 00	23 00
Rose, Mrs. E. H., Estate		
Slaves......2	....	6 00
Rose, A. B.		
Real Estate............10,000	140 00	
Interest on Bonds, &c......1,200	30 00	
Dividends......300	7 50	
Slaves......5	15 00	
Carriage......1	30 00	
Horses......2	20 00	242 50
Rose, Jas. L., in trust		
Real Estate............1,700	23 80	
Slaves......9	27 00	50 80
Rosenbluth, S.		
Stock of Goods......2,000	....	28 00
Rosis, Joseph		
Stock of Goods......150	2 10	
Slave......1	3 00	5 10

			TAXES.
Ross, Estate J.			
Real Estate	46,000	644 00	
Slaves	14	42 00	
Carriage	1	30 00	
Horses	3	30 00	
Dog	1	2 00	748 00
Ross, Harriet C.			
Real Estate	1,800	25 20	
Slaves	6	18 00	43 20
Ross, Ann and M. Henry			
Real Estate	24,500	....	343 00
Ross, Mary M.			
Real Estate	4,000	56 00	
Slaves	2	6 00	62 00
Rothmahler, E. B.			
Slave	1	....	3 00
Roulain, Estate A.			
Real Estate	14,000	....	196 00
Roumillat, J.			
Stock of Goods	400	....	5 60
Rouse, Amelia and children			
Real Estate	2,000	....	28 00
Rouse, Wm. M.			
Stock of Goods	1,000	14 00	
Slave	1	3 00	17 00
Rout, Estate Wm. Geo.			
Real Estate	17,000	238 00	
Slaves	5	15 00	253 00
Roux, Ann H.			
Slave	1	....	3 00
Rowelt, Richard			
Commissions	420		10 50
Roye, N. A.			
Real Estate	6,000	84 00	
Slaves	8	24 00	108 00
Ruddock, Theo. D.			
Real Estate	3,500	....	49 00
Rudulph, Jane			
Real Estate	18,000	....	252 00
Ruff, O. C.			
Slaves	7	....	21 00
Ruff & Dowie			
Stock of Goods	13,000	....	182 00
Ruffio, C. II.			
Real Estate	3,000	....	42 00

			TAXES
Rumpel, G. H.			
Real Estate	2,000		28 00
Rumph, Mrs. G H.			
Real Estate	3,700		51 80
Runcken, Henry			
Real Estate	8,000		112 00
Russ, Mary P.			
Slave	1		3 00
Russ, Sarah			
Slave	1		3 00
Russell, H. P			
Slaves	3	9 00	
Commissions	6,000	150 00	159 00
Russell, Estate Eliza			
Real Estate	2,000		28 00
Russell & Co.			
Real Estate	5,000		70 00
Russell, John			
Real Estate	12,500	175 00	
Interest on Bonds, &c	107	2 68	
Dividends	140	3 50	
Horse	1	10 00	191 18
Russell & Jones			
Stock of Goods	20,000	280 00	
Shipping	250	1 88	281 88
Rutherford, Lucy			
Slaves	3		9 00
Rutherford, Estate			
Real Estate	3,000		42 00
Rutjes, A. J.			
Real Estate	11,000	154 00	
Stock of Goods	1,000	14 00	
Slaves	6	18 00	186 00
Rutledge, E. C.			
Interest on Bonds, &c	2,113	52 83	
Slaves	3	9 00	61 83
Rutledge, Mrs. A. A.			
Interest on Bonds, &c	3,022	75 55	
Slaves	2	6 00	81 55
Rutledge, B H.			
Real Estate	15,000	210 00	
Slaves	3	9 00	
Income	4,890	122 27	341 27
Rutledge, Mrs. Charles			
Slaves	2		6 00

		TAXES.

Rutledge, Maria and children
 Real Estate..................12,000   168 00
 Slaves..........................10   30 00   198 00

Rutledge, John
 Slaves...........................2   6 00
 Carriage.........................1   30 00
 Horses...........................2   20 00
 Dog..............................1   2 00   58 00

Rutledge, F., Trustee
 Slave............................1   3 00

Ryan, Thomas
 Real Estate..................20,000   280 00
 Slaves...........................7   21 00
 Carriage.........................1   30 00
 Horses...........................2   20 00
 Dogs.............................2   4 00   355 00

Ryan, Thomas and Son
 Carriage.........................1   20 00
 Commissions..................4,000   100 00   120 00

Ryan, William B.
 Real Estate...................5,000   70 00

Ryan, W K.
 Real Estate...................6,000   84 00
 Slaves...........................6   18 00
 Carriage.........................1   30 00
 Commissions..................3,000   75 00
 Horses...........................2   20 00
 Dog..............................1   2 00   229 00

Ryan, Elizabeth H.
 Slaves...........................8   24 00

Ryan, Miss E. M.
 Slaves...........................5   15 00

Ryan, Estate Elizabeth
 Slaves..........................12   36 00
 Carriage.........................1   20 00
 Horse............................1   10 00
 Dog..............................1   2 00   68 00

Ryan, Thomas E.
 Stock of Goods...............500   7 00
 Slaves...........................2   6 00
 Horses...........................3   30 00
 Dog..............................1   2 00   45 00

Ryan, Mary T.
 Real Estate...................3,000   42 00
 Slaves...........................3   9 00   51 00

		TAXES.
Ryan, William		
Real Estate.................3,400	47 60	
Slaves 6	18 00	
Dogs............................2	4 00	69 60
Ryan, John		
Slaves 2	....	6 00
Ryan, John and wife		
Real Estate.................5,500	77 00	
Slaves 2	6 00	83 00
Ryan, John S.		
Real Estate................20,000	280 00	
Slaves..........................7	21 00	
Carriage.......................1	20 00	
Income.....................3,000	75 00	
Horses 2	20 00	416 00
Royal, S. M.		
Slave 1	....	3 00
Sachtleben, Augustus		
Real Estate.................4,000	....	56 00
Sack, William M.		
Real Estate.................1,500	....	21 00
Sage, William M.		
Slaves..........................3	9 00	
Carriage.......................1	20 00	
Horse 1	10 00	
Dogs............................2	4 00	43 00
Sahlmon, C.		
Real Estate.................6,000	84 00	
Slave 1	3 00	87 00
Sahlmon, Estate H.		
Real Estate.................6,000	....	84 00
Salcedo, Antonio		
Stock of Goods..........3,000	42 00	
Dog 1	2 00	44 00
Salinas, A. J.		
Real Estate................18,000	252 00	
Slaves 10	30 00	
Carriage.......................1	20 00	
Commissions.............2,000	*50 00	352 00
Salmond, Ann C.		
Slave 1	....	3 00
Saloman, Miss A. L.		
Real Estate.................3,500	....	49 00
Saltar, Mrs. J. C.		
Real Estate.................5,300	74 20	
Slaves 4	12 00	86 20

			TAXES
Saltus, children of F W			
Slaves	7		21 00
Saltus, children of S. W			
Real Estate	4,000		56 00
Salvo, James			
Real Estate	3,700	51 80	
Slave	1	3 00	54 80
Salvo, Francis, Trustee			
Real Estate	2,800	39 20	
Slave	1	3 00	42 20
Sams, Dr. D. D.			
Income	1,700		42 50
Samson, Joseph			
Real Estate	2,500	35 00	
Slaves	5	15 00	50 00
Sanders, Miss Anna H.			
Real Estate	3,000		42 00
Sanders, Mrs. S.			
Real Estate	8,000	112 00	
Slave	1	3 00	115 00
Sanders, Samuel			
Real Estate	3,000	42 00	
Slave	1	3 00	45 00
Sanders, Thomas L.			
Slaves	8	24 00	
Carriage	1	20 00	
Horse	1	10 00	54 0
Sanders, William T.			
Real Estate	20,000	280 00	
Slaves	3	9 00	
Carriage	1	15 00	
Horse	1	10 00	314 0
Sanders, J. A.			
Real Estate	3,700	51 80	
Slaves	16	48 00	
Carriage	1	20 00	
Horses	2	20 00	139 8
Sanders, Laura and children			
Real Estate	6,000		84 0
Sanders, Mrs. E. E.			
Real Estate	4,000	56 00	
Slaves	2	6 00	
Carriage	1	20 00	
Horse	1	10 00	92 0

			TAXES.
Sanders, Frances N.			
Slaves	2		6 00
Sanders, T. and G.			
Slaves	6	18 00	
Carriage	1	20 00	
Horse	1	10 00	
Dogs	4	8 00	56 00
Sanders, Anna H.			
Real Estate	14,000	196 00	
Slave	1	3 00	199 00
Sangster, Sabina E.			
Real Estate	4,000	56 00	
Slaves	24	72 00	
Dog	1	2 00	130 00
Sass, J. K.			
Dividends	100	2 50	
Slaves	6	18 00	
Carriage	1	20 00	
Horses	2	20 00	
Dog	1	2 00	62 50
Sass, Octavia M.			
Slaves	5		15 00
Sassard, Captain John			
Slave	1	3 00	
Shipping	10,000	75 00	78 00
Sassard, Robert			
Slaves	3		9 00
Savage, Joseph			
Slave	1		3 00
Savage, Estate Miss S. H.			
Slave	1		3 00
Sawadseke, J M.			
Stock of Goods	500		7 00
Scanlan, Trust Estate Eliza			
Real Estate	2,500		35 00
Scanlan, S. E.			
Slaves	2		6 00
Schafer, H.			
Stock of Goods	6,000		84 00
Schaffner, Dr. John F.			
Real Estate	10,500		147 00
Scheper, H.			
Stock of Goods	200		2 80

			TAXES.
Schirmer, Jacob F			
Real Estate	13,200	184 80	
Interest on Bonds, &c.	600	15 00	
Slaves	18	54 00	
Carriage	1	20 00	
Annuity	400	10 00	
Horse	1	10 00	293 80
Schirmer, William C.			
Real Estate	4,000	56 00	
Slaves	4	12 00	
Carriage	1	20 00	
Horse	1	10 00	98 00
Schirmer, Jacob S.			
Real Estate	6,000	84 00	
Slaves	6	18 00	
Income	1,900	47 50	149 50
Schirmer, Cecilia D. B.			
Slaves	4		12 00
Schirmer, Estate W H.			
Slaves	3		9 00
Schirer, Mary C.			
Real Estate	5,000		70 00
Schlepegrell, C. J			
Real Estate	7,000		98 00
Schmetzer, George C.			
Real Estate	2,500	35 00	
Slaves	2	6 00	
Carriage	1	20 00	
Horses	2	20 00	81 00
Schmidt, John H.			
Real Estate	1,800	25 20	
Slaves	2	6 00	31 20
Schmidt, Estate John W			
Real Estate	11,000		154 00
Schmidt, A.			
Real Estate	3,500	49 00	
Stock of Goods	800	11 20	60 20
Schmidt, heirs of J. W			
Real Estate	10,000		140 00
Schmidt, Ursula			
Real Estate	2,000		28 00
Schmidt, Estate J. W., Jr.			
Real Estate	2,500	35 00	
Slaves	2	6 00	41 00
Schnaars, Dederick			
Stock of Goods	300		4 20

		TAXES.
Schnaars, F.		
Stock of Goods..................500		7 00
Schneider, William		
Stock of Goods..................500	....	7 00
Schnierle, John		
Real Estate.....................25,000	350 00	
Slaves................................19	57 00	407 00
Schnierle, John, Trustee		
Slaves..................................2	....	6 00
Schnierle, William		
Real Estate.....................27,000	....	378 00
Schuboe, F		
Slave....................................1	....	3 00
Schreiner, J H.		
Real Estate.....................23,000	322 00	
Stock of Goods..................2,200	30 80	
Slaves..................................5	15 00	
Carriage...............................1	20 00	
Horse..................................1	10 00	397 80
Schroder, Henry		
Stock of Goods..................500	7 00	
Dog.....................................1	2 00	9 00
Schroder, Brothers		
Stock of Goods..................6,500	91 00	
Slaves..................................5	15 00	
Dog.....................................1	2 00	108 00
Schroder, H.		
Stock of Goods..................400	5 60	
Dog.....................................1	2 00	7 60
Schroder, H.		
Stock of Goods..................450	....	6 30
Schroder, H. C.		
Stock of Goods..................500	7 00	
Dog.....................................1	2 00	9 00
Schroder, Ferdinand		
Real Estate........................700	....	9 80
Schroder, Jacob		
Stock of Goods..................3,500	....	49 00
Schroder, H. W		
Slaves..................................6	....	18 00
Schroder, Mrs. E.		
Real Estate.....................2,500	....	35 00
Schuckmann, L.		
Real Estate.....................6,500	....	91 00

		TAXES.
Schuckmann, P		
Stock of Goods......2,000		28 00
Schulken, F.		
Real Estate......5,000	70 00	
Slaves......3	9 00	79 00
Schulte, J. H.		
Real Estate......4,000	56 00	
Interest on Bonds, &c......390	9 75	
Slave......1	3 00	
Dog......1	2 00	70 75
Schulze, John W		
Stock of Goods......500		7 00
Schur, B.		
Stock of Goods......500	7 00	
Slaves......2	6 00	13 00
Schwartz, H.		
Real Estate......1,000	14 00	
Dog......1	2 00	16 00
Schwecke, D. H.		
Real Estate......4,000	56 00	
Stock of Goods......300	4 20	60 20
Schwettmann, C. F		
Real Estate......6,000	84 00	
Stock of Goods......2,000	28 00	
Dog......1	2 00	114 00
Schwing, Estate C.		
Real Estate......19,500	273 00	
Interest on Bonds, &c......700	17 50	
Slaves......13	39 00	
Dog......1	2 00	331 50
Schwing, Sophia		
Stock of Goods......1,000		14 00
Schwitzer, Otto		
Stock of Goods......800	11 20	
Dog......1	2 00	13 20
Scockevick, John		
Slave......1		3 00
Scott, B. T.		
Slaves......2		6 00
Scott, Margaret		
Real Estate......7,000	98 00	
Slaves......7	21 00	119 00
Scott, Mary		
Slaves......5		15 00

		TAXES.

Screven, Mrs. M. F.
    Slaves....................................4 .... 12 00

Screven, R. E.
    Real Estate....................3,500   49 00
    Slave..................................1   3 00
    Commissions....................800   20 00   72 00

Seabrook, Mary Ann
    Slaves..................................17 .... 51 00

Seabrook, Edward M., Trustee
    Slaves....................................2 .... 6 00

Seabrook, William
    Real Estate..................10,000 140 00
    Slaves..................................3   9 00
    Carriage............................1   30 00
    Horses..............................2   20 00 199 00

Seabrook, A.
    Real Estate....................2,500   35 00
    Slaves................................16   48 00   83 00

Seabrook, S. S.
    Slave..................................1 .... 3 00

Sebring, Edward
    Real Estate..................15,500 217 00
    Slaves................................15   45 00
    Carriage............................1   30 00
    Shipping....................4,000   30 00
    Horses..............................3   30 00 352 00

Sebring, E., and others
    Real Estate....................2,000 .... 28 00

Sebring & Edgerton
    Slave..................................1 .... 3 00

Seckendorff, J.
    Stock of Goods..............1,000 .... 14 00

Seedorff, Henry C.
    Real Estate..................11,500 161 00
    Horses..............................2   20 00 181 00

Seedorff, John
    Stock of Goods................600 .... 8 40

Seel, Charles
    Stock of Goods................600 .... 8 40

Seel, Lewis
    Real Estate....................4,400   61 60
    Slaves..................................7   21 00   82 60

			TAXES.
Seignious, Charles W			
Real Estate	61,600	862 40	
Stock of Goods	600	8 40	
Slaves	37	111 00	981 80
Seignious, F. P			
Real Estate	17,500	245 00	
Stock of Goods	500	7 00	
Slaves	11	33 00	
Carriage	1	20 00	
Horse	1	10 00	315 00
Seixas, Estate D. C.			
Interest on Bonds, &c	2,240	56 00	
Dog	1	2 00	58 00
Seixas, Estate Isaac			
Real Estate	500		7 00
Seixas, Mrs. H. D.			
Interest on Bonds, &c	297 50	7 43	
Slave	1	3 00	10 43
Seligman, Morris, in trust			
Slaves	3	9 00	
Annuity	120	3 00	
Dog	1	2 00	14 00
Selvey, Joseph			
Real Estate	140		1 96
Semcke, J E.			
Real Estate	5,500		77 00
Semken, W			
Stock of Goods	400		5 60
Sergeant, Mrs. M. A.			
Slave	1		3 00
Seyle, P W			
Real Estate	725	10 15	
Slaves	4	12 00	
Horse	1	10 00	
Dog	1	2 00	34 15
Seyle, F O.			
Real Estate	2,500		35 00
Seymour, Ann			
Real Estate	1,800		25 20
Seymour, R. W			
Real Estate	10,000	140 00	
Slaves	16	48 00	
Income	1,000	25 00	213 00
Seymour, R. W., Trustee of C. H. Bernard			
Real Estate	68,400		957 60

			TAXES.
Seymour, R. W., Trustee			
Slaves.....................14			42 00
Seymour, Miss E. A. G.			
Slaves........................7			21 00
Shachte, John			
Real Estate................30,500	427	00	
Slaves......................11	33	00	460 00
Shackelford, Mrs. E. S.			
Real Estate.................5,000	70	00	
Interest on Bonds, &c............1,204	30	10	
Slaves 14	42	00	142 10
Shackelford, J M.			
Interest on Bonds, &c.............297			7 43
Shackelford, Mrs. M., in trust			
Interest on Bonds, &c............1,145	25	63	
Slave..........................1	3	00	28 63
Shaffer, Estate F.			
Real Estate.................15,000	210	00	
Slaves 17	51	00	
Carriage......................1	20	00	281 00
Shalloe, Michael			
Stock of Goods...............5,000			70 00
Shanahan, M.			
Real Estate 900			12 60
Shanklin, Mrs. C. A.			
Interest on Bonds, &c.............655	16	37	
Slaves........................2	6	00	22 37
Shaper, J. H.			
Real Estate................3,000	42	00	
Stock of Goods..............1,200	16	80	
Dog...........................1	2	00	60 80
Shaw, J			
Stock of Goods 7,500	....		105 00
Shecut, Estate L. A.			
Real Estate................4,000	56	00	
Slaves........................4	12	00	
Dog..........................1	2	00	70 00
Shepherd, William A.			
Real Estate................1,200	....		16 80
Shepherd, W			
Real Estate..................200	....		2 80
Sheppard, Mary S.			
Slaves 3	....		9 00
Sheppard, Estate James			
Real Estate................3,000	....		42 00

17

                                                          TAXES.
Sheridan, John
    Real Estate..........................1,800   25 20
    Dog 1   2 00   27 20
Sheridan, James
    Real Estate............................300   4 20
Shier, C. P
    Interest on Bonds, &c.............885   22 13
    Slaves..10   30 00   52 13
Shier, Dr. B. F
    Slaves 3   9 00
    Carriage 1   20 00
    Income 200   5 00
    Horse 1   10 00   44 00
Shields, Trust Estate C.
    Real Estate.............................600   ....   8 40
Shingler, W P
    Real Estate........................62,500   875 00
    Slaves..9   27 00
    Carriage 1   30 00
    Horse 1   10 00   942 00
Shingler Brothers
    Real Estate..........................8,000   112 00
    Income...................................4,000   100 00   212 00
Shirer, Harriet
    Real Estate..........................1,500   21 00
Shirer, J B.
    Real Estate..........................1,100   15 40
    Dog 1   2 00   17 40
Shokes, John C.
    Real Estate..........................1,800   25 20
    Dog 1   2 00   27 20
Shokes, H. C.
    Horse...1   10 00
Shoolbred, Mrs. Jane
    Slaves 16   ....   48 00
Shroudy, Eliza
    Real Estate..........................3,000   42 00
    Slaves 5   15 00   57 00
Shuler, Estate Isham
    Slaves 5   ....   15 00
Siedenburg, F. W
    Stock of Goods......................300   ....   4 20
Siegling, John, Trustee
    Slaves..7   21 00

			TAXES
Siegling, John			
Real Estate	39,900	558 60	
Stock of Goods	8,000	112 00	
Slaves	10	30 00	
Dog	1	2 00	702 60
Siegling, John, President German Friendly Benevolent Society			
Real Estate	6,000	....	84 00
Sifley, Caroline A.			
Real Estate	14,000	....	196 00
Sifley, H. R., and others			
Real Estate	1,500	....	21 00
Sifley, John, and wife			
Real Estate	5,000	....	70 00
Sifley, John			
Real Estate	1,500	....	21 00
Sigwald, C. B.			
Stock of Goods	800	11 20	
Slave	1	3 00	14 20
Sigwald, Estate Mrs. E. A.			
Real Estate	1,800	....	25 20
Sigwald, Henry W			
Real Estate	3,000	42 00	
Slave	1	3 00	45 00
Silcox, D. H.			
Real Estate	26,500	371 00	
Stock of Goods	26,000	364 00	
Slaves	8	24 00	
Shipping	2,575	19 31	
Horse	1	10 00	
Dog	1	2 00	790 31
Silcox, D. H., Trustee			
Real Estate	6,000	84 00	
Slaves	5	15 00	99 00
Simmons, D. J.			
Slave	1	....	3 00
Simmons, Mrs. C. R.			
Slaves	6	....	18 00
Simmons, J. A.			
Real Estate	7,000	98 00	
Slaves	2	6 00	104 00
Simmons, Rev. D. L.			
Carriage	1	20 00	
Horse	1	10 00	30 00

		TAXES.
Simms, W G.		
Real Estate..........................4,000	56 00	
Slaves..................................4	12 00	68 00
Simonds, A.		
Slave..................................1		3 00
Simons Brothers		
Stock of Goods....................14,500	203 00	
Slaves..................................3	9 00	212 00
Simons, William		
Interest on Bonds, &c..............112	2 80	
Slaves..................................6	18 00	
Carriage..............................1	20 00	
Horse..................................1	10 00	50 80
Simons, William, Guardian		
Interest on Bonds, &c............3,000		75 00
Simons, Ann		
Real Estate.........................12,000	168 00	
Slaves..................................11	33 00	
Carriage..............................1	30 00	
Horses.................................2	20 00	251 00
Simons, K. L.		
Slaves..................................10	....	30 00
Simons, Harris		
Slave..................................1		3 00
Simons, Catherine M.		
Real Estate..........................4,000	56 00	
Slaves..................................6	18 00	74 00
Simons, John C.		
Real Estate.........................11,000	154 00	
Slaves..................................4	12 00	166 00
Simons, James		
Real Estate.........................10,000	140 00	
Slaves..................................7	21 00	
Carriage..............................1	30 00	
Carriage..............................1	20 00	
Income...............................5,000	125 00	
Horse..................................1	10 00	346 00
Simons, James, Guardian		
Real Estate..........................2,000	....	28 00
Simons, James & Dr. G. W Wescott		
Real Estate..........................1,000	....	14 00
Simons, Edward		
Slave..................................1	....	3 00

			TAXES.
Simons, Keating L.			
Real Estate	4,000	56 00	
Slaves	2	6 00	62 00
Simons, Thomas Y.			
Real Estate	11,300	158 20	
Slaves	5	15 00	
Income	5,000	125 00	298 20
Simons, Thomas Y., Trustee Roand and children			
Real Estate	8,000	112 00	
Slaves	34	102 00	214 00
Simons, Thomas Y., Trustee			
Real Estate	2,500		35 00
Simons. Thomas Y., Trustee			
Slaves	3		9 00
Simons, Thomas G., Sr.			
Real Estate	9,000 00	126 00	
Interest on Bonds, &c.	3,489 28	87 23	
Slaves	15	45 00	
Carriage	1	30 00	
Carriage	1	20 00	
Horses	3	30 00	338 23
Simons, T. Grange, Jr.			
Real Estate	10,000	140 00	
Interest on Bonds, &c.	105	2 63	
Slaves	11	33 00	175 63
Simons, T. G. and Sons			
Commissions	4,911 45		122 78
Simons, S. Y.			
Dividends	182	4 55	
Slaves	2	6 00	10 55
Simons, John H.			
Real Estate	18,000	252 00	
Slaves	22	66 00	
Dog	1	2 00	320 00
Simons, H.			
Stock of Goods	1,500	21 00	
Dog	1	2 00	23 00
Simons, L. & B. B. Davidson			
Real Estate	6,000		84 00
Simonton, J. R., in trust			
Slaves	8	24 00	
Dogs	2	4 00	28 00
Simonton, J. R., Trustee			
Slaves	4		12 00

		TAXES.
Simonton, C. H.		
Real Estate............8,000	112 00	
Slaves 5	15 00	
Income............3,500	87 50	
Dog............1	2 00	216 50
Simonton, C. H., Trustee		
Real Estate............4,000	56 00	
Slaves........5	15 00	
Dog............1	2 00	73 00
Simpson, Miss C.		
Slaves............3		9 00
Sinclair, Margaret		
Interest on Bonds, &c............140	3 50	
Slaves............6	18 00	
Carriage............1	20 00	
Horse............1	10 00	51 50
Singer, I. M. & Co.		
Stock of Goods............5,000	....	70 00
Sinkler, Mrs. James		
Slaves............9	....	27 00
Sires, Francis		
Real Estate............1,200	16 80	
Interest on Bonds, &c............200	5 00	
Slave............1	3 00	24 80
Sires, J. F		
Real Estate............2,500	....	35 00
Sires, Trust Estate M. M.		
Real Estate............2,000	28 00	
Slave............1	3 00	31 00
Skeen, Elizabeth S.		
Real Estate............600	....	8 40
Skeen, Trust Estate Elizabeth S.		
Slaves............2		6 00
Skrine, Dr. T. C., Trustee		
Real Estate............1,200		16 80
Skrine, W A., Trustee		
Slave............1	....	3 00
Skrine, W A.		
Slaves............2	....	6 00
Sloman, Elizabeth and Ann		
Real Estate............5,000	70 00	
Slave............1	3 00	
Carriage............1	20 00	
Horse............1	10 00	103 00

		TAXES.
Sloman, John		
Slave 1		3 00
Small, Jacob		
Real Estate............30,000	420 00	
Slaves......................18	54 00	
Carriage.......................1	15 00	
Horse 1	10 00	
Dog 1	2 00	501 00
Smith, Thomas H.		
Real Estate................800	11 20	
Slave 1	3 00	14 20
Smith, P F.		
Real Estate..............8,000	112 00	
Interest on Bonds, &c......455	11 38	
Slaves 11	33 00	156 38
Smith, Charlotte		
Real Estate..............8,500	119 00	
Slave 1	3 00	122 00
Smith & Porter		
Real Estate..............1,500		21 00
Smith, Thomas P		
Real Estate.............10,000	140 00	
Slaves..........................6	18 00	
Carriage 1	30 00	
Horses.........................2	20 00	
Dog 1	2 00	210 00
Smith's daughters, W S.		
Real Estate.............5,500	77 00	
Slaves........................14	42 00	119 00
Smith, Theodore A.		
Slave 1	3 00	
Dog 1	2 00	5 00
Smith, Mrs. James E.		
Slaves 2	6 00	
Dogs 2	4 00	10 00
Smith, C. B.		
Slave 1		3 00
Smith, Margaret M.		
Real Estate.............5,000	70 00	
Slaves.........................5	15 00	85 00
Smith, Estate William M.		
Slaves.......................10	30 00	
Dog 1	2 00	32 00
Smith, Estate R.		
Slaves 15		45 00

		TAXES.
Smith, S. E. and C. L.		
Slaves........4	....	12 00
Smith, Julius C.		
Slave........1	3 00	
Dogs 4	8 00	11 00
Smith, Mrs. Julius		
Slave 1	....	3 00
Smith, Mrs. E. M., Guardian W M. and J. M.		
Slaves........3	....	9 00
Smith, Elizabeth A.		
Real Estate........1,200	....	16 80
Smith, Miss M. M.		
Slave........1	....	3 00
Smith, Mrs. E. P		
Real Estate........15,000	210 00	
Carriage........1	30 00	
Horses........2	20 00	260 00
Smith, Estate Sarah		
Real Estate........18,000	....	252 00
Smith, Estate B.		
Real Estate........7,000	....	98 00
Smith, Ann F.		
Slaves........3	....	9 00
Smith, Elizabeth B.		
Real Estate........4,000	56 00	
Slaves........2	6 00	
Dog........1	2 00	64 00
Smith, James		
Slaves........8	....	24 00
Smith, Elizabeth D.		
Real Estate........3,000	....	42 00
Smith, Angus		
Real Estate........1,500	....	21 00
Smith & Dulin		
Commissions........7,000	....	175 00
Smith, Mrs. E. L.		
Slaves........10	....	30 00
Smith, Susan M.		
Slaves........6	....	18 00
Smith, Emma Sarah		
Real Estate........6,000	84 00	
Interest on Bonds, &c........1,529	38 23	
Slaves........4	12 00	
Carriage........1	30 00	
Horses........2	20 00	184 23

			TAXES.
Smith, James			
Interest on Bonds,&c	210	5 25	
Slaves	11	33 00	
Dog	1	2 00	40 25
Smith, Sarah L.			
Slaves	5		15 00
Smith, Elizabeth			
Real Estate	7,000	98 00	
Slave	1	3 00	101 00
Smith, J. J. Pringle			
Slaves	5	15 00	
Carriage	1	20 00	
Horses	2	20 00	55 00
Smith, W B.			
Real Estate	35,000	490 00	
Interest on Bonds, &c	2,500	62 50	
Slaves	12	36 00	
Carriage	1	30 00	
Shipping	3,000	22 50	
Horses	2	20 00	661 00
Smith, W B. & Co.			
Stock of Goods.	12,000	168 00	
Income	8,500	212 50	380 50
Smith, William Wragg			
Real Estate	10,000	140 00	
Slaves	7	21 00	161 00
Smith, W J.			
Real Estate	7,000	98 00	
Slave	1	3 00	
Carriage	1	20 00	
Horse	1	10 00	131 00
Smith, R. F., Trustee			
Real Estate	5,000	....	70 00
Smith, Estate R. F.			
Real Estate	26,000	....	364 00
Smith, William Walton			
Slave	1	....	3 00
Smith, Rosina			
Real Estate	1,200	....	16 80
Smith, Mary			
Interest on Bonds, &c	72	1 81	
Slaves	2	6 00	7 81
Smith, Mary G.			
Slaves	2	....	6 00

			TAXES.
Smith, P A., Trustee of E. Smith and children			
Real Estate...................1,800	....		25 20
Smith, Eliza F.			
Real Estate...................8,000	112 00		
Slaves 7	21 00	133 00	
Smith, Estate Quintan			
Real Estate...................4,000	56 00		
Slaves 8	24 00	80 00	
Smith, William C.			
Real Estate...................3,500	49 00		
Slaves 5	15 00		
Dog 1	2 00	64 00	
Smith, Josiah E.			
Slaves 5	....	15 00	
Smith, Sarah L.			
Slaves 3	....	9 00	
Smith, William J., Trustee			
Slave 1	....	3 00	
Smyth, Trust Estate Mrs. M. M. A.			
Real Estate..................18,000	252 00		
Interest on Bonds, &c.............303	7 58		
Slaves 6	18 00		
Carriage 1	30 00		
Carriage 1	20 00		
Horses 3	30 00		
Dogs 2	4 00	361 58	
Smyth, Rev. Thomas and Mrs. M. M. A., joint heirs			
Real Estate..................15,000	....	210 00	
Smyth, A.			
Stock of Goods...............1,500	....	21 00	
Smyzer, H.			
Real Estate...................3,000	....	42 00	
Snowden, Mrs. J. S.			
Real Estate...................8,000	112 00		
Slaves 5	15 00	127 00	
Snowden, Estate L. A.			
Slaves 2	....	6 00	
Snowden, Dr. William			
Real Estate...................3,000	42 00		
Slaves 8	24 00		
Carriage 1	20 00		
Income 500	12 50		
Horse 1	10 00	108 50	
Snowden, Estate William J. O.			
Slaves 4	....	12 00	

			TAXES.
Snowden, P G.			
Slaves	2		6 00
Society, Southern Baptist Publication			
Stock of Goods	5,500		77 00
Sollee, H., Trustee			
Slaves	3		9 00
Sollee, Caroline A.			
Slaves	7		21 00
Solomons, Catherine			
Real Estate	1,000		14 00
Solomons, J. R.			
Real Estate	4,000	56 00	
Slaves	3	9 00	
Income	1,000	25 00	90 00
Sommers, E.			
Real Estate	10,000	140 00	
Slaves	4	12 00	152 00
Soubeyroux, Honora			
Stock of Goods	150		2 10
Sparnick, H.			
Real Estate	4,000		56 00
Spaulding, Rev. A. T.			
Real Estate	3,250	45 50	
Slaves	4	12 00	57 50
Spear, James E.			
Stock of Goods	35,000	490 00	
Slave	1	3 00	
Dog	1	2 00	495 00
Spears, Trustee Mrs. C. P			
Interest on Bonds, &c	186	4 65	
Slaves	5	15 00	19 65
Speissegger, Theodore C.			
Real Estate	3,000	42 00	
Slaves	4	12 00	54 00
Speissegger, Theodore C., Trustee			
Slaves	5		15 00
Speissegger, Thomas W			
Real Estate	3,000	42 00	
Stock of Goods	500	7 00	49 00
Spence, Thompson & Co.			
Commissions	1,080		27 00
Spencer, Seth			
Commissions	800		20 00
Spencer, Seth, Trustee			
Slave	1		3 00

			TAXES.
Spillman, A.			
Stock of Goods	3,000	42 00	
Slave	1	3 00	45 00
Spillman, John			
Real Estate	1,200		16 80
Sprague, J. W			
Real Estate	12,000		168 00
Spratt, L. W			
Real Estate	9,900	138 60	
Income	1,000	25 00	
Dog	1	2 00	165 60
Spring, Catherine			
Real Estate	600		8 40
Springer, Mrs. M. A.			
Slaves	6		18 00
Stackley, John			
Real Estate	4,500	63 00	
Stock of Goods	1,500	21 00	84 00
Stall, Estate Frederick			
Real Estate	1,300 00	*18 20	
Interest on Bonds, &c	183 03	4 59	22 79
Stall, John R.			
Real Estate	26,900		376 60
Stall, William C.			
Real Estate	1,500	21 00	
Stock of Goods	400	5 60	
Slave	1	3 00	29 60
Stall, Mrs. C. M.			
Slave	1		3 00
St. Amand, A., Trustee			
Real Estate	29,500		413 00
St. Amand, Estate J. A.			
Real Estate	3,000	42 00	
Slaves	2	6 00	
Dog	1	2 00	50 00
St. Amand, M. W., Guardian			
Interest on Bonds, &c	1,141 98		28 54
St. Amand, A.			
Carriage	1	20 00	
Horse	1	10 00	
Dog	1	2 00	32 00
St. Amand, A., Trustee for Aimar			
Interest on Bonds, &c	819		20 48
Starr, Estate Edwin P			
Real Estate	36,000		504 00

269

		TAXES.
Starr, Robt. C.		
Real Estate............2,000	....	28 00
Starr, Sarah C.		
Real Estate............2,000	....	28 00
Starr, Trust Estate Caroline E.		
Real Estate............1,800	....	25 20
Steed, Ella		
Real Estate............700	....	9 80
Steedman, Susan M.		
Slaves............2	....	6 00
Steedman, Wm. B., in trust		
Real Estate............4,000	56 00	
Slaves............8	24 00	80 00
Steedman, Wm. B., in trust		
Real Estate............6,000	84 00	
Slaves............8	24 00	108 00
Steedman, Wm. K.		
Real Estate............5,000	70 00	
Interest on Bonds, &c............1,519	37 97	
Slaves............7	21 00	128 97
Steedman, Estate Chas. J		
Real Estate............800	....	11 20
Steele, Dr. E. C.		
Real Estate............9,000	126 00	
Slaves............12	36 00	
Carriage............1	20 00	
Horse............1	10 00	192 00
Steele, Walter, & Co.		
Stock of Goods............8,000		112 00
Steffins, Geo. W		
Real Estate............3,000	42 00	
Stock of Goods............5,000	70 00	
Slave............1	3 00	115 00
Steiber, J		
Slave............1		3 00
Stein, John F		
Real Estate............1,200	16 80	
Slave............1	3 00	19 80
Steinmeyer, John H.		
Real Estate............36,000	504 00	
Slaves............40	120 00	
Carriage............1	30 00	
Carriage............1	20 00	
Shipping............2,000	115 00	
Horses............3	30 00	
Dogs............2	4 00	723 00

	TAXES	
Stenmeyer, John F		
Real Estate................12,300	172 20	
Slaves.........................5	15 00	
Carriage........................1	20 00	
Horses...........................2	20 00	
Dog...............................1	2 00	229 20
Steinmeyer, Estate M. C.		
Real Estate..................800	11 20	
Slaves..............................5	15 00	26 20
Stellges, John		
Real Estate.................1,000	14 00	
Dog................................1	2 00	16 00
Stelling, John, and Estate H. Doscher		
Real Estate..................8,800	....	123 20
Stelling, John		
Real Estate..................3,500	....	49 00
Stelling, E. H.		
Stock of Goods..............300	4 20	
Slave...............................1	3 00	
Horse..............................1	10 00	17 20
Stemmermann, A.		
Real Estate..................4,100	57 40	
Stock of Goods..............500	7 00	
Dog................................1	2 00	66 40
Stender, Henry		
Real Estate..................9,200	128 80	
Stock of Goods.............1,000	14 00	
Slave...............................1	3 00	
Carriage...........................1	20 00	
Horse..............................1	10 00	175 80
Stenley, E. and C.		
Real Estate..................6,000	....	84 00
Stent, "The Misses"		
Real Estate..................5,000	70 00	
Slave...............................1	3 00	73 00
Stevens, Sarah		
Slaves..............................4	....	12 00
Stevens, C. H.		
Real Estate.................24,600	344 40	
Slaves.............................15	45 00	
Carriage...........................1	30 00	
Carriage...........................1	20 00	
Horses.............................3	30 00	
Dog...............................1	2 00	471 40
Stevens, P. F.		
Real Estate..................2,000	....	28 00

			TAXES.
Stevens, Mary S.			
Real Estate	5,000	70 00	
Interest on Bonds, &c	420	10 50	
Slaves	3	9 00	89 50
Stevenson, Wellington			
Slaves	2	6 00	
Dog	1	2 00	8 00
Stevenson, W., Trustee			
Slaves	2		6 00
Stewart, Martha			
Real Estate	20,000	280 00	
Slaves	7	21 00	301 00
Stewart, Miss C. A.			
Real Estate	4,000	56 00	
Slave	1	3 00	59 00
Stuart, Jane			
Real Estate	1,800	25 20	
Slaves	7	21 00	46 20
Stiles, C. W			
Real Estate	4,400	....	61 60
Stillman, Sarah R.			
Slaves	2	....	6 00
Stock, Ann S.			
Interest on Bonds, &c	384	....	9 60
Stock, John Y			
Real Estate	8,000	112 00	
Slaves	8	24 00	
Dogs	2	4 00	140 00
Stocker, James M.			
Stock of Goods	3,000	42 00	
Income	2,000	50 00	92 00
Stocker, James M., Trustee			
Real Estate	1,600	....	22 40
Stocking, D. S.			
Slaves	3	....	9 00
Stockman, Laura			
Real Estate	3,500	49 00	
Stock of Goods	300	4 20	
Slave	1	3 00	56 20
Stoddard, E. B. & Co.			
Real Estate	2,500	35 00	
Stock of Goods	67,500	945 00	
Slave	1	3 00	983 00

			TAXES.
Stone, R. G.			
Slaves	6	18 00	
Carriage	1	20 00	
Horse	1	10 00	48 00
Stone, Miss M.			
Real Estate	4,500	63 00	
Slaves	4	12 00	
Carriage	1	20 00	
Horse	1	10 00	105 00
Stone, Miss M. E.			
Slaves	3		9 00
Stoney & Wiltberger			
Real Estate	10,000	140 00	
Stock of Goods	6,500	91 00	231 00
Stoney, S. D. and wife, in trust			
Real Estate	5,000	70 00	
Slaves	6	18 00	
Shipping	2,000	15 00	
Horse	1	10 00	
Dog	1	2 00	115 00
Stoney, Estate Elizabeth			
Real Estate	4,500	63 00	
Slaves	8	24 00	87 00
Stoney, Theodore			
Real Estate	9,400	131 60	
Slaves	4	12 00	
Carriage	1	15 00	
Commissions	5,851	146 28	304 88
Stoney, Samuel D., Trustee			
Slaves	2		6 00
Stoppelbein, L. E.			
Real Estate	2,200	30 80	
Slave	1	3 00	33 80
Stoy, J. W			
Dog	1		2 00
Storer, Michael			
Real Estate	1,500		21 00
Stratton, William			
Stock of Goods	200	2 80	
Slaves	2	6 00	
Dog	1	2 00	10 80
Strauss, B.			
Stock of Goods	3,000		42 0C
Strain, James			
Slave	1		3 00

		TAXES.
Streckfuss, John F.		
Real Estate............8,500	119 00	
Stock of Goods............500	7 00	126 00
Street, H. T.		
Real Estate............25,000	350 00	
Slave............1	3 00	
Carriage............1	30 00	
Horses............2	20 00	
Dog............1	2 00	405 00
Street & West		
Stock of Goods............5,000	70 00	
Commissions............2,588	64 70	
Dog............1	2 00	136 70
Strobel, M. D.		
Real Estate............6,000	84 00	
Interest on Bonds, &c............210	5 25	89 25
Strobel, B. M.		
Real Estate............8,000	112 00	
Slaves............2	6 00	
Dogs............2	4 00	122 00
Strobel, Mary J		
Real Estate............4,000	56 00	
Slaves............4	12 00	68 00
Strobel, Mary G.		
Real Estate............3,500	49 00	
Slaves............3	9 00	58 00
Strobel & Phillips		
Stock of Goods............700		9 80
Strobel, Mrs. A. D., in trust		
Real Estate............13,500	189 00	
Slave............1	3 00	
Dog............1	2 00	194 00
Strohecker, H. F.		
Real Estate............39,500	553 00	
Stock of Goods............12,000	168 00	
Carriage............1	20 00	
Horse............1	10 00	
Dog............1	2 00	753 00
Strohecker, B. A. G.		
Slaves............4	....	12 00
Strohecker, Dr. E. L.		
Real Estate............13,000	....	182 00
Strohecker, Mrs. H.		
Real Estate............10,000	140 00	
Slaves............7	21 00	161 00

		TAXES.
Strohecker, Mrs. H., Guardian of George		
Slave...1	....	3 00
Strohecker, Mrs. H., Guardian of L.		
Slaves...3	....	9 00
Strohecker, J. P		
Slave...1	....	3 00
Strohecker, J P., C. C. & O. E.		
Real Estate...13,000	....	182 00
Strohecker, Charles C.		
Slaves...3	....	9 00
Strong, C.		
Stock of Goods...100	....	1 40
Stroub, Estate Catharine		
Real Estate...1,200	....	16 80
Struss, E.		
Stock of Goods...500	....	7 00
Suares, J. E.		
Real Estate...3,000	42 00	
Stock of Goods...6,000	84 00	126 00
Suares, Harriet		
Real Estate...1,200	....	16 80
Sullivan, Grace O.		
Real Estate...22,000	308 00	
Slaves...2	6 00	314 00
Sullivan, Mary T.		
Real Estate...4,200	58 80	
Slaves...2	6 00	64 80
Sussdorff, G.		
Real Estate...4,000	....	56 00
Surtis, Thomas		
Real Estate...2,000	....	28 00
Sweeney, Miss E. M.		
Real Estate...2,000	28 00	
Slave...1	3 00	31 00
Swift, Thomas B.		
Slave...1		3 00
Swinton, William H.		
Dog...1	....	2 00
Swinton, William H., Trustee of Hamlin		
Real Estate...2,500	35 00	
Slaves...2	6 00	41 00
Swinton, Estate William H.		
Slaves...15	....	45 00

			TAXES.
Swinton, Mary C			
Real Estate	4,000	56 00	
Carriage	1	20 00	
Horse	1	10 00	86 00
Syfan, C. T. W			
Real Estate	1,200		16 80
Symes, S. A. and children			
Real Estate	5,500	....	77 00
Symons, John			
Real Estate	5,500	77 00	
Horses	4	40 00	117 00
Symes & Hernandez			
Stock of Goods	16,000	....	224 00
Taber, W R.			
Real Estate	3,500	49 00	
Slaves	3	9 00	
Carriage	1	20 00	
Horse	1	10 00	88 00
Taft, Davis			
Slaves	14	....	42 00
Taft, A. R. & Co.			
Real Estate	11,000	154 00	
Slaves	7	21 00	
Carriage	1	30 00	
Income	5,000	125 00	
Horses	2	20 00	250 00
Taft, A. R., Trustee			
Slaves	4		12 00
Taglierani, M.			
Slaves	2		6 00
Taglierani, M. & Co.			
Stock of Goods	600		8 40
Talbird, John E.			
Slaves	2		6 00
Talbird & Henerey			
Real Estate	8,000		112 00
Tannlunson, A.			
Real Estate	8,000	112 00	
Stock of Goods	800	11 20	
Slaves	6	18 00	141 20
Tarrant, Trust Estate Mary			
Real Estate	1,400	....	19 60
Tavel, R. A.			
Real Estate	11,000	154 00	
Interest on Bonds, &c	140	3 50	157 50

			TAXES.

Taylor, James H.
    Real Estate 11,000   154 00
    Commissions 500   12 50
    Horse 1   10 00   176 50

Taylor, Jane
    Slave 1   3 00

Taylor, T. B.
    Slaves 7   21 00

Taylor, Thomas R.
    Real Estate 6,000   84 00
    Stock of Goods 1,200   16 80   100 80

Taylor, Mary S.
    Real Estate 500   ....   7 00

Teague, J. N.
    Slaves 3   9 00
    Dog 1   2 00   11 00

Teasdale, R. H.
    Slave 1   3 00

Tenhet, Isabella
    Real Estate 1,000   14 00

Tennent, Estate Ann M.
    Real Estate 8,000   112 00
    Interest on Bonds, &c 1,600   40 00
    Slaves 8   24 00
    Carriage 1   20 00
    Horse 1   10 00   206 00

Tennent, J. S.
    Real Estate 13,000   182 00
    Slaves 13   39 00
    Carriage 1   30 00
    Horses 2   20 00   271 00

Tennent, C.
    Slaves 4   12 00

Tennent, E. S.
    Real Estate 10,000   140 00
    Dividends 10   25
    Slaves 17   51 00   191 25

Tew, Emily J
    Slave 1   3 00

Thackum, F. Postell
    Real Estate 3,300   46 20
    Slave 1   3 00   49 20

			TAXES
Thames, J E.			
Real Estate	4,500	63 00	
Slaves	2	6 00	
Dog	1	2 00	71 00
Tharin, Edward C.			
Carriage	1	20 00	
Horse	1	10 00	
Dog	1	2 00	32 00
Tharin, Edward C., Trustee			
Slave	1		3 00
Thauss, Frederick W			
Real Estate	2,000	28 00	
Stock of Goods	200	2 80	30 80
Thayer, Emery			
Real Estate	13,000		182 00
Thayer, Dewing & Co.			
Stock of Goods	35,000		490 00
Thayer, T. Heyward			
Real Estate	1,500	21 00	
Slave	1	3 00	24 00
Thayer, T. Heyward, Trustee			
Slaves	2		6 00
Thayer, E., Agent			
Real Estate	5,000		70 00
Thayer, Estate Mrs. S. C.			
Real Estate	2,800		39 20
Thayer, William, in trust			
Slaves	7	21 00	
Dog	1	2 00	23 00
Thee, John H.			
Real Estate	13,000	182 00	
Stock of Goods	600	8 40	
Slaves	2	6 00	196 40
Theiling, F W., Jr.			
Stock of Goods	500		7 00
Theiling, Frederick W			
Stock of Goods	500	7 00	
Dog	1	2 00	9 00
Theus, Catharine			
Slave	1		3 00
Thole, C. F			
Stock of Goods	400	5 60	
Slave	1	3 00	8 60

TAXES.

Thomas, S.
    Real Estate..........................8,000   112 00
    Slaves 4   12 00   124 00

Thomas, S., Trustee
    Slaves 5   ....   15 00

Thomas, Dr. F. Gaillard
    Slaves 9   27 00

Thomas, William
    Stock of Goods....................4,000   ....   56 00

Thomas, Jane M.
    Real Estate..........................7,000   98 00
    Slaves 5   15 00   113 00

Thomlinson, R.
    Real Estate..........................6,000   84 00
    Slaves 7   21 00
    Carriage....................................1   20 00
    Horse 1   10 00
    Dogs 2   4 00   139 00

Thompson, William
    Real Estate..........................5,500   77 00
    Slaves 7   21 00   98 00

Thompson, Estate George
    Real Estate........................39,200   548 80
    Interest on Bonds, &c...............847   21 18
    Slaves 16   48 00   617 98

Thompson, Estate Ann M.
    Real Estate..........................9,000   126 00
    Slaves 2   6 00   132 00

Thompson, Trust Estate Jane M.
    Real Estate........................25,000   350 00
    Slaves......................................4   12 00   362 00

Thompson, Estate H. T. and Louisa C.
    Real Estate..........................5,000   70 00
    Slaves......................................2   6 00   76 00

Thompson, Estate P S.
    Interest on Bonds, &c...............402   10 05
    Slaves......................................4   12 00   22 05

Thompson, John B. and A. E.
    Real Estate..........................4,500   ....   63 00

Thompson, Thomas
    Real Estate..........................1,000   ....   14 00

Thompson, William
    Real Estate..........................3,700   ....   51 80

			TAXES.
Thomson, John			
Real Estate	8,000	112 00	
Interest on Bonds, &c	210	5 25	
Shipping	800	6 00	123 25
Thomson, John & Co.			
Stock of Goods	5,000	70 00	
Slave	1	3 00	73 00
Thomson, Estate John			
Real Estate	3,500	....	49 00
Thorpe, Joseph			
Real Estate	1,500	....	21 00
Thouron, Joseph A.			
Slaves	2	....	6 00
Thurston, Mrs. E. E.			
Real Estate	3,600	50 40	
Slaves	13	39 00	89 40
Thurston, Edward N.			
Real Estate	15,000	210 00	
Interest on Bonds, &c	3,002	75 05	
Slaves	5	15 00	
Carriage	1	30 00	
Carriage	1	20 00	
Horses	2	20 00	
Dogs	2	4 00	374 05
Thwing, Trust Estate Isabella			
Real Estate	4,000		56 00
Tidemann, John N.			
Real Estate	4,700	65 80	
Stock of Goods	1,700	23 80	
Slaves	2	6 00	
Carriage	1	20 00	
Horse	1	10 00	
Dog	1	2 00	127 60
Tidymann, Estate Philip T.			
Real Estate	8,000	112 00	
Slaves	8	24 00	
Carriage	1	30 00	
Horses	2	20 00	186 00
Tiedemann, Otto			
Real Estate	22,500	315 00	
Stock of Goods	3,000	42 00	
Interest on Bonds, &c	180	4 50	
Slaves	9	27 00	
Dogs	2	4 00	392 50
Tiencken, H. W			
Stock of Goods	500	....	7 00

		TAXES.
Tiencken, L. C.		
Stock of Goods........300	....	4 20
Tiencken, John		
Real Estate........3,500	49 00	
Stock of Goods........700	9 80	
Dog........1	2 00	60 80
Tietjen, Claus		
Stock of Goods........600		8 40
Tilton, Rebecca		
Real Estate........1,600	22 40	
Slave........1	3 00	25 40
Timmons, Eliza		
Real Estate........3,000	....	42 00
Timothy, Estate Ann		
Slaves........3	....	9 00
Tobias, Estate Isaac		
Real Estate........2,000	28 00	
Slave........1	3 00	31 00
Tobias, A. L.		
Real Estate........3,500	49 00	
Slaves........9	27 00	
Carriage........1	20 00	
Dog........1	2 00	98 00
Tobias, Joseph L.		
Slaves........2	6 00	
Horse........1	10 00	16 00
Tobias' Sons, A.		
Real Estate........18,600	260 40	
Stock of Goods........10,000	140 00	
Slave........1	3 00	
Income........9,000	225 00	628 40
Tobias, Mrs. E.		
Real Estate........17,000	....	238 00
Tobias, V J., Trustee		
Slave........1	....	3 00
Tobin, Richard		
Real Estate........6,000	....	84 00
Todd, E. W		
Slave........1	....	3 00
Togno, Madam R. A.		
Real Estate........15,000		210 00
Tolla, John		
Real Estate........4,560	....	63 84

			TAXES.
Touyes, Lewis			
Stock of Goods	300	4 20	
Horse	1	10 00	14 20
Toomer, Miss E. O.			
Slaves	4		12 00
Toomer, Mary P			
Real Estate	8,000	112 00	
Slaves	7	21 00	133 00
Toomer, N. L.			
Slaves	2		6 00
Toomer, H. L.			
Real Estate	11,000	154 00	
Slaves	19	57 00	
Carriage	1	30 00	
Carriage	1	20 00	
Horses	3	30 00	291 00
Toomer, Mrs. A. E.			
Slaves	4	12 00	
Dog	1	2 00	14 00
Toomer, T. S., Trustee			
Slave	1		3 00
Torre, John C., della			
Carriage	1	20 00	
Horses	2	20 00	40 00
Torre della & Co.			
Real Estate	19,000	266 00	
Slaves	7	21 00	287 00
Torrent, John			
Real Estate	4,000	56 00	
Slave	1	3 00	
Carriage	1	20 00	
Horses	4	40 00	119 00
Torry, Ann W			
Slaves	8		24 00
Touhy, Mrs. B. L.			
Real Estate	21,000	294 00	
Slaves	3	9 00	303 00
Toumey, John			
Carriage	1	20 00	
Horse	1	10 00	
Dog	1	2 00	32 00
Toussiger, Eliza			
Real Estate	3,000	42 00	
Slave	1	3 00	45 00

282

		TAXES.
Townsend, Arnold & Co.		
Real Estate...............45,000	....	630 00
Trapier, Paul		
Slave.................................1		3 00
Trapier, W H.		
Slaves.................................10	....	30 00
Trapmann, W. H.		
Real Estate.................12,000	168 00	
Interest on Bonds, &c 500	12 50	
Slaves...........................6	18 00	
Carriage........................1	20 00	
Shipping....................6,500	48 75	
Horse 1	10 00	
Dog.............................1	2 00	279 25
Trapmann, W H., Trustee		
Real Estate.................6,000	84 00	
Interest on Bonds, &c............420	10 50	
Slave...........................1	3 00	97 50
Traxler, Ann		
Slaves...........................4	....	12 00
Trenholm, George A. and others		
Real Estate.................80,000	1,120 00	
Slave 1	3 00	1,123 00
Trenholm, Charles L.		
Real Estate.................10,000	140 00	
Slaves.........................4	12 00	
Carriage........................1	30 00	
Horses.........................4	40 00	222 00
Trenholm, George A.		
Real Estate.................24,000	336 00	
Slaves.........................14	42 00	
Carriage........................1	30 00	
Carriage........................1	20 00	
Horses.........................4	40 00	468 00
Trenholm, W. L.		
Real Estate.................11,000	154 00	
Slaves.........................2	6 00	
Carriage........................1	30 00	
Horses.........................2	20 00	
Dogs 2	4 00	214 00
Trenholm, C. L., G. A. and W B. Burden		
Real Estate.................120,000	1,680 00	
Slave...........................1	3 00	1,683 00
Trenholm, C. L. and G. A. and T. D. Wagner		
Real Estate.................8,500	....	119 00

	TAXES.

Trenholm, E. L.
 Real Estate........................18,000 252 00
 Carriage.................................1 30 00
 Horses....................................4 40 00 322 00

Trescot, George F., Trustee
 Slaves.....................................4 12 00

Trescot, Sarah
 Real Estate.........................3,000 42 00
 Slaves....................................4 12 00 54 00

Triest, Joseph
 Stock of Goods...................1,000 14 00
 Slave......................................1 3 00
 Carriage.................................1 20 00
 Horse.....................................1 10 00 47 00

Trott, W G.
 Real Estate.........................6,500 91 00
 Stock of Goods...................3,350 46 90
 Dog..1 2 00 139 90

Trott, Emily M.
 Real Estate............................500 7 00
 Slave......................................1 3 00 10 00

Trott, Elizabeth J
 Slaves....................................4 .... 12 00

Trotti, Estate Caroline
 Slave.....................................1 .... 3 00

Trout, T. B.
 Real Estate.........................5,700 79 80
 Stock of Goods...................2,500 35 00
 Slaves....................................3 9 00
 Carriage.................................1 20 00
 Shipping.............................4,200 31 50
 Horse.....................................1 10 00
 Dog..1 2 00 187 30

Trout, T. B., Trustee
 Real Estate.........................3,500 49 00

Trout, W
 Real Estate.........................5,000 .... 70 00

Trow, Mrs. A. W
 Stock of Goods......................500 .... 7 00

Trumbo, C. C.
 Real Estate.......................28,500 399 00
 Slaves...................................10 30 00
 Carriage.................................1 20 00
 Horses....................................4 40 00 489 00

			TAXES.
Tucker, Miss A. A.			
Slaves	2	6 00	
Carriage	1	20 00	
Horse	1	10 00	36 00
Tucker, Harriet S.			
Slaves	3		9 00
Tudor, Frederick			
Real Estate	30,000	420 00	
Stock of Goods	3,000	42 00	462 00
Tumelty, Mary			
Stock of Goods	500		7 00
Tunis, Mary			
Slaves	2	6 00	
Dog	1	2 00	8 00
Tupper, T., Senr.			
Real Estate	6,500	91 00	
Slaves	11	33 00	124 00
Tupper, T. and Sons			
Stock of Goods	10,000	140 00	
Commissions	12,000	300 00	440 00
Tupper, T., Jr.			
Real Estate	5,000	70 00	
Slaves	4	12 00	82 00
Tupper, James			
Real Estate	15,500	217 00	
Slaves	9	27 00	
Carriage	1	30 00	
Horses	2	20 00	
Dog	1	2 00	296 00
Tupper, James, Trustee Edwards			
Real Estate	770		10 78
Tupper, Samuel Y.			
Real Estate	5,000	70 00	
Slaves	4	12 00	
Carriage	1	20 00	
Horse	1	10 00	
Dog	1	2 00	114 00
Turnbull, Anna B.			
Real Estate	9,000	126 00	
Slaves	5	15 00	
Carriage	1	30 00	
Horses	2	20 00	191 00
Turnbull, Amey			
Real Estate	3,000	42 00	
Slaves	3	9 00	51 00

		TAXES.
Turnbull, Mrs. Andrew		
Slaves....................7	21 00	
Carriage..................1	30 00	
Horses 2	20 00	
Dog........................1	2 00	73 00
Turner, Mrs. Mary E.		
Slaves 6		18 00
Turner, S. C.		
Horse 1		10 00
Turpin, Estate of, and Meverick		
Real Estate..........2,500		35 00
Tweed, Ellen		
Real Estate..........1,500	21 00	
Slave 1	3 00	24 00
Tylee, Cornelia S.		
Slave 1		3 00
Ufferhardt, Wm.		
Real Estate..........4,000	56 00	
Dog 1	2 00	58 00
Ufferhardt & Campsen		
Stock of Goods.....13,000	182 00	
Interest on Bonds, &c.......52	1 30	
Dog........................1	2 00	185 30
Ufferhuslo, Charles		
Real Estate..........1,500		21 00
Ultermahl, Mary O.		
Real Estate..........1,200		16 80
Valentine, S.		
Real Estate..........5,000	70 00	
Slaves 6	18 00	88 00
Vance, Francis L.		
Slave 1		3 00
Vandelken, Estate H.		
Real Estate..........1,400		19 60
Vanderhorst, Elias		
Real Estate........100,000	1,400 00	
Slaves....................7	21 00	
Carriage..................1	30 00	
Carriage..................1	20 00	
Horses 4	40 00	1,511 00
Vanderlippe, Frederick		
Real Estate..........1,500	21 00	
Slaves 2	6 00	27 00
Van Ness, M. L.		
Slaves....................5		15 00

		TAXES.

Vannoy, Mary E.
 Slaves.........................8   ....   24 00

Van Schaack, Peter, Trustee
 Real Estate...................6,000   ....   84 00

Van Schaack & Grierson
 Stock of Goods..............6,330   ....   88 62

Van Winkle, John
 Stock of Goods..............8,000   ....   112 00

Van Wyck, Mrs. L. A.
 Real Estate...................8,700   ....   121 80

Vardell, W G.
 Carriage..........................1   20 00
 Horses.............................2   20 00   40 00

Varner, Henry
 Real Estate...................1,500   ....   21 00

Vaux, Mrs. C. A.
 Interest on Bonds, &c........350   8 75
 Slaves............................8   24 00   32 75

Venning, M. H.
 Slaves...........................3   ....   9 00

Venning, Martha
 Slaves...........................4   ....   12 00

Venning, John
 Real Estate...................6,000   ....   84 00

Venning, J. M.
 Real Estate.................74,600   1,044 40
 Interest on Bonds, &c......3,950   98 75
 Slaves............................6   18 00
 Carriage..........................1   20 00
 Income..........................450   11 25
 Horse............................1   10 00
 Dog..............................1   2 00   1,204 40

Venning, Mrs. Robert
 Slaves...........................7   ....   21 00

Ventee, Ann
 Slave............................1   ....   3 00

Verdier, Caroline
 Slave............................1   ....   3 00

Verdier, Mrs. Caroline
 Slave............................1   ....   3 00

Verdier, Mrs. C. B.
 Slaves...........................3   ....   9 00

Verdier, Miss Isbell
 Slave............................1   ....   3 00

			TAXES.
Verdier, Miss E.			
Slave	1		3 00
Veronee, Samuel J B.			
Real Estate	400		5 60
Veuve, Ulysse			
Stock of Goods	300		4 20
Vidal, James			
Real Estate	5,000	70 00	
Slaves	10	30 00	
Carriage	1	20 00	
Horse	1	10 00	130 00
Vincent, Hugh E.			
Real Estate	13,800	193 20	
Stock of Goods	7,000	98 00	
Slaves	3	9 00	
Horse	1	10 00	310 20
Vincent, Hugh E. & D. B.			
Real Estate	1,500	21 00	
Shipping	9,000	67 50	88 50
Vincent, Mrs. C.			
Slaves	11		33 00
Vlaceth, Nicholas			
Stock of Goods	300		4 20
Vogelsang, Meno			
Real Estate	13,500	189 00	
Slaves	24	72 00	261 00
Voight, C.			
Stock of Goods	1,700	23 80	
Dog	1	2 00	25 80
Vollers, J. H.			
Stock of Goods	1,800		25 20
Von Dohlen, A.			
Real Estate	14,000	196 00	
Stock of Goods	1,500	21 00	
Slaves	4	12 00	
Horse	1	10 00	239 00
Von Eitzen, H. H.			
Stock of Goods	500		7 00
Von Glahn, A.			
Real Estate	400		5 60
Von Glahn, B.			
Real Estate	7,500		105 00
Von Glahn, C.			
Stock of Goods	500	7 00	
Dog	1	2 00	9 00

		TAXES.
Von Glahn, M.		
Stock of Goods....................800		11 20
Von Hadlen, C.		
Stock of Goods....................1,100		15 40
Von Hollen, H. W		
Stock of Goods....................1,000		14 00
Von Hollen, John		
Stock of Goods....................1,200		16 80
Von Holnitz, H.		
Real Estate....................5,000	70 00	
Stock of Goods....................300	4 20	
Dog....................1	2 00	76 20
Von Santen, F		
Stock of Goods....................7,500		105 00
Von Soosten, M.		
Stock of Goods....................500	7 00	
Horses....................2	20 00	
Dog....................1	2 00	29 00
Von Sprecken, F		
Slaves....................2	6 00	
Dog....................1	2 00	8 00
Voss, Frederick		
Horse....................1	10 00	
Dog....................1	2 00	12 00
Wacker, L.		
Stock of Goods....................300	....	4 20
Wagener, J C.		
Stock of Goods....................800		11 20
Wagner, Samuel J.		
Real Estate....................2,000	28 00	
Interest on Bonds, &c....................112	2 80	
Slaves....................5	15 00	45 80
Wagner, S. J., Trustee of Enslow		
Real Estate....................13,900	194 60	
Slaves....................5	15 00	209 60
Wagner, S. J., Trustee		
Slaves....................2		6 00
Wagner, A. C.		
Slave....................1		3 00
Wagner, J B., for James Maebeth		
Slaves....................7		21 00
Wagner, Estate Dr. John		
Slaves....................3	....	9 00

			TAXES.
Wagner, T. D., Trustee of Mrs. Moses			
Real Estate	13,000		182 00
Wagner, T. D., for self and Mrs. George Wagner			
Real Estate	16,400	229 60	
Slaves	6	18 00	
Carriage	1	30 00	
Horses	2	20 00	297 60
Wagner, Effingham			
Real Estate	10,000	140 00	
Slaves	10	30 00	
Carriage	1	30 00	
Horses	2	20 00	
Dog	1	2 00	222 00
Wagner, Mary C.			
Real Estate	3,500		49 00
Waldron, Egleston & Co.			
Stock of Goods	17,000		238 00
Walker, J. E.			
Real Estate	29,500		413 00
Walker, A. W and Estate C. S. Walker			
Real Estate	12,000		168 00
Walker, W S. and D A.			
Real Estate	12,000	168 00	
Slaves	14	42 00	
Shipping	1,250	9 38	
Horse	1	10 00	229 38
Walker, Evans & Co.			
Real Estate	24,000	336 00	
Stock of Goods	18,000	252 00	
Slaves	2	6 00	594 00
Walker, Joseph, Agent			
Stock of Goods	8,000		112 00
Walker, John C., in trust			
Slaves	2		6 00
Walker, Joseph F., in trust			
Real Estate	7,000	98 00	
Slaves	4	12 00	110 00
Walker, G.			
Slaves	7	21 00	
Horse	1	10 00	31 00
Walker, R. T.			
Commissions	2,100		52 00
Walker, Jane			
Real Estate	9,000	126 00	
Slaves	5	15 00	141 00

19

			TAXES.
Walker, William H.			
Real Estate	31,000	434 00	
Slaves	12	36 00	
Carriage	1	20 00	
Horse	1	10 00	500 00
Walker, James			
Real Estate	37,000	518 00	
Stock of Goods	15,000	210 00	
Commissions	4,000	100 00	828 00
Walker, George W., in trust			
Real Estate	6,000	84 00	
Slaves	6	18 00	102 00
Walker, James			
Real Estate	300		4 20
Walker, H. P			
Real Estate	4,000	56 00	
Slaves	6	18 00	
Carriage	1	20 00	
Income	1,000	25 00	
Horse	1	10 00	129 00
Walker, H. P., Trustee			
Real Estate	4,000	56 00	
Slaves	5	15 00	71 00
Walker, Mrs. E. J			
Real Estate	6,000	....	84 00
Walker, Mary E., Executrix			
Interest on Bonds, &c	240	6 00	
Slaves	5	15 00	21 00
Walker, Estate James M.			
Slaves	2	....	6 00
Walker, E. B.			
Slave	1	....	3 00
Wallace, Andrew			
Real Estate	10,000		140 00
Wallace, Estate Andrew			
Real Estate	1,200	....	16 80
Wallace, Thomas			
Real Estate	11,500	161 00	
Stock of Goods	10,000	140 00	
Slaves	6	18 00	
Dogs	3	6 00	325 00
Walpole, J L.			
Slaves	4	....	12 00

			TAXES.
Walpole, H. E.			
Real Estate	4,000	56 00	
Slaves	4	12 00	
Carriage	1	20 00	
Horse	1	10 00	
Dogs	2	4 00	102 00
Walpole, J B. L.			
Slaves	3		9 00
Walsh, Thomas V and Joseph F			
Slave	1		3 00
Walsh, Patrick			
Slave	1		3 00
Walter, Mary G.			
Interest on Bonds, &c	143	3 58	
Dividends	40	1 00	4 58
Walter, Trust Estate George H. and E. R.			
Real Estate	7,500	105 00	
Dog	1	2 00	107 00
Walter, G. H., Trustee			
Slave	1		3 00
Walton, J. M.			
Real Estate	5,000	70 00	
Slaves	6	18 00	
Dog	1	2 00	90 00
Ward, Mrs. J. D.			
Real Estate	20,000	280 00	
Interest on Bonds, &c	506	12 65	
Slaves	15	45 00	
Carriage	1	30 00	
Carriage	1	20 00	
Annuity	5,000	125 00	
Horses	3	30 00	542 65
Ward, the Misses			
Real Estate	2,500	35 00	
Slaves	4	12 00	47 00
Ward, Estate John			
Real Estate	3,000		42 00
Ward, Miss M. M.			
Real Estate	6,500	91 00	
Slaves	2	6 00	97 00
Ward, Mrs. E. J. and M. M.			
Slaves	7		21 00
Wardlaw, Walker & Co.			
Commissions	25,000		625 00

			TAXE
Wardlaw, W A.			
Real Estate............12,000	168	00	
Slaves..................5	15	00	
Carriage................1	20	00	
Horse...................1	10	00	213 0
Waring, Thomas R.			
Real Estate............11,500	161	00	
Slaves.................25	75	00	
Carriage................1	30	00	
Horses..................2	20	00	
Dogs....................2	4	00	290 0
Waring, Estate J. L.			
Slave...................1			3 0
Waring, M. A.			
Real Estate............7,000	98	00	
Slaves..................5	15	00	113 0
Waring, Mrs. P H.			
Real Estate............5,000	70	00	
Slaves.................11	33	00	103 0
Waring, Thomas			
Real Estate............12,000	168	00	
Interest on Bonds, &c....1,400	35	00	
Slaves..................5	15	00	218 0
Waring, Thomas, Trustee			
Slave...................1			3 0
Waring, Thomas, Trustee Mrs. Bulow			
Real Estate............4,000	56	00	
Slaves..................5	15	00	
Dog.....................1	2	00	73 0
Waring, Dr. H. S.			
Slaves..................8	24	00	
Carriage................1	20	00	
Income................500	12	50	
Horse...................1	10	00	66 50
Waring, Dr. J B.			
Real Estate............8,000	112	00	
Slave...................1	3	00	115 0
Waring, Dr. Morton			
Slave...................1			3 00
Waring, Estate J. J.			
Slaves..................3			9 00
Waring, J. H., Trustee Lockwood			
Real Estate............3,500	49	00	
Slaves..................9	27	00	76 00
Warley, Miss Ann E.			
Interest on Bonds, &c...35			88

			TAXES.
Warnken, H. G.			
Slave	1		3 00
Warnken, Peter, (a minor)			
Real Estate	1,200		15 80
Warren, B. W			
Slaves	2		6 00
Warren, Elizabeth			
Slave	1		3 00
Warren, Thomas J., Trustee			
Real Estate	4,000	56 00	
Slaves	16	48 00	104 00
Washington, Trust Estate T. N.			
Slaves	16		48 00
Waterman, C.			
Slaves	6		18 00
Waterman, John			
Slaves	6		18 00
Waterman, C., Trustee			
Slave	1		3 00
Watson, James S.			
Real Estate	5,000		70 00
Watson, Estate Captain			
Real Estate	4,000		56 00
Watts, Mrs. S.			
Stock of Goods	2,500		35 00
Wayne, Daniel G.			
Real Estate	15,000	210 00	
Slaves	10	30 00	
Carriage	1	20 00	
Horse	1	10 00	270 00
Weatherhorn, M.			
Stock of Goods	200	2 80	
Horse	1	10 00	12 80
Webb, Miss Susan P.			
Slaves	11		33 00
Webb & Sage			
Stock of Goods	55,000	770 00	
Shipping	600	4 50	
Dog	1	2 00	776 50
Webb, Mrs. C. H.			
Slaves	14	42 00	
Carriage	1	20 00	
Horse	1	10 00	72 00
Webb, Walter			
Real Estate	3,500		49 00

		TAXE
Webb, Mary M.		
Slaves 17		51 (
Webb, William L.		
Interest on Bonds, &c.........35	88	
Slaves 2	6 00	
Carriage 1	20 00	
Horses 2	20 00	
Dog 1	2 00	48 (
Webb, Eliza A., No. 1		
Real Estate 9,000	126 00	
Interest on Bonds, &c.......385	9 63	
Slaves 9	27 00	
Carriage 1	30 00	
Horses 2	20 00	212 (
Webb, Eliza A., No. 2		
Slaves................10	....	30 (
Webb, William L., in trust		
Slave 1	....	3 (
Webb, Thomas L.		
Real Estate 9,800	137 20	
Slaves 4	12 00	
Carriage 1	30 00	
Carriage 1	20 00	
Horses 3	30 00	
Dogs 2	4 00	233 '
Webb, Susan L., in trust		
Slave 1	....	3 (
Webb, Samuel		
Real Estate 1,400	....	19 (
Weber, Charlotte		
Real Estate 2,500	....	35 (
Webster, S. C.		
Carriage 1	15 00	
Income 500	12 50	
Horse 1	10 00	37
Webster, Trust Estate S. C.		
Slaves 5	15 00	
Carriage 1	30 00	
Horses 2	20 00	65
Wedding, Christian		
Real Estate 1,100		15
Wedemeyer, Beta		
Stock of Goods 500	....	7

			TAXES.
Weed, Jane			
Real Estate	2,500	35 00	
Interest on Bonds, &c	167	4 18	
Slaves	7	21 00	60 18
Weghe, John L.			
Slave	1		3 00
Wehlers, Estate J C.			
Real Estate	2,000		28 00
Wehmann, F.			
Stock of Goods	1,500	21 00	
Slaves	4	12 00	
Dog	1	2 00	35 00
Weiles, John			
Slaves	6		18 00
Weinburg, Miss F.			
Stock of Goods	500		7 00
Weiskopf, Leopold			
Real Estate	1,500	21 00	
Stock of Goods	800	11 20	32 20
Weisenger, Charles			
Real Estate	25,500		357 00
Weisenger, Leonard			
Real Estate	26,000		364 00
Weisenger, Dorothea			
Real Estate	13,500	189 00	
Slaves	6	18 00	207 00
Weiters, Otto, Agent			
Stock of Goods	650		9 10
Welch, R. M.			
Real Estate	6,000	84 00	
Stock of Goods	15,000	210 00	
Slaves	2	6 00	
Dog	1	2 00	302 00
Welch, M. C.			
Real Estate	1,200	16 80	
Dog	1	2 00	18 80
Welch, Sarah E.			
Slaves	6		18 00
Weldon, John			
Real Estate	4,500		63 00
Welling's children, Samuel			
Real Estate	1,000		14 00
Wells, Estate J. F.			
Real Estate	6,500	91 00	
Interest on Bonds, &c	800	20 00	111 00

TAXES.

Wellsman, James
   Real Estate..................35,500   497 00
   Slaves 9   27 00
   Carriage..............................1   30 00
   Shipping 53,000   397 50
   Commissions......................400   10 00   961 50

Wellsman, James, Agent
   Slave 1   3 00

Wenholtz, F
   Real Estate......................4,500   63 00

Werner, D.
   Real Estate......................5,000   70 00
   Stock of Goods..................600   8 40   78 40

Werner, Herman
   Stock of Goods..................500   ....   7 00

Werson, Sarah A.
   Real Estate......................3,500   ....   49 00

Wescoat, William
   Slaves....................................4   ....   12 00

Wescott, Dr. G. W
   Real Estate....................11,000   154 00
   Slaves 7   21 00
   Carriage..............................1   15 00
   Income..............................2,000   50 00
   Horse 1   10 00   250 00

West, Charles H.
   Real Estate....................19,000   266 00
   Slaves................................7   21 00
   Shipping.......................24,410   183 08
   Dog.....................................2   4 00   474 08

West, C. H. and Son
   Stock of Goods 12,500   175 00

West, Charles H., Jr.
   Real Estate......................6,000   84 00
   Slaves 7   21 00
   Carriage..............................1   20 00
   Horse..................................1   10 00   135 00

West, P
   Real Estate......................3,000   42 00
   Slave..................................1   3 00
   Carriage..............................1   15 00   60 00

West, Trust Estate Mrs. E. E.
   Slaves..................................9   27 00

Westendorff, James S.
   Real Estate 150   2 10
   Slaves 4   12 00   14 10

		TAXES.
Westendorff, C. W., Agent		
Slaves 2	....	6 00
Westendorff, C. P. L., Agent		
Slaves 3		9 00
Westerlund, C. T.		
Slave 1	3 00	
Shipping 3,500	26 25	29 25
Weston, Francis		
Real Estate......................15,500	217 00	
Slaves 31	93 00	
Carriage 1	30 00	
Horses 3	30 00	370 00
Weston, Estate Dr. Paul		
Real Estate......................15,000	....	210 00
Weyman, Ann C.		
Real Estate........................3,000		42 00
Weyman, Estate F H.		
Slaves 5		15 00
Whaley, Wm.		
Real Estate......................18,000	252 00	
Slaves 16	48 00	
Carriage 1	30 00	
Income 4,890 89	122 27	
Horses 2	20 00	472 27
Whaley, Wm.. Trustee T. C. and F W Mitchell		
Real Estate........................1,700	23 80	
Slaves 5	15 00	
Dogs 2	4 00	42 80
Whaley, John B.		
Slave 1		3 00
Whaley, B. J.		
Real Estate........................7,500	105 00	
Interest on Bonds, &c............300	7 50	
Slaves 4	12 00	
Carriage 1	20 00	
Income 2,000	50 00	
Horse 1	10 00	
Dog 1	2 00	206 50
Wharves, Commercial		
Real Estate....................100,000	....	1,400 00
Wharf, Boyce & Co.'s		
Real Estate....................120,000	1,680 00	
Slaves 2	6 00	1,686 00
Wharf, Southern		
Real Estate......................60,000		840 00

		TAXES.
Wharf, Brown & Co.'s		
Real Estate..................90,000	1,260 00	
Slaves..................2	6 00	1,266 00
Wharves, Owners of Adger's		
Real Estate..................135,000	1,890 00	
Slaves..................2	6 00	
Horses..................2	20 00	1,916 00
Wharton, Thos. J.		
Real Estate..................5,500	77 00	
Slaves..................3	9 00	86 00
Wharton & Petsch		
Real Estate..................11,000	154 00	
Slaves..................6	18 00	
Carriage..................1	20 00	
Horse..................1	10 00	202 00
Wharton, G. C.		
Real Estate..................6,800	95 20	
Slaves..................10	30 00	
Horse..................1	10 00	135 20
Wharton, Jane K.		
Real Estate..................5,400		75 60
Wheeler, Geo.		
Slaves..................8		24 00
Whelan, Peter		
Slaves..................4	....	12 00
Whilden, Wm. G.		
Real Estate..................8,500	119 00	
Carriage..................1	20 00	
Dog..................1	2 00	141 00
Whilden, W G., in trust		
Slave..................1		3 00
Whilden, Mrs. A. C.		
Slaves..................3		9 00
Whilden, Miss A. C.		
Slave..................1		3 00
Whilden, Joseph		
Real Estate..................2,200	30 80	
Slave..................1	3 00	33 80
Whilden, Joseph, Trustee		
Slave..................1		3 00
Whilden, B. F.		
Slave..................1	3 00	
Dog..................1	2 00	5 00
Whilden, B. F., Trustee		
Slave..................1	....	3 00

			TAXES.
Whipple, James			
Real Estate	3,000		42 00
Whitaker, Mary			
Real Estate	6,000		84 00
Whitaker, Wm.			
Horse	1		10 00
White, James			
Real Estate	8,300	116 20	
Slaves	7	21 00	
Carriage	1	20 00	157 20
White, Robert			
Real Estate	6,000	84 00	
Stock of Goods	2,500	35 00	119 00
White, Dr. Thomas G.			
Slaves	3		9 00
White, Wm. T.			
Real Estate	14,000	196 00	
Slaves	14	42 00	
Horse	1	10 00	
Dogs	2	4 00	252 00
White, A. J			
Real Estate	40,400	565 60	
Dividends	200	5 00	
Slaves	14	42 00	
Carriage	1	30 00	
Commissions	2,500	62 50	
Horses	3	30 00	
Dog	1	2 00	737 10
White, A. J., Trustee E. B. White, wife and children.			
Real Estate	7,000	98 00	
Slaves	16	48 00	146 00
White, Edward B.			
Real Estate	12,000	168 00	
Carriage	1	20 00	
Income	500	12 50	210 50
White, Estate John B.			
Slaves	6		18 00
White, Dr. Octavius A.			
Real Estate	5,000	70 00	
Slaves	5	15 00	
Carriage	1	15 00	
Income	1,000	25 00	125 00
White, Edwin J			
Slave	1	3 00	
Dog	1	2 00	5 00

		TAXES.

White, E. John
    Slave................1   3 00

White, Estate W J.
    Real Estate............2,500   35 00
    Slaves................2   6 00   41 00

White, James H.
    Real Estate............7,700   107 80
    Slaves................3   9 00   116 80

White, Jane M.
    Real Estate............15,000   210 00
    Slaves................13   39 00
    Dog...................1   2 00   251 00

White, Mrs. E. B.
    Slaves................4   ....   12 00

White, Sarah and Caroline
    Real Estate............7,000   98 00
    Interest on Bonds, &c....374   9 35
    Slaves................5   15 00
    Carriage..............1   20 00
    Horse.................1   10 00   152 35

White, George
    Slaves................3   ....   9 00

White, Dr. C. G.
    Real Estate............3,500   49 00

White, W W., in trust
    Real Estate............1,500   21 00

White, Mrs. A. E.
    Slaves................4   12 00
    Dog...................1   2 00   14 00

White, J Thomas H.
    Real Estate............16,000   224 00
    Slaves................20   60 00
    Carriage..............1   30 00
    Horses................2   20 00
    Dog...................1   2 00   336 00

Whiting, Zelia
    Real Estate............8,500   119 00
    Slave.................3   9 00   128 00

Whiting, E. M., Trustee
    Real Estate............2,800   ....   39 20

Whiting, E. M., Guardian
    Slave.................1   3 00

Whitney, Mary A.
    Real Estate............12,700   177 80
    Slave.................1   3 00   180 80

		TAXES.
Whitney, T. A.		
Real Estate 7,000	98 00	
Slaves............9	27 00	
Carriage............1	20 00	
Income............2,000	50 00	
Horse............1	10 00	205 00
Whitney, F. H.		
Real Estate............10,000	140 00	
Slaves............7	21 00	
Carriage............1	20 00	
Horses............2	20 00	201 00
Whitridge, Dr. J. B.		
Slaves............2		6 00
Whittemore, C.		
Real Estate............4,000	56 00	
Slaves............10	30 00	
Carriage............1	20 00	
Horse............1	10 00	116 00
Whittemore, L. and children		
Real Estate............8,000	112 00	
Interest on Bonds, &c............14	35	
Slave............1	3 00	115 35
Whittemore, L. B.		
Horses............2	20 00	
Dog............1	2 00	22 00
Whitty, Estate Edward		
Real Estate............4,500		63 00
Whyte, Joseph		
Real Estate............6,100	85 40	
Slaves............3	9 00	94 40
Wickenberg, F R.		
Real Estate............4,000	56 00	
Slaves............3	9 00	
Carriage............1	30 00	
Horses............2	20 00	115 00
Wiebens, H.		
Stock of Goods............400		5 60
Wiedeau, Jacob		
Real Estate............1,500	....	21 00
Wiemer, George		
Slave............1		3 00
Wienges, Estate Conrad		
Real Estate............4,500	....	63 00

		TAXES.

Wienges, Jacob
 Real Estate.....................28.600 300 40
 Interest on Bonds, &c..............400 10 00
 Slaves...................................7 21 00
 Carriage................................1 20 00
 Horse...................................1 10 00 361 40

Wienges, Conrad M.
 Real Estate........................8,000 112 00
 Slaves...................................3 9 00 121 00

Wienges, G. W
 Real Estate.......................1,800 25 20

Wienges, G. W., in trust
 Slave...................................1 3 00

Wienholtz, F
 Real Estate........................8,000 112 00
 Stock of Goods.....................500 7 00 119 00

Wienholtz, Estate J P
 Real Estate......................12,000 168 00

Wigfall, Eliza M.
 Interest on Bonds, &c..............998 24 95
 Slaves...................................7 21 00 45 95

Wigg, William Hazard
 Slaves...................................7 21 00

Wightman, John T.
 Real Estate......................13,000 182 00
 Slave....................................1 3 00 185 00

Wilber, W G.
 Real Estate........................2,000 .... 28 00

Wilbur, M. E.
 Slaves...................................2 .... 6 00

Wilbur, T. A.
 Real Estate........................4,500 63 00
 Slaves...................................5 15 00 78 00

Wilbur, W W
 Slaves...................................3 9 00
 Dog......................................1 2 00 11 00

Wilbur & Son
 Commissions.....................2,000 .... 50 00

Wilbur, M. B.
 Slaves...................................4 .... 12 00

Wiley, Estate William
 Real Estate.......................1,200 .... 16 80

Wiley, L. M.
 Real Estate......................23,000 .... 322 00

		TAXES.
Wiley, Samuel		
Stock of Goods 1,500	21 00	
Slaves 4	12 00	
Carriage 1	20 00	
Commissions 1,300	32 50	
Horse 1	10 00	
Dog 1	2 00	97 50
Wiley, James		
Real Estate 4,000	56 00	
Stock of Goods 3,000	42 00	
Slave 1	3 00	
Horse 1	10 00	111 00
Wilkening, J. H.		
Stock of Goods 500	7 00	
Slave 1	3 00	10 00
Wilkes, Mrs. C.		
Real Estate 9,700	135 80	
Slaves 16	48 00	
Carriage 1	30 00	
Horses 2	20 00	
Dog 1	2 00	235 80
Wilkie, Anna C.		
Slaves 12		36 00
Wilkie & Shier		
Stock of Goods 4,500	63 00	
Horse 1	10 00	73 00
Wilkie, Caroline, in trust		
Slaves 2		6 00
Wilkins, B. G.		
Real Estate 10,000	140 00	
Slaves 8	24 00	
Carriage 1	30 00	
Shipping 1,500	11 25	
Horses 2	20 00	
Dogs 3	6 00	231 25
Wilkins, Martin L.		
Income 1,240		31 00
Wilkins, Mrs. E. B.		
Real Estate 7,000	98 00	
Interest on Bonds, &c 1,962	49 05	
Slaves 21	63 00	
Carriage 1	30 00	
Horses 2	20 00	260 05

		TAXES.
Wilkinson, James W		
Real Estate...........12,000	168 00	
Interest on Bonds, &c...........1,050	26 25	
Slaves...........10	30 00	
Income...........2,500	62 50	
Dogs...........2	4 00	290 75
Wilkinson, Mrs. E.		
Real Estate...........9,000	126 00	
Interest on Bonds, &c...........966	24 15	
Slaves...........11	33 00	
Dog...........1	2 00	185 15
Williams, G. W		
Real Estate...........13,000	182 00	
Slaves...........9	27 00	
Carriage...........1	30 00	
Horses...........2	20 00	
Dog...........1	2 00	261 00
Williams, G. W & Co.		
Real Estate...........37,200	520 80	
Stock of Goods...........80,000	1,120 00	
Slave...........1	3 00	1,643 80
Williams, Farrow & Co.		
Commissions...........4,224 51		105 61
Williams & Brown		
Stock of Goods...........1,500	....	21 00
Williams, H. H.		
Real Estate...........5,500		77 00
Williams, W B.		
Real Estate...........8,000	112 00	
Slaves...........9	27 00	
Horse...........1	10 00	149 00
Williams, E. H.		
Slave...........1		3 00
Williams, Harriet H.		
Real Estate...........12,700	177 80	
Slaves...........5	15 00	192 80
Williams, William H.		
Real Estate...........1,500	....	21 00
Williams, Henry		
Real Estate...........13,700	191 80	
Slaves...........3	9 00	
Carriage...........1	20 00	220 80
Williamson, Jane		
Slaves...........8		24 00
Williamson, John		
Real Estate...........4,400		61 60

			TAXES.
Williman, A. B.			
Interest on Bonds, &c	100	2 50	
Slave	1	3 00	5 50
Williman, Assigned Estate, Christopher			
Real Estate	3,200		44 80
Williman, Jacob, Trustee			
Slaves	19		57 00
Williman, Estate Elizabeth			
Slaves	4		12 00
Willing, Susan and children			
Real Estate	2,000		28 00
Willington, A. S.			
Real Estate	19,500	273 00	
Interest on Bonds, &c	595	14 88	
Slaves	14	42 00	
Carriage	1	30 00	
Horses	2	20 00	
Dog	1	2 00	381 88
Willington, A. S. & Co.			
Slaves	2		6 00
Willis, John G.			
Real Estate	12,000	168 00	
Stock of Goods	5,400	75 60	
Slaves	3	9 00	
Dog	1	2 00	254 60
Willis, Henry, Sen.			
Real Estate	12,000	168 00	
Slaves	3	9 00	
Carriage	1	20 00	
Income	500	12 50	
Horse	1	10 00	
Dog	1	2 00	221 50
Willis, Henry, Jr.			
Real Estate	4,000	56 00	
Income	500	12 50	68 50
Willis, E.			
Slave	1	3 00	
Dog	1	2 00	5 00
Wilmans, A. F.			
Slave	1		3 00
Wilmans & Price			
Real Estate	10,000	140 00	
Stock of Goods	23,000	322 00	462 00
Wilson, Estate Angus			
Real Estate	5,000		70 00

			TAXES.
Wilson, Sarah L., in trust			
Real Estate	10,000	140 00	
Slaves	3	9 00	149 00
Wilson, Mrs. S. F S.			
Real Estate	115,700	1,619 80	
Slaves	13	39 00	
Carriage	1	30 00	
Horses	2	20 00	1,708 80
Wilson, J M.			
Real Estate	8,000	112 00	
Slaves	14	42 00	
Dog	1	2 00	156 00
Wilson, James M., Trustee			
Slave	1		3 00
Wilson, Wm. A.			
Real Estate	2,500	....	35 00
Wilson, Mrs. S. A. and children			
Slave	1	....	3 00
Wilson, Jane J. C.			
Slaves	2	....	6 00
Wilson, Mary E.			
Real Estate	2,500	35 00	
Slaves	7	21 00	56 00
Wilson, Mary E.			
Interest on Bonds, &c	262	6 55	
Slaves	7	21 00	27 55
Wilson, Estate Thomas			
Slaves	10	....	30 00
Wilson, Isaac M., Agent			
Slave	1		3 00
Wilson, William M.			
Slaves	4	12 00	
Dog	1	2 00	14 00
Wilson, Samuel			
Real Estate	8,000	112 00	
Slaves	7	21 00	
Carriage	1	20 00	
Horse	1	10 00	
Dog	1	2 00	165 00
Wilson, Abram			
Slaves	7	21 00	
Dog	1	2 00	23 00
Wilson, Abraham			
Slaves	37	....	111 00

			TAXES.
Wilson, John			
Real Estate	10,900	152 60	
Stock of Goods	1,500	21 00	
Slaves	8	24 00	
Carriage	1	20 00	
Dog	1	2 00	219 60
Wilson, A. B., in trust			
Real Estate	4,000	56 00	
Slaves	3	9 00	65 00
Wilson, Hugh, Jr.			
Slaves	13	39 00	
Carriage	1	30 00	
Horses	3	30 00	99 00
Wilson, Hugh, Sr.			
Real Estate	13,000	182 00	
Carriage	1	30 00	
Horses	2	20 00	232 00
Wilson, John R.			
Slaves	10	30 00	
Carriage	1	20 00	
Horses	2	20 00	
Dogs	3	6 00	76 00
Wilson, Sarah J.			
Real Estate	10,000	140 00	
Slaves	4	12 00	152 00
Wilson, Mrs. Charity			
Real Estate	8,000	112 00	
Slaves	4	12 00	124 00
Wilson, Estate B. H.			
Slave	1		3 00
Wiltberger, Mrs. E. E.			
Slaves	6	18 00	
Dog	1	2 00	20 00
Wincey, Mrs. R.			
Real Estate	1,600		22 40
Wing, Robert			
Real Estate	3,300	46 20	
Stock of Goods	300	4 20	50 40
Winkler, Rev. E. T.			
Interest on Bonds, &c	105	2 63	
Slaves	5	15 00	17 63
Winslow, Edward			
Slaves	10		30 00
Winter, Rebecca G.			
Slave	1		3 00

			TAXES
Winter, John			
Stock of Goods	500	7 00	
Slave	1	3 00	
Dog	1	2 00	12 0
Winningham, L. W			
Slaves	4		12 0
Winthrop, Dr. H.			
Real Estate	7,000	98 00	
Slaves	20	60 00	
Carriage	1	20 00	
Income	1,000	25 00	
Horse	1	10 00	
Dog	1	2 00	215 0
Winthrop, Dr. H., in trust			
Slaves	9	....	27 0
Winthrop, Elizabeth			
Real Estate	2,000	28 00	
Interest on Bonds, &c.	140	3 50	31 5
Winthrop, Jane			
Real Estate	2,000	28 00	
Interest on Bonds, &c.	140	3 50	
Slave	1	3 00	34 5
Winthrop, Francis			
Slave	1		3 0
Winthrop, Joseph A.			
Real Estate	10,000	140 00	
Slaves	2	6 00	146 0
Winthrop, Joseph & Son			
Commissions	3,000	....	75 0
Wirth, J			
Real Estate	4,500	63 00	
Stock of Goods	300	4 20	
Dog	1	2 00	69 2
Withers, William			
Real Estate	8,000	112 00	
Slave	1	3 00	
Carriage	1	20 00	
Horse	1	10 00	145 0
Withers, Caroline			
Slaves	2		6 0
Withers, M. R.			
Slaves	7		21 0
Withington, Martha			
Real Estate	1,500	21 00	
Slaves	2	6 00	27 0

			TAXES.
Witsell, John			
Slave	1	3 00	
Dog	1	2 00	5 00
Witsell, Trustee Mrs.			
Slaves	6		18 00
Wittchen, John F.			
Real Estate	8,000	112 00	
Slaves	8	24 00	136 00
Wittchen, H.			
Real Estate	3,500	49 00	
Slaves	2	6 00	55 00
Wohlers, John C.			
Real Estate	6,800	95 20	
Stock of Goods	2,000	28 00	
Dog	1	2 00	125 20
Wolken, H.			
Stock of Goods	400		5 60
Wood, Mrs. S.			
Real Estate	12,000		168 00
Wood, Mary			
Real Estate	6,500		91 00
Wood, Daniel			
Real Estate	5,200	72 80	
Slaves	2	6 00	78 80
Woodside, Samuel A.			
Real Estate	1,000		14 00
Woodward, Peter			
Real Estate	6,500		91 00
Woodworth, Eliza			
Real Estate	2,000	28 00	
Slaves	5	15 00	43 00
Woody, J. T.			
Slave	1		3 00
Woolf, Sarah			
Real Estate	13,000		182 00
Wotton, Mrs. C. P M.			
Real Estate	3,300		32 20
Wragg, Dr. William T.			
Real Estate	10,000	140 00	
Interest on Bonds, &c.	490	12 25	
Slaves	17	51 00	
Carriage	1	30 00	
Carriage	1	20 00	
Income	4,000	100 00	
Horses	3	30 00	383 25

		TAXE
Wragg, Estate Thomas L.		
Real Estate........................16,200	226 80	
Slave...1	3 00	229 ?
Wragg, Mrs. M. A.		
Interest on Bonds, &c................500	12 50	
Slaves..12	36 00	
Carriage..................................1	30 00	
Horses.....................................2	20 00	98 ?
Wragge, J. H. F.		
Real Estate........................1,600	22 40	
Dog...1	2 00	24 ?
Wrede, John H.		
Stock of Goods...................7,000	....	98 (
Wrede, C. W		
Real Estate........................8,000	....	112 (
Wright, Eliza		
Real Estate........................5,500	....	77 (
Wright, Mrs. C. F.		
Stock of Goods......................700	....	9 ?
Wright, Jane R.		
Real Estate........................2,500	....	35 (
Wuhrmann, Lilienthal & Klatte		
Stock of Goods...................5,000	....	70 (
Wurthmann, Estate H.		
Real Estate........................6,400	....	89 (
Wyatt, S. & Co.		
Real Estate........................6,000	84 00	
Commissions.,....................5,000	125 00	209 (
Yates, Rev William B.		
Slaves..................................11	33 00	
Carriage...............................1	20 00	
Horse....................................1	10 00	
Dog.......................................1	2 00	65 (
Yates, J D.		
Real Estate........................1,200	16 80	
Interest on Bonds, &c................400	10 00	26 ?
Yates, J. D., Trustee E. A. and children		
Real Estate........................5,000	70 00	
Slaves....................................7	21 00	91 (
Yates, J. D., Trustee White		
Real Estate........................1,000	....	14 (
Yates, J D., Trustee Long and children		
Slaves....................................7	....	21 (

		TAXES.	
Yates, J Legare			
Real Estate	6,000	84 00	
Slaves	3	9 00	93 00
Yates, W J			
Real Estate	6,000		84 00
Yates, Dr. William			
Slaves	4	12 00	
Carriage	1	20 00	
Horse	1	10 00	42 00
Yates, Trust Estate Caroline L.			
Real Estate	4,500		63 00
Yancorich, Sylvester			
Real Estate	600		8 40
Yeadon, Richard			
Real Estate	23,100 00	323 40	
Interest on Bonds, &c.	6,300 00	157 50	
Dividends	18 75	46	
Slaves	5	15 00	
Carriage	1	30 00	
Carriage	1	20 00	
Income	1,313	32 83	
Horses	3	30 00	609 19
Yeadon, R., Trustee			
Slave	1		3 00
Yeadon, Mary V			
Slaves	13		39 00
Yeadon, Steedman			
Real Estate	1,500	21 00	
Slaves	3	9 00	
Carriage	1	20 00	
Horse	1	10 00	60 00
You, Mary L.			
Slave	1		3 00
You, Mrs. M. A. and family			
Real Estate	6,000	84 00	
Interest on Bonds, &c.	415	10 37	94 37
Young, Louis			
Slaves	3		9 00
Young, Robert A.			
Stock of Goods	500	7 00	
Slaves	3	9 00	
Dog	1	2 00	18 00
Young, H. E.			
Slave	1	3 00	
Income	1,588	39 70	42 70

		TAXES.
Young, children of William		
Slaves....................................2	....	6 00
Young, William		
Slaves....................................2	....	6 00
Zacharias, E.		
Stock of Goods....................300	....	4 20
Zanoguena, Sebastian		
Real Estate..........................160	2 24	
Stock of Goods....................850	11 90	
Slaves......................................3	9 00	
Carriage...................................1	20 00	
Horse.......................................1	10 00	53 14
Zealy, Joseph		
Slave..1		3 00
Zehe, H.		
Real Estate.......................3,700	....	51 80
Zehe, John H.		
Stock of Goods....................500	....	7 00
Zerbst, John D.		
Stock of Goods....................500	7 00	
Dog..1	2 00	9 00
Zerbst, G. H.		
Real Estate.......................4,000	56 00	
Stock of Goods....................400	5 60	
Dog..1	*2 00	63 60
Zernow, John		
Real Estate..........................600	8 40	
Stock of Goods....................500	7 00	15 40
Zylstra, Charlotte		
Slaves......................................4	....	12 00

TAX ON PROPERTY

PAID BY

PERSONS OF INDIAN DESCENT

AND

FREE PERSONS OF COLOR.

			TAXES.
Aiken, William			
Real Estate	1,200		16 80
Aiken, Estate Carter			
Real Estate	300		4 20
Allen, Jane			
Slave	1		3 00
Alston, Thomas			
Horse	1		10 00
Ancrum, Susan			
Real Estate	1,800		25 20
Anderson, Nelson			
Real Estate	2,500		35 00
Artson, Martha			
Slave	1		3 00
Aspinall, Nicholas			
Real Estate	300		4 20
Aspinall, Mary			
Real Estate	2,000		28 00
Attels, Thomas			
Real Estate	300		4 20
Austin, Samuel			
Real Estate	1,500	21 00	
Slaves	6	18 00	39 00
Bamfield, Estate Joseph			
Real Estate	1,500		21 00
Baring, Joseph			
Real Estate	900		12 60
Barnet, Sarah			
Real Estate	400		5 60
Barnwell, Sarah			
Real Estate	400		5 60
Barron, Esther			
Real Estate	3,000		42 00
Bascom, Warly			
Horses	2		20 00
Bateman, Estate Isaac			
Real Estate	1,500		21 00
Baxter, Amos			
Real Estate	2,900	40 60	
Slave	1	3 00	43 60
Baxter, Amos, Trustee			
Slaves	13		39 00
Bennet, Catherine			
Real Estate	1,200		16 80

		TAXES.
Bennet, Sarah		
Real Estate ...300		4 20
Bentham, Ann		
Slaves ...4		12 00
Bentham, William H. (Indian)		
Real Estate ...500		7 00
Benson, Estate H.		
Real Estate ...200		2 80
Benson, George		
Real Estate ...200		2 80
Berney, J. A.		
Real Estate ...3,000		42 00
Berry, Moses		
Real Estate ...220		3 08
Berry, William		
Real Estate ...1,000		14 00
Berry, William, Trustee		
Slaves ...4		12 00
Bethune, Charles		
Real Estate ...300		4 20
Bing, Gordon		
Real Estate ...400		5 60
Blake, Prince		
Horse ...1		10 00
Blake, Ephraim		
Horse ...1		10 00
Boag, Celia A.		
Real Estate ...1,500		21 00
Bowen, Martha		
Slaves ...2		6 00
Bonneau, Jennett		
Real Estate ...1,000	14 00	
Slave ...1	3 00	17 00
Brailsford, Frederick		
Slave ...1		3 00
Brady, Francis		
Horse ...1		10 00
Brown, Ann		
Real Estate ...200		28 00
Brown, Malcom		
Real Estate ...9,100	127 40	
Slaves ...4	12 00	
Horse ...1	10 00	149 40

			TAXES.
Brown, Peter			
Real Estate	1,000	14 00	
Slave	1	3 00	17 00
Brown, Julia			
Stock of Goods	100	....	1 40
Buchanan, Diana			
Real Estate	1,500		21 00
Burckmeyer, Ellen			
Real Estate	1,200		16 80
Burke, Mary			
Real Estate	1,600	....	22 40
Burke, Louisa			
Slaves	2	....	6 00
Campbell, Mary			
Real Estate	4,500	63 00	
Slaves	5	15 00	78 00
Campbell, Estate Nichodemus			
Real Estate	500	....	7 00
Canmand, Estate Francis			
Real Estate	4,800	....	67 20
Carroll, James			
Real Estate	1,200		16 80
Castiva, Mary			
Slave	1		3 00
Chase, Matilda			
Real Estate	1,200	16 80	
Slaves	3	9 00	25 80
Chever, Joseph			
Real Estate	1,000	....	14 00
Chion, Susan			
Real Estate	1,000	....	14 00
Christopher, Nancy			
Real Estate	1,000	....	14 00
Cleveland, John			
Real Estate	800	....	11 20
Cleveland, Christiana			
Slaves	2		6 00
Cobb, Gideon			
Real Estate	2,000	....	28 00
Cochran, Thomas			
Real Estate	1,500	....	21 00
Cole, Thomas			
Real Estate	1,200	....	16 80

		TAXES.
Cole, Agnes		
Real Estate....................1,000	....	14 00
Collins, Estate R. H.		
Slaves.................................2		6 00
Conner, Ann		
Slaves 3		9 00
Cooler, Estate Archy		
Real Estate...................1,800	....	25 20
Cooper, Rebecca		
Slave 1	....	3 00
Cordes, Lucretia		
Real Estate....................4,100		57 40
Cornwell, Amelia L. (Indian)		
Slaves 4		12 00
Cox, Daniel		
Real Estate......................900	....	12 60
Crimmell, Margaret		
Real Estate...................1,800	....	25 20
Crosby, Mary		
Real Estate......................600	....	8 40
Dart, William		
Real Estate...................1,400	....	19 60
David, Lawrence, Trustee		
Slave 1	....	3 00
Davis, Rebecca		
Real Estate...................1,200	....	16 80
Deas, Estate Eliza W		
Real Estate...................1,200	16 80	
Slave.....................................1	3 00	19 80
Deas, Eliza C.		
Real Estate...................2,000	....	28 00
Deas, Jane		
Real Estate...................1,000		14 00
Deas, R. L.		
Real Estate...................1,600	....	22 40
Decoster, Louisa R.		
Real Estate...................3,000	42 00	
Slaves 5	15 00	57 00
Decoster, W B.		
Real Estate...................1,700	23 80	
Slaves...................................3	9 00	32 80
Delarge, John		
Real Estate...................2,000	....	28 00

		TAXES.

Deletta, A.
 Real Estate..................2,000 28 00
 Slaves....................3 9 00 37 00

Deliessline, A.
 Real Estate..................2,000   28 00

Demar, Samuel T.
 Real Estate..................2,000 28 00
 Slaves....................2 6 00 34 00

Dereef, R. E. (Indian)
 Real Estate..................23,000 322 00
 Slaves....................14 42 00
 Commissions..................400 10 00
 Horse....................1 10 00 384 00

Dereef, Joseph (Indian)
 Real Estate..................16,000 224 00
 Slaves....................6 18 00 242 00

Dereef, Joseph, Trustee
 Real Estate..................3,000   42 00

Dereef, J M. F
 Real Estate..................3,700 51 80
 Commissions..................300 7 50 59 30

Dereef, J. M. F., Trustee
 Real Estate..................1,500   21 00

Dereef, R. E., Jr.
 Real Estate..................2,500   35 00

Dereef, R. E., Trustee
 Slaves....................4   12 00

Desverney, Isabella and children
 Real Estate..................1,200   16 80

Dewees, W E. (Indian)
 Real Estate..................1,800   25 20

Dingle, Moses
 Real Estate..................200   2 80

Douglas, Margaret
 Real Estate..................1,200   16 80

Drayton, Paul B.
 Real Estate..................600   8 40

Drayton, Sarah
 Real Estate..................2,000   28 00

Duncan, Robert
 Slave....................1   3 00

Duprat, Estate Ann
 Real Estate..................3,000   42 00

			TAXES.
Duprat, Elizabeth			
Slaves	12		36 00
Echard's children, H. A.			
Real Estate	600		8 40
Eden, William			
Real Estate	1,200		16 80
Edwards, Estate Jacob			
Real Estate	1,000		14 00
Eggart, M. J.			
Real Estate	2,000		28 00
Elfe, Maria			
Real Estate	800	11 20	
Slave	1	3 00	14 20
Elfe, E. J.			
Real Estate	1,500		21 00
Elwig, Rebecca			
Real Estate	1,000	14 00	
Slave	1	3 00	17 00
Elwig, William			
Horse	1		10 00
Emmerly, William			
Real Estate	500		7 00
Evans, Friday			
Real Estate	600	8 40	
Slaves	2	6 00	14 40
Fanning, Thomas			
Slave	1		3 00
Fennick, John			
Real Estate	700		9 80
Ferrette, Virginia			
Real Estate	8,500	119 00	
Slaves	6	18 00	137 00
Ferrette, Charles			
Horse	1		10 00
Ferguson, James			
Real Estate	300		4 20
Fields, Sarah M.			
Real Estate	1,500		21 00
Firman, Mary			
Real Estate	3,500		49 00
Ford, William			
Real Estate	1,000		14 00
Ford, Ann			
Real Estate	400		5 60

			TAXES.

Fordham, Henry
 Real Estate..........................500 7 00
 Slave.........................1 3 00 10 00
Fordham, Martha
 Real Estate........................2,500 .... 35 00
Forrest, Ann
 Real Estate........................6,000 84 00
 Slaves.........................3 9 00 93 00
Fox, Elizabeth (Indian)
 Slave.........................1 .... 3 00
Francis, John L.
 Real Estate........................11,600 162 40
 Slaves.........................7 21 00 182 40
Francis, William H.
 Real Estate........................1,500 .... 21 00
Francis, Ann
 Real Estate........................2,000 28 00
 Slaves.........................2 6 00 34 00
Franklin, Amelia
 Slaves.........................3 .... 9 00
Frost, Emma
 Real Estate..........................500 .... 7 00
Frost, Estate H. M.
 Real Estate........................2,000 .... 28 00
Garden, Elias, (Indian)
 Real Estate........................14,000 196 00
 Slaves.........................3 9 00
 Horses.........................2 20 00
 Dog.........................1 2 00 227 00
Gardener, Mary Ann, (Indian)
 Slaves.........................2 .... 6 00
Gaskin, Sarah
 Slave.........................1 .... 3 00
Gibbs, Leander
 Real Estate........................1,200 .... 16 80
Gist, Juber
 Real Estate........................1,500 .... 21 00
Givins, Sarah
 Real Estate........................1,500 21 00
 Slaves.........................3 9 00 30 00
Glenn, Estate George
 Real Estate........................1,500 .... 21 00
Glover, Catharine
 Real Estate........................1,200 .... 16 80

			TAXES.
Glover, George A.			
Real Estate	1,200		16 80
Gorden, John			
Real Estate	1,800		25 20
Gonzales, Hannah			
Real Estate	3,000	42 00	
Slaves	3	9 00	51 00
Graddick, H. T.			
Real Estate	1,000		14 00
Grant, Alfred			
Real Estate	2,000	28 00	
Slaves	4	12 00	40 00
Grant, Ann			
Real Estate	1,800	25 20	
Slave	1	3 00	28 20
Grant, Phillis			
Real Estate	200		2 80
Grant, James			
Horse	1		10 00
Green, J J.			
Real Estate	3,500		49 00
Gregory, Sarah E.			
Real Estate	500		7 00
Greggre, Aberdeen			
Real Estate	1,000		14 00
Gough, Trust Estate Clarinda			
Real Estate	300		4 20
Haig, Edwin			
Real Estate	1,500		21 00
Hampton, Daphney			
Real Estate	2,500		35 00
Hargraves, Robert			
Slave	1		3 00
Harney, Robert H.			
Real Estate	8,450	118 30	
Commissions	150	3 75	122 05
Harper, Jack			
Real Estate	1,000		14 00
Harrison, Richard			
Real Estate	5,000	70 00	
Commissions	150	3 75	73 75
Hatt, Estate James F.			
Real Estate	3,800		53 20

			TAXES.
Hazell, Peter			
Real Estate	2,500	35 00	
Horse	1	10 00	45 00
Hedley, Eugenia			
Real Estate	3,000		42 00
Hedley, Theresa			
Real Estate	2,000	28 00	
Slave	1	3 00	31 00
Hill, Rose			
Real Estate	400		5 60
Hill, John			
Real Estate	100		1 40
Hoff, John			
Real Estate	2,400	33 60	
Slave	1	3 00	36 60
Holmes, Susan A.			
Real Estate	2,000	28 00	
Slaves	2	6 00	34 00
Holmes, Emeline P			
Real Estate	300		4 20
Holmes, E. P and Moses Dingle			
Real Estate	400		5 60
Holmes, Thomas M.			
Slaves	3	9 00	
Horse	1	10 00	19 00
Holmes, William L.			
Real Estate	750		10 50
Holmes, Sarah A.			
Real Estate	1,800		25 20
Holmes, William, Trustee			
Slaves	3		9 00
Holloway, C. H.			
Real Estate	5,500	77 00	
Slave	1	3 00	80 00
Holloway, R.			
Real Estate	9,200	128 80	
Slave	1	3 00	131 80
Holloway, R. W			
Real Estate	1,000		14 00
Holloway, James			
Real Estate	1,500		21 00
Holloway, Samuel D.			
Real Estate	3,835		53 69
Holloway, Elizabeth			
Real Estate	8,300		116 20

		TAXES.
Holloway, Mary		
Real Estate................900	....	12 60
Holloway, F. P		
Slaves.....................2	....	6 00
Holloway, Cornelius		
Real Estate..............1,000	14 00	
Slaves.....................2	6 00	20 00
Holton, Margaret		
Real Estate..............2,500	....	35 00
Hopkins, Cynthia		
Real Estate..............1,200	16 80	
Slave......................1	3 00	19 80
Houston, Robert		
Real Estate..............2,000	....	28 00
Howard, Robert		
Real Estate.............33,900	474 60	
Slaves.....................5	15 00	
Commissions............150	1 75	491 35
Howard & Ancrum		
Real Estate..............2,500	....	35 00
Howard, Sarah (Indian)		
Real Estate..............1,200	....	16 80
Huger, Estate C. & R.		
Real Estate..............1,900	....	26 60
Ingliss, William		
Real Estate..............3,000	....	42 00
Ingliss, Guy		
Real Estate..............1,100	....	15 40
Jackson, William		
Real Estate................600	8 40	
Slaves.....................2	6 00	14 40
James, Henry		
Real Estate................950	....	13 13
James, Daniel		
Real Estate................100	....	1 40
Johnson, Sally		
Real Estate..............5,500	77 00	
Slaves.....................4	12 00	89 00
Johnson, J. D.		
Real Estate..............4,000	56 00	
Slaves.....................3	9 00	65 00
Johnson Elizabeth		
Real Estate..............1,300	....	18 20
Johnson, Mary S.		
Slave......................1	....	3 00

			TAXES.
Johnson, Louisa			
Real Estate	1,000		14 00
Johnson and P Poinsett, Trustee			
Slave	1		3 00
Johnston, James			
Real Estate	7,300	72 20	
Slaves	10	30 00	102 20
Jones, Charlotte			
Real Estate	2,000		28 00
Jones, Joshua			
Real Estate	3,800		53 20
Jones, Ellen			
Real Estate	1,200		16 80
Judah, John			
Horse	1		10 00
Judah, Harriet			
Real Estate	1,400		19 60
Keath, Fanny			
Real Estate	1,500		21 00
Kinloch, Estate Richmond			
Real Estate	2,000		28 00
Kinloch, B. K.			
Horse	1		10 00
Koechler, Estate Jacob			
Real Estate	2,600	36 40	
Slaves	5	15 00	51 40
Lafarge, Emily			
Real Estate	3,000		42 00
Langdon, Edmund			
Real Estate	4,000		56 00
Lawrence, Sarah			
Real Estate	1,500		21 00
Lawrence, Mary			
Real Estate	500		7 00
Lawrence, Edward			
Real Estate	2,000		28 00
Legare, Charles			
Real Estate	2,950		41 30
Legare, Jacob			
Real Estate	1,200		16 80
Legare, Julia			
Slave	1		3 00
Legare, Sarah			
Real Estate	1,000		14 00

			TAXES.
Lesesne, Thomas			
Real Estate	1,000		14 00
Levy, James			
Real Estate	170		2 38
Lewis, John			
Real Estate	200		2 80
Lewis, John M.			
Real Estate	400		5 60
Lewis, John			
Horse	1		10 00
Lewis, Eugenia			
Real Estate	200		2 80
Lewis, Phœbe			
Slaves	11		33 00
Lincoln, Sarah			
Real Estate	2,600	36 40	
Slaves	3	9 00	45 40
Lubett, Caroline			
Real Estate	5,000	70 00	
Slaves	4	12 00	82 00
Lucas, George			
Real Estate	3,200		44 80
Main, Francis			
Real Estate	1,000		14 00
Martin, Sarah			
Real Estate	1,500		21 00
Martineau, Abraham			
Real Estate	1,800		25 20
Mason, Jane			
Real Estate	1,500		21 00
Mathews, Henry			
Real Estate	600		8 40
Mathews, John B. (Indian)			
Real Estate	5,500	77 00	
Slave	1	3 00	80 00
Mathews, S.			
Real Estate	200		2 80
Mathews, Joseph C.			
Real Estate	500		7 00
Mathews, Peter B.			
Real Estate	4,400	61 60	
Slaves	7	21 00	82 60
Mathews, Estate Phœbe			
Slave	1		3 00

			TAXES.
Maxwell, Thomas B.			
Slaves	2		6 00
Maxwell, James R.			
Real Estate	1,000		14 00
Maxwell, Thirza			
Real Estate	1,200		16 80
Maxwell, S. J.			
Real Estate	2,300		32 20
Mazyck, Peter			
Real Estate	600		8 40
Miles, Sylvia			
Real Estate	1,200		16 80
Miller, Eliza			
Real Estate	1,200		16 80
Miller, Wm.			
Real Estate	1,200		16 80
Mishow, Elizabeth			
Real Estate	500		7 00
Mitchell, Wm. Boone			
Real Estate	2,000	28 00	
Horse	1	10 00	38 00
Mitchell, W B.			
Real Estate	700		9 80
Mitchell, Ann (Indian)			
Real Estate	4,600	64 40	
Slave	1	3 00	67 40
Mitchell, Harriet (Indian)			
Real Estate	2,000		28 00
Mitchell, Estate S.			
Real Estate	1,500		21 00
Mitchell, Wm.			
Real Estate	400		5 60
Moore, Maria C.			
Real Estate	8,500	119 00	
Slaves	5	15 00	134 00
Morris, John			
Real Estate	1,700	23 80	
Slaves	5	15 00	38 80
Morrison, Robert			
Real Estate	1,800		25 20
Motte, Douilla and children			
Real Estate	5,000		70 00
Moultrie, Emily			
Real Estate	400		5 60

			TAXES.
Moultrie's children, Robert			
Real Estate	1,000		14 00
Murley, H.			
Real Estate	1,800		25 20
Mushington, Mary			
Real Estate	1,500		21 00
McBeth's children, J.			
Real Estate	800		11 20
McCall, Emma			
Real Estate	6,700	93 80	
Slaves	2	6 00	99 80
McKinlay, Wm.			
Real Estate	25,320		354 48
McKinlay, Wm. and A.			
Real Estate	6,000		84 00
McKinlay, Geo.			
Real Estate	3,500	49 00	
Slaves	2	6 00	55 00
McLean, Stephen			
Real Estate	3,500	49 00	
Slave	1	3 00	
Horse	1	10 00	62 00
McVicar, Louisa			
Real Estate	4,200	58 80	
Slaves	5	15 00	73 80
McNillaye, Estate Eliza			
Slave	1		3 00
Naylor, Ellen			
Real Estate	500		7 00
Nelson, Hanna			
Real Estate	5,800	81 20	
Slaves	2	6 00	
Horse	1	10 00	97 20
Nelson, Charlotte			
Real Estate	1,800		25 20
Osburn, W R.			
Real Estate	1,200		16 80
Owens, Henry			
Slaves	2		6 00
Palmer, Emma			
Slaves	2		6 00
Palmer, Edward			
Slaves	2		6 00

			TAXES.
Parker, Sylvia			
Real Estate	2,500		35 00
Parsons, Mary H.			
Slaves	3		9 00
Pawley, Rebecca			
Real Estate	1,200		16 80
Pencil, Margaret			
Slave	1		3 00
Peronneau, Emma			
Real Estate	100		1 40
Perry, Estate Robert			
Real Estate	3,500	49 00	
Slave	1	3 00	52 00
Perry, Isaac			
Horses	2		20 00
Perry, Francis			
Slave	1		3 00
Phillips, Anna			
Real Estate	600		8 40
Pincell, Wm. B.			
Real Estate	800		11 20
Plumeau, Francis			
Slaves	4		12 00
Plumet, Elizabeth			
Real Estate	2,000		28 00
Poinsett, Paul			
Real Estate	1,200		16 80
Pritchard, Josephine			
Real Estate	400		5 60
Pritchard, Catherine			
Real Estate	50		70
Purvis, Wm.			
Real Estate	1,950		27 30
Quash, Martha			
Real Estate	2,500		35 00
Ranor, Catherine			
Slaves	5		15 00
Richardson, Nelson			
Real Estate	2,100		29 40
Rivers, Thomas			
Real Estate	800		11 20
Roberts, Isaac			
Real Estate	300		4 20

                                                                    TAXES.
Rollins, William
    Real Estate..........................3,000   42 00
    Slave 1   3 00
    Commissions 175   4 38
    Horse 1   10 00   59 38
Ryan, Augustus (Indian)
    Real Estate..........................3,500   49 00
    Horse 1   10 00   59 00
Sasportas, J. A.
    Real Estate..........................6,700   93 80
    Slaves 5   15 00
    Horse 1   10 00   118 80
Sasportas, F C.
    Real Estate..........................2,000   28 00
    Slaves 2   6 00   34 00
Seymour, W N. (Indian)
    Real Estate..........................1,200   16 80
    Slave......................................1   3 00   19 80
Shirtliff, Elizabeth
    Real Estate..........................1,000   ....   14 00
Simms, Mary Ann
    Slave......................................1   ....   3 00
Simms, J J.
    Slaves....................................2   ....   6 00
Shrewsbery, Ann
    Real Estate..........................2,500   ....   35 00
Shrewsbery, George
    Real Estate..........................5,500   77 00
    Slaves 12   36 00
    Carriage 1   20 00
    Horses....................................2   20 00   153 00
Simmons, Isabella D.
    Real Estate..........................1,500   ....   21 00
Skirving, William
    Real Estate..........................3,500   ....   49 00
Small, Catherine
    Real Estate..........................1,000   ....   14 00
Small, Maria
    Real Estate..........................300   ....   4 20
Small, Richard
    Real Estate..........................3,500   49 00
    Slave 1   3 00   52 00
Small, Thomas R.
    Real Estate..........................7,300   102 20
    Slaves 3   9 00   111 20

		TAXES.
Small, Thomas, and James Bright		
Slaves........7		21 00
Small, Thomas R., and John Holmes		
Slaves........3		9 00
Small, Thomas R., and F Disvenier, Trustees		
Slave........1		3 00
Smith, Emily		
Slave........1		3 00
Spencer, Catherine		
Real Estate........1,000		14 00
Steedman, Mary		
Slave........1		3 00
Steele, Catherine E.		
Slave........1		3 00
Steinmitz, Nancy		
Real Estate........1,500		21 00
Steward, Mary Ann		
Real Estate........2,500		35 00
Steward, Nancy		
Real Estate........250		3 50
St. Marks, Francis		
Real Estate........11,550	161 70	
Slaves........3	9 00	170 70
St. Marks, William		
Real Estate........1,950		27 50
Stroub, M. A.		
Slave........1		3 00
Swinton, R.		
Real Estate........600		8 40
Taylor, Estate Elizabeth		
Real Estate........1,600		22 40
Theus, Thomas		
Real Estate........1,200		16 80
Thorne, Rebecca		
Real Estate........4,000	56 00	
Slaves........2	6 00	62 00
Thorne, Philip		
Real Estate........2,000		28 00
Thorne, John		
Real Estate........900		12 60
Toomer, Robert		
Real Estate........1,800		25 20
Trazvant, Diana		
Real Estate........800		11 20

		TAXES.	
Trescott, Harriet			
Real Estate............3,800	46 20		
Slave............1	3 00		
Carriage............1	20 00		
Horse............1	10 00	79 20	
Vessey, Sarah			
Slaves............4		12 00	
Walker, Betsey			
Real Estate............2,000	28 00		
Slaves............2	6 00	34 00	
Walker, Trust Estate Ann J			
Real Estate............2,500	35 00		
Slaves............2	6 00	41 00	
Walker, Jane			
Real Estate............800	....	11 20	
Wall, E. P			
Real Estate............1,500	....	21 00	
Washington, Jim			
Real Estate............1,500	....	21 00	
Watkins, Trust Estate Rebecca			
Real Estate............1,000		14 00	
Weston, Maria			
Real Estate............40,075	561 05		
Slaves............14	42 00		
Horse............1	10 00	613 05	
Weston, Jacob			
Real Estate............11,600	162 40		
Slaves............2	6 00		
Horse............1	10 00	178 40	
Weston, Jacob, in trust			
Real Estate............2,000		28 00	
Weston, Jacob, in trust L. Burke			
Real Estate............2,000		28 00	
Weston, Jacob, Trustee			
Slaves............7		21 00	
Weston, Samuel			
Real Estate............9,300	130 20		
Slave............1	3 00	133 20	
Weston, Samuel, Trustee			
Slaves............2	....	6 00	
Weston, Samuel, Trustee			
Slaves............8	....	24 00	
Weston, Harriet			
Real Estate............3,000	42 00		
Slave............1	3 00	45 00	

			TAXES.
Weston, Sarah			
Real Estate	1,500		21 00
Weston, S. and W B. Clark's children			
Real Estate	3,500		49 00
Weston, Sarah H.			
Slave	1		3 00
Weston, Firman J			
Real Estate	1,500		21 00
Weston, Estate John			
Real Estate	3,500		49 00
White, Joseph			
Real Estate	2,500		35 00
Wig, Elizabeth			
Real Estate	600		8 40
Wigfall, Paul			
Real Estate	2,500		35 00
Wightman, Estate Ann Jane			
Real Estate	3,500	49 00	
Slaves	2	6 00	55 00
Wilkinson, Mary			
Real Estate	1,200		16 80
Wilkinson, Richard			
Real Estate	1,800	25 20	
Slaves	3	9 00	34 20
Wilkinson, Paul			
Real Estate	300		4 20
Wilkinson, F L.			
Real Estate	5,400	75 60	
Slaves	4	12 00	
Horses	2	20 00	107 60
Wilkinson, Edward			
Real Estate	2,200		30 80
Wilkinson, F. L. and John Gordon			
Real Estate	300		4 20
Williams, James			
Slaves	2		6 00
Williams, Ann			
Slave	1		3 00
Wilson, Joshua			
Real Estate	5,200	72 80	
Horse	1	10 00	82 80
Wilson, Ann			
Real Estate	600		8 40

			TAXES.
Wilson, John			
Real Estate	2,000	28 00	
Slave	1	3 00	31 00
Wilson, Willoughby			
Slave	1	....	8 00
Wilson, Warley			
Real Estate	500	....	7 00
Winret, Sarah			
Stock of Goods	100	....	1 40

RATES OF TAXATION

UNDER THE ORDINANCE OF 1860, TO RAISE SUPPLIES.

Real Estate..................................$ 1 40 per cent.
Stock of Goods............................ 1 40 "
Interest on Bonds, &c.................. 2 50 "
Dividends.................................... 2 50 "
Slaves... 3 00 each.
Carriages drawn by Two Horses.... 30 00 "
Carriages drawn by One Horse...... 20 00 "
Sulkeys and Chairs...................... 15 00 "
Gross Income.............................. 2 50 per cent.
Commissions............................... 2 50 "
Annuities.................................... 2 50 "
Premiums of Insurance................ 1 25 "
Capital Stock of all Gas-light Companies....... 50 "
Capital in Shipping...................... 75 "
Gross Receipts of all Commercial Agencies.... 2 50 "
Horses and Mules........................ 10 00 each.
Dogs... 2 00 "

www.ingramcontent.com/pod-product-compliance
Lightning Source LLC
Chambersburg PA
CBHW021156230426
43667CB00006B/422